COLLE

312713

Date Due

JANUA LINGUARUM

STUDIA MEMORIAE
NICOLAI VAN WIJK DEDICATA

edenda curat

C. H. VAN SCHOONEVELD

INDIANA UNIVERSITY

SERIES MINOR

21

1970

MOUTON

THE HAGUE · PARIS

COLLECTANEA LINGUISTICA

ESSAYS IN GENERAL AND GENETIC LINGUISTICS

by

N. E. COLLINGE
UNIVERSITY OF TORONTO

1970

MOUTON

THE HAGUE · PARIS

LIBRARY OF CONGRESS CATALOG CARD NUMBER: 76-129298

Printed in The Netherlands by Mouton & Co., Printers, The Hague.

PREFACE

Historical linguistics and general linguistics have had a long divorce this century, though overtures of rapprochement have been more frequent recently. But they do each other so much good as to outweigh the feeling among general theorists that historical study is no more than a minute subdivision of the general field, and the delusion of some historians that they alone touch reality. These essays have a foot in both doors. If they seem merely programmatic, that is because they seek only to provoke thought, not codify it. If not everywhere is there great depth, shallow waters at least run wide.

Two of the chapters which follow are reprints of somewhat inaccessible papers; one, though accessible more readily, has seemed to regain relevance recently. The rest are new, but composed over several years, not always with complete demarcation of interest. It has not been possible to take account of any work of others which has appeared after the end of 1967 (except for references to forthcoming material, if then known).

My gratitude to those who have helped me to form ideas or to follow lines of enquiry is shown, I hope adequately, in scattered footnotes. I am especially indebted to Professor H. M. Hoenigswald, whose reading of the proofs has saved me from many errors. I should also wish to thank Mouton and Co., and their Editor Professor C. H. van Schooneveld, for accepting this volume in their *Janua Linguarum* series. For inadequacies of deep argument and inelegancies of surface expression, blame me.

April, 1969   N. E. COLLINGE

CONTENTS

1. PHONETIC SHIFTS AND PHONEMIC ASYMMETRIES[1]

Several scholars have speculated on the effects of operational systems on items of language history. Phonetic shifts have been interpreted in terms of remedying "crowding of the oral space" or of "filling gaps in the sound system". One thinks of the names of Mildred Pope, Martinet, Juilland and Haudricourt, and Ruipérez; and set against them, as opponents of the overuse of the factor of "structural pressure", Galton and Lasso de la Vega. A recent adherent of the notion contented himself therefore with observing that "phonetic developments do in fact frequently have the effect of resolving asymmetries in the phonological system". But these consequential developments may well be absent when there seems to be a crying need for their intervention, and even appear to promote successive and fresh asymmetries. Nor do scholars adequately distinguish between phonetic groupings with natural (physiological) symmetry and phonemic systems with functional (mathematical) symmetry. W. S. Allen, whose is the commendably cautious remark quoted above, has used the systemic principle of equal spacing to explain neatly the aperture shift and rearrangement in the long mid vowels of Attic-Ionic Greek, when secondary long vowels entered from contraction or lengthening of the short mid the shifts as numbered) (as in the first figure on page 10).

But apart from other similar and quite unresolved asymmetries in But apart from other similar and quite unresolved asymmetries in the ancient Greek system, Modern Greek (with a relevant historical connexion), without significant aperture-difference between long

[1] Originally published in *Proceedings of the Fourth International Congress of Phonetic Sciences*, edited by Antti Sovijärvi and Pentti Aalto (The Hague, Mouton & Co., 1962), pp. 563-566.

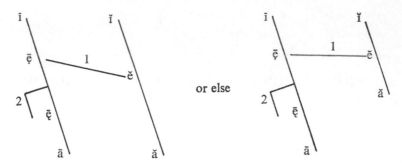

and short vowels and with stress-conditioned quantity, clearly
tolerates PHONETIC asymmetry with no signs of distress:

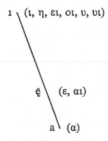

Phonemically, here is no asymmetry but only three equipollent
terms in an inventory. Phonemic asymmetry must mean either
uneven frequency of occurrence of individual terms or imbalance
(e.g. numerical) between distributionally similar sub-systems. To
return to Attic-Ionic, awareness of sound-difference, not of the
frequency-difference, is suggested by the purely graphic evidence
(and in Mod. Gk. uneven frequency is tolerated in respect of /i/),
while numerical imbalance was actually produced by and kept
after the shift, with four terms in the long system against three
in the short in this sector. Admittedly Allen speaks of 'phonological'
(and not phonemic) symmetry, in tune with the common British
preference for disregarding distributional counters in favour of
accurate description of the sounds, especially in their place of
realisation in the utterance, and of handling them as functional
elements by stressing the perceptual aspect. But then the *pattern*

remains the same as in phonetic analysis, and meets the same objections to 'systemic causation' of shifts.

Another examples may make this clear. There may be a point in examining together the Attic-Ionic shifts of $\bar{\varrho} > \bar{u}$ (c. 350 B.C. $- \breve{o} > \breve{u}$ is very uncertain and ignored in what follows) and $\breve{u} \rightarrow \breve{\imath}$ (date unknown but had moved by 350; classical result probably [y].[2] If systemic connexion is presumed as it has been, this means, both phonetically and phonologically, that

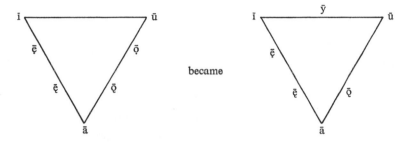

became

creating and leaving an asymmetry (even if $\bar{\varrho}$ was subsequently somewhat closed); and this new long vowel system stood beside the short system

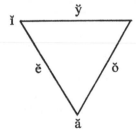

with toleration of comparative crowding of the front oral space and narrowing of perceptual frontiers in the long system, and not even like placement of gaps. In one sector, it may be admitted that in terms of perceptual efficiency

[2] Possibly a front vowel, lip-rounded. But it is easier to cite it as central, as allowing most symmetry (and it might have been [ʉ] or [ɨ]).

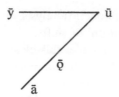

is better than an interim form

but this does not entitle us to speak of symmetry.

Phonemically the position is worse: /ā/ǭ/ǭ/ū/ passes to /ā/ǭ/ū/ȳ/, via either (1) /ā/ǭ/ō/ȳ/ or (2) /ā/ǭ/ū/. If (1), no improvement in either frequency-symmetry or sub-systemic balance was achieved by either stage of shift. If the less likely (2), we cannot detect, in the absence of oral record, whether /ū/ really was overloaded and felt to be so; and if it was, how were the original members of that phoneme extricated for passing to /ȳ/? And why was the achieved balance with the equivalent sector of the short vowel system (each of three terms temporarily?) at once thrown away?

It is, of course, possible to allow schematic pattern to phonemes also, by stressing their essential phonetic exponence and (as does Martinet) by using componential analysis to plot their relative positioning in terms of the distinctive features of which they are made up. But the objections remain: the appearance of the opposition of the presence/absence of a given feature in one place in the schema is no guarantee that it WILL appear in another place where, as regards phonetic balance, it COULD.

These pragmatic considerations suggest that if there is a scale of belief ranging from full acceptance of systemic control of sound-shifts to utter denial of such causation, the truth is probably nearer to the latter end of the scale.

2. PATTERN IN LINGUISTICS

Language is regularly, almost boringly, described as patterned activity; it would be tedious to collect examples. The word 'pattern', with no discernible lexical overtones, appears freely and innocently whenever any sort of configuration of linguistic items or events is characterized as a whole.[1] Halliday (1964, 305) calls it 'a general, non-technical name for all the organization, at all levels, that is a crucial property of language as such'. Hence attempts to give a theoretical or even a practical definition of 'pattern' in any such context are extremely rare. Linguists are readier to ask what patterns are basic, or how patterns interact, than to question the scope of the term itself. If any self-conscious use exists, however, it is worth seeking out; and Hockett's '*Course*' (1958), a more or less canonical isagoge even in this era of formal theory, is as good a point of departure as any for a terminological drag-hunt. His application of the term is threefold:

(1) — on p. 109 — he establishes 'the principle of neatness of pattern', with immediate reference to descriptive phonology, and with maximal symmetry as the *summum bonum*.[2] Here pattern = INTERNAL RESPONSION; i.e. one envisages, in each sector of description, a master shape plus coherent and matching sub-shapes.

[1] Absence of precision over 'pattern' is confirmed by a glance at the indexes of textbooks. Entries range from 'pattern: *passim*' (e.g. Strang, 1962) to no citation at all (e.g. Bloomfield, 1935). Lamb's (1966, 12f.) four types of pattern are essentially configurations. This present attempt to pin 'pattern' down was first presented as a lecture in Newcastle upon Tyne in May 1965, and profited much from the comments of Barbara Strang, Niels Lyhne Jensen and B. J. Sims.

[2] Symmetry may be regarded as a function of analysis. So Haugen (1962, 648f.) declares "symmetry is merely a way of stating that the same distinctive feature occurs at more than one place in the system".

(2)   — on p. 157 — he introduces the notion of 'recurrent patterns', with immediate reference to grammar, as the explanation of speakers' ready acceptance of new sentences.   The argument proceeds to constituent analysis, but his basic observation is the mainspring of generative grammar.   And the highest pattern-level is subsequently called a 'construction' (p. 164).   Here pattern = EXTERNAL RESPONSION; i.e. one envisages an identity, greater or less, of whole shapes.

(3)   — on pp. 334 ff. — he speaks of 'overall pattern', this being the totality of productive and receptive habits of speakers whose idiolects have some common core.   Here pattern = A TOTALITY OF OPERATIONAL ELEMENTS, an available pool of which any two listed items are not necessarily functionally co-existent (cf. especially his figure 39.5).

Clearly, here are three substantially different usages.   The first founders on two rocks: (a) from a synchronic point of view, languages tolerate much asymmetry and non-integration and under-employment (although the items which carry these characteristics probably have, on average, consistently shorter individual lives than the equivalent integrated specimens at each level); and (b) it is a diachronic commonplace that languages become both more tidy and less tidy, and move with equal frequency in either direction;[3] and the processes interplay.   To take a random example: in hypothetical conditional sentences in Latin, the formal application of the tenses of the subjunctive and the contextual organization of time-reference move towards (but do not finally reach) a one-to-one terminal congruence in a three-term system, and do so visibly in the transition from pre-Plautine to post-Plautine usage.[4]   On the

[3]   Which is simply another reflection of the practical absence of universals in language history, an absence made very clear by the reports of Hoenigswald and Cowgill in Greenberg (1963).

[4]   This rests on the simple view, namely that originally e.g. *faciam* serves for both future and present reference (two functions with one exponent), and *facerem, fecissem* both serve for past reference (one function, two exponents): the valor-difference (if any) of the latter pair is, arguably, of a durative/non-durative aspectual type.   But, were it not for the partially aoristic function and form-history of the Latin 'perfect', it would be easier (and always has been fashionable, off and on, since Varro) to set up two superimposed systems, one

other hand, in Greek, the linked verb-form scatter πείϲομαι, πέπονϑα, ἔπαϑον reduces almost to chaos the close ablaut responsion of the inherited root syllables *k^uenth-, *k^uonth-, *k^unth-. Symmetry, then, is to be rejected both as a descriptive ideal (as it is championed most recently by Kemp Malone, 1962) and as a historical aid. Lehmann went so far as to say, in defence of the historical usefulness of symmetry, "the forms we reconstruct will have to be symmetrical ... and from non-symmetrical patterns in our reconstructions we may be able to reconstruct earlier forms of the language" (1954, 103; the reference being to the proto-language under description).[5] On all this it is relevant to look back to chapter 1 above. Against Lehmann especially one may point to the neat Latin correspondences *ĕmit/ēmit*, *fŭgit/fūgit* etc., or *mŏuet/mōuit*, *sĕdet/sēdit*, *uĭdet/uīdit*, which offer a stem-form relation between present and perfect tenses so regular as to discourage deeper digging (indeed, the alternating duration-feature of the root vowel even disregards conjugational frontiers). In fact, an earlier stage seems to show *ĕm/ēm* but *fŭg/foug*, and sets *mŏue/mŏue* against *sĕde/sĕsd* against *uĭde/uoid* — the pattern now shot to pieces. And the contrasting evolution of the classical Latin forms of the declension of subjunctive *sim* and indicative *sum* is a cautionary tale for pattern enthusiasts.

---

of time reference and one of perfectivity/imperfectivity, for all the formally distinct 'tenses'. Then the picture of the development mentioned above is from position (1):—*faciam/fecerim* = impf/pf. system imposed on fut. + pres. reference; *facerem/fecissem* = impf./pf. system imposed on past reference — to position (2): *faciam/fecerim* = impf./pf. system imposed on future reference only; *facerem* = monosystemic exponent of present time reference only; *fecissem* = monosystemic exponent of the past time reference only. Then the movement is seen as an improvement of the efficiency of time reference combined with a 'skewing' of this particular aspect application; the example is one of simultaneous tidying and untidying (and a new system may be settling on the debris of two old ones). As a replacement example (of mere tidying) one may offer the reduction of the actual and potential complications of IE gender to the two-term, syntactically regular, arrangement of Romance.

[5] Lehmann elsewhere (1962, 179) uses 'pattern' in Hockett's second sense, in the virtually traditional collocation 'pattern-practice', for what is often called 'structure-drill'.

It is worth noting that Lehmann envisages patterns which are not symmetrical. Yet the inference seems to be that responsion is crucial in the sense that:

(a) it is the operational basis, and so it 'carries' the anomalies;
(b) it is what is worth describing;
(c) it can suggest what is, especially historically, worth looking for.

This last consideration makes one think of predictive asymmetries elsewhere, notably in the realm of physics. The search for, and the theoretical handling of, elementary particles is conducted largely in terms of patterning (e.g. 'for every particle there is an anti-particle', 'mirror-images', etc.). This approach is justified by such empiric corroborations as the discovery, in February 1964, of the $\Omega-$ particle, the prediction of which rested on a pattern grouping of baryons of 3/2 spin within a matrix defined in one (vertical) dimension by hypercharge $(-2 \rightarrow +1)$ and in the other (horizontal) by 'I-spin component' $(-3/2 \rightarrow +3/2)$. This gave the figure:

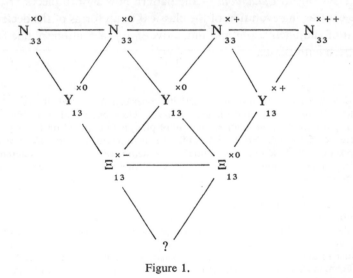

Figure 1.

wherein '?' forecast an occupant of this apex-cell (with the characteristics of negative charge, 3/2 spin, and around 3,350 electron-masses) — and this turned up as $\Omega-$.[6]

The interesting thing is that, while this pattern must be held to exist in nature, the physicist has to permutate and manipulate his matrices (based on properties) before he can reproduce it, and may fashion many sterile patterns on the way. For not all patterns predict; or, more correctly, patterns vary in their power of prediction, according to the suggestive placing of apparent gaps. One might point to the matrices which can handle the apparent syllable structure of proto-Indo-European, as understood since de Saussure; and one might note that, if we use the differential axes ⟨presence/absence of peak vowel⟩ and ⟨values of the non-peak element⟩ nothing more is predictable by the (morphologically prompted) inclusion of '*e?*' ($=$ /e:/) than the independent existence of the coefficient '?' (subsequently established as the famous 'laryngeal'), while if the second axis is varied to ⟨scale of stability and/or consistency of the non-peak element in comparative reflexes⟩ a greater delicacy of forecast is achieved, in that the predicted element will now occupy a cell so placed (alongside *n*, no doubt) as to assign to it articulatory fringe status in its probable phonetic exponence (i.e. a non-buccal, low integration, type).[7]

Householder (1965, 22) speculates that in subatomic physics the properties (mass, charge, spin etc.) exist, while the particles themselves (muon, proton, pi meson etc.) are not 'things' but merely bundles of properties; then 'decay' is a metaphor for the de- and re-combining of properties, 'spatial reshufflings'. Householder's

[6] The SU₃ theory, to which an introduction may be sought from any recent treatise on particle-physics. On pattern-seeking in science generally, see R. M. W. Dixon's rather simplicistic account (*Linguistic Science and Logic*, [The Hague, 1963], 11 ff.). There may be a further analogue in the theory that some of the now proliferating particles are 'excited states' of previously known ones. For instance, one may reject will/wish as the *Grundbedeutung* of the PIE non-indicative finite verb forms (against Kroll), in favour of a tolerant, 'low-energy' valor like Sweet's 'non-assertion' of Gonda's 'visualization'. Then, for their undeniable presence in non-bound clause structures, will/wish can be manifestations of 'high-energy' behaviour.

[7] See chapter 5, *passim*. It is the gratuitous introduction of external responsion pattern which fictitiously increases the apparent integration and promotes a multiplicity of laryngeals.

point is equally intriguing for linguists. If a distinctive feature matrix is to be regarded as more real than the phonemes which fill its cells or are specified by its '+' or '−' entries in whole columns, then an acoustic shape is more real than an entity which some call a 'heuristic fiction' and others show to be a mental response-area — and who will quarrel with that? And if 'charge' and 'mass' are reasonably analogous to such spectrographically established features as 'acuteness' and 'compactness', are we on the brink of an inter-discipline parallelism of some consequence? In particular, in view of longstanding suspicion about the adequacy of e.g. biological models in historical linguistics,[8] is there anything compelling in the application of geometrical models? It is note-worthy that the pattern-prediction of the physicists presumes a geometrical economy; that is, the suppletion of ⌄⁷ is held as certain to be ⌄˙˙⁷ and not ⌄˙˙⁷ or the like, the realization of the whole shape being limited in terms of direction and plane (and even oddly limited within the range of regular shapes, e.g. to either triangles or hexagons, for such appears to be the case in particle physics). To put this positively, however, linguists should ask themselves whether they accept that systems must be, at some stage at least in their evolution, regularly developed to the full extent of their geometrical economy. The answer probably is that systems are not necessarily so developed, and that the geometrical compulsion, if it exists, in users of linguistic systems would seem (by the evidence of many an analysis of this or that sector of this or that language) to be satisfied by *potential* regularity of shape, hexagons manqués and so forth. Man, paradoxically, would not have pro-gressed as a tool-user had he not always had a high tolerance of physical imperfection in his tools.[9]

---

[8]   Cf. Lehmann (1962, 142), who sees the application of geometry and biology as equally over-simplicistic. As to the biological model, however, Stevick (1963) has a defence worth studying.

[9]   No purpose is served by regurgitating here the much-chewed arguments for and against the idea that pattern — or any structure or system — is an extrane-ous imposition on the data and has its roots in the analyst's mind. As what Householder would call 'an old God's truth man', I see no pattern of analysis justified unless it truthfully reflects the data (whether or not these include the

In the current survey of educated (spoken) English usage a matrix presentation is achieved by combining the dimensions of ⟨basic structure⟩ and ⟨differential 'features' (manifested, potential or transformational)⟩ — so that, after *I know/say/think/believe/* etc., *that he is Adj* is permutated with *him to be Adj/ he is to be Adj/ his being Adj* etc. (see chapter 7, p. 150), a gradience is achieved which permits the relative placing of the basic structures in terms of operational similarity and flexibility: but the clarity of the pattern is interrupted by an isolated plus in a field of minuses, or vice versa, arising from e.g. the fact that *he is said to be foolish* is an acceptable sentence but **I say him to be foolish* is not.[10] Adroit reshuffling will remove that unexpected anomaly only at the expense of introducing others (e.g. deriving from *I like him to be foolish* as against **he is liked to be foolish*). There is no point in taking evading action. The similarity network which links structures has holes in it; why should we expect it not to? Gaps in the pattern are part of the pattern; and if this emasculates the pattern so much the worse for any theory which mistakenly assigns power, descriptive or predictive, where it does not belong. Gap-shifting, by pattern-pressure, is arbitrary.

Moreover, if a neat tetragonic arrangement like

$$/p/\text{——}/b/$$
$$/p^h/\text{——}/b^h/$$

is to be established within many consonantal macro-systems (and for a similar vocalic pattern in Icelandic, see Haugen, 1962, 649), and if we are to set beside it /p/—/b/, as does Jakobson, there

$$\begin{array}{c} | \diagup \\ /p^h/ \end{array}$$

can scarcely be an argument from geometry against the suspect

---

tacit knowledge of the language user). That the data themselves are "impressed with patterns, generally incomplete, by our pattern-making minds" (Entwistle, 1953. viii) is no ground, especially in view of the incompleteness, for a sophistic θέσις versus φύσις dichotomy. And even if it were, true θέσις rests on φύσις, as Plato said: you cannot efficiently impress what is not naturally inherent.

[10] See in particular Quirk (1965), and (for example) try inserting *hopes* as a 'finite' into the matrix in his table 5.

(and Jakobson would say non-existent)[11] arrangement /p/—/b/.

$$/b^h/$$

Yet there may be many a hidden warning that users of language systems 'see' no such obvious geometric shapes at all. In the Greek sub-systems of stops such as /p/—/b/, the term 'middle', by

$$/p^h/$$

the dictates of this pattern, would seem by geometry to be expected to attach itself to /p/ — in fact it is /b/ which is so designated.[12]

So far, then, 'pattern' would seem to possess the power of revealing a potential geometry without ensuring its actuality; of classifying phenomena into regularities and anomalies without claiming uniqueness for, or predicating falsity of, any particular classification; and of 'predicting' that an evolutionary process will be found to have occurred, with no more than a 50% chance of verification.[13]

Hockett's second application of 'pattern' is more immediately intelligible. It corresponds to what is probably in general usage the normal meaning of the term. The implications of this normal usage will be considered presently. Meanwhile, it may be worth exploring a possible relationship between this kind of 'pattern' and that examined above. It is at least arguable that an externally responsive syntagmatic pattern (whether phonotactic, syntactical or collocational) may induce some 'internal responsion'. A syntactical structure, if expressed as a 'syntagmeme', to take one example, may import wholly or partially its own shape-converse. In view of what we have seen of 'internal' patterns, this tendency

---

[11]   Non-existent because it falls foul of one of what Sebeok has called Jakobson's 'universal implications'. See Jakobson (1957, 23; 1962, 526). But Madurese (East Java) has been credited with voiceless, voiced and voiced aspirated stops, and these varieties only; see Alan M. Stevens, *Language* 41 (1965), 294 fn. 1.

[12]   See Collinge (1963, 232-235).

[13]   Hockett's first type of pattern could presumably include non-symmetrical, but still articulated, geometrical shapes, such as the 'golden section' which underlies much classical architecture and plastic art, and which has recently been imported into the analysis of Latin poetry by George E. Duckworth. But the formula $m/M = M/M + m = 0.618$ does not seem to be the basis of any linguistic system or structure known to me.

will be spasmodic. As for T-grammar, the most obviously 'shaped' figure, a recurrent 'Phrase-marker', will not have one sector mirrored by another, e.g. as if the sector

were mirrored by

unless it happens by coincidence that such mirroring is part of the data — i.e. not in English grammar unless and until *VO* becomes a regular sentence-form, equally as frequent as *SV* (though this is itself, in that form, uncommon — see Quirk, 1965, 207). For all the universalizing tendency of such grammars, a P-marker is essentially idiosyncratic; Latin usage, for example, is immaterial here. (But, to keep to transformations for the moment, there is no sense in trying, either by maintaining and manipulating the optional/obligatory status of T-rules or by doctoring the lexicon-entries of grammatical elements, to preclude sentences like *who rumours it?*[14] while generating the type *it is rumoured that they will*

---

[14] To ignore it is to ignore a potential recurrence-pattern which may very well influence native speakers (even jokes like *if it's feasible let's fease it* are a strong support for the set-conditioned mental analogue interpretation of transformational analysis). That a sentence is absent is a limited statement which sets arbitrary bounds (usually defined in terms of 'aberrations') to modes and registers of a language, bounds which are much less defensible than within a taxonomic framework (for a systems-and-structures, or scale-and-category, grammar is less explicit but more prescriptive and potentially proscriptive than a generative one). A pan-idiolectal, pan-dialectal, pan-modal description ('overall pattern'), for all its inherent falsity, is a logical, even if impractical, necessity within a complete intuition-sensitive grammar; and such a pan-pattern is the current basis of the transformationalists' phonology.

soon marry. Not only does the former type occur (under special conditions): it is also more unmistakably 'T-derived', by native speakers, then most other sentences of the language, and its aberrant status is better handled by a frequency scale or the like. Thus the passive transformation as presented in early Chomskian grammar stands revealed as merely the more or less frequent form of a potentially symmetrical pattern of (two-way) active⇔passive 'T-rules'.[15] This is a matter of not ignoring pattern in the data — even potential pattern — but it touches on the intuitions which transformational analysis seeks to articulate, and which new Chomskian 'base component dummies' tend to obscure (cf. Chomsky, 1965).

A similar and perhaps more powerful argument for attraction of patterns of type 2 to type 1 can be applied to patterns of morphology, as a simple example will show. Recently familiar is one concept of the *lexeme*, established as having the same relation to *word* at the lexical level as has morpheme to morph, and phoneme to allophone, at their respective levels (so by Lyons 1963, 11f.; cf. Matthews, 1965). (In passing however, one cannot help expressing surprise at the readiness with which this concept embraces an analogy deriving from an extremely simple-minded version of taxonomic analysis — and this of the 'crude parallelism' variety, far removed from the subtleties of such 'strata-operators' as Pike or Lamb.) As a word is an ordered structure (or '*n*-tuple') of morphemes, a lexeme must be a set of such structures (or '*n*-tuples') sharing at least one morpheme which would itself appear (tacitly rather than explicitly in the work of those who use this concept) to be a lexical element — that is, an element selected for contextual or referential reasons which are not necessarily ultimately definable purely in terms of co-occurrences within the structure of the

---

[15]   This system argues that priority should be assigned, within an ordered set of rules, to a sentence-form only on the basis of comparative frequency of occurrence and only with reference to the behaviour of individual utterances. The notion of 'kernel' sentences is scarcely defensible, either as establishing a typical base-form or as purporting to judge which of two given sentences is prior and which the transform. But this danger has been seen, unidirectional and 'optional' transformationalism is dead, and kernels are no longer insisted upon, except interpretatively; see Chomsky, 1965.

immediate sentence or paragraph/paraphone or of their transforms. The result is that the lexeme is reasonably regarded both as the universal minimal semantic unit and, for inflexional languages which respond to a traditional WP analysis, as the crucial grammatical unit, in terms of which, for example, the morphological component of a generative grammar can be stated (cf. Matthews, 1965, 1966). For a language like Latin the relevant formula may be said to be $M_L{\frown}M_{G(1-n)}$, and the relevant shape something like

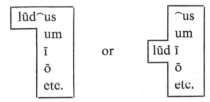

Now it is often said that pure arbitrariness decides whether we build our paradigms by 'endings' rather than by 'stems'; or that if any special consideration operates here it is that of convenience, in that grammatical morphemes operate in closed systems of relatively few terms. (This consideration has even greater weight when co-existent systems are disentangled, an occasional but rather artificial device in handling an inflexional language.) But nothing gainsays the reverse procedure — that is, a formula $M_{L(1-}{\frown}M_G$ leading to a shape like

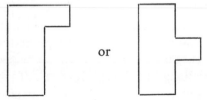

Indeed, there are two good reasons for accepting this alternative: (1) traditional inflexion-grammar rests on both shapes, presentation being by paradigm-types ('declension' and 'conjugation'). Since Remmius Palaemon's subdivision of nominal and verbal items according to the form of genitive singular or 2 sing. present indicative respectively, the display has involved the 'anti-lexemic' shapes

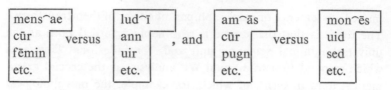

(2) grammatical distinctions may be deduced from shapes of this
second type. For instance, the classes Noun and Adjective are
morphologically distinguishable either in terms of the contrast
between the relation of

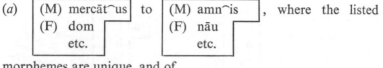

morphemes are unique, and of

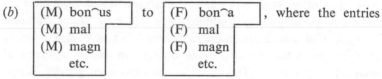

of one shape repeat those of the other;[16] or else in terms of the
revealing double-entry within one shape which makes

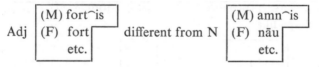

One may therefore propose that this shape, responsive to that of
the lexeme, be recognized — and presumably named, if we are to be
analogical, something like 'morphologeme'. To be sure, there is
nothing new about it. Apollonius Dyscolus (in his work on syntax,
section II 2 in Uhlig's 1910 edition) states a parallelism in the
system of person (+ number) as between pronoun and verb, like
that in the system of case as between pronoun and noun. For the

[16] *Seruos/a, dominus/a* etc. are equivocal, their class being a matter for
syntactical determination alone. Even syntactically the two classes (N and
Adj) are largely fused (cf. *iuris consultus* (uncertain class), alongside *iuris
peritus* (Adj) and *iuris defensor* (N), or phrases like *patre nullo, matre serua* etc.).

latter he cites the lexemic 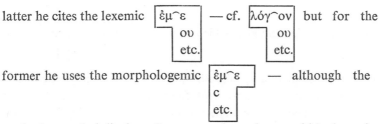 — cf. λόγ͡ον but for the

former he uses the morphologemic ἐμ͡ε — although the

equivalent verbal display of person and number would be lexemic, and this (pronoun-verb) systemic equation is a contextual coincidence, or at least an arbitrariness. We may note, in passing, that the morphologeme and the lexeme are both *shapes* (a fact obscured when a particular 'quotative' form, e.g. *equus*, is cited as THE lexeme: cf. Matthews, 1966, 173), whereas the morpheme is essentially a functional inventory. This underlines the danger of wanting lexeme and morpheme to behave like theoretical counterparts. It is possible, in terms of set theory, to define the morphological component of the grammar of an inflected language as the Cartesian product of the sets ⟨lexical inventory⟩ and ⟨grammatical markers⟩; this can be reformulated as either the lexemic or the morphologemic inventory, and the shapes of either type will suffice. But for the purposes of historians both shapes are essential; for example, the type of analogical evolution[17] which reduces ἕπομαι, *ἕτεται, ἑπόμεθα etc. to 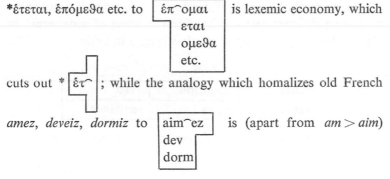 is lexemic economy, which

cuts out *ἐτ͡; while the analogy which homalizes old French

amez, deveiz, dormiz to aim͡ez is (apart from *am > aim*)
dev
dorm

---

[17]   Robins (1957, 75) usefully defines analogy as "the reformation of phonological forms under inter-level pressure of congruence with the majority patterns of grammatically or semantically (contextually) cognate and associated forms in the language".

morphologemic economy, which cuts out * 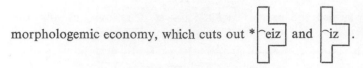 eiz and iz .

That this shape-duality should induce an internally responsive pattern (i.e. cause a movement from the second to the first of Hockett's types) may be a special property of inflecting languages, in the classical typological sense of that term. What is more, we may have here a typological diagnostic, in that neither shape operates in an isolating language and the morphologeme is obviously de trop and useless in an agglutinative language. Finally, in programmed instruction the lexeme operates in transformational drills, the morphologeme in substitution drills.

Another essentially geometric (i.e. essentially type 1) pattern-analysis, but importing its own special connexion with mathematical concepts, is the so-called matrix display recently (1966, 367-376) favoured by Pike (but not only by him). This kind of network or bi-ordinate presentation may introduce a welcome 'field theory' for the generalization of WP grammar; but arithmetical operations with whole matrices are conspicuously avoided by linguists, and even as a deployment of the interrelations of a language's categories a matrix has many hidden snares.[18] It is often, if well balanced, too coarse-meshed for part of the data (a defect which is not cured by having different matrices at different levels of structure). In Varro's simple quaternary word-class system in Latin:

	+ case	− case
+ tense	participle	verb
− tense	noun	remainder

the group 'remainder' confounds adverbs, conjunctions, pronouns

---

[18]   For instance, the pyramid figure by means of which Pike (1962, 235) displays the Ixil clause system is said to represent clause-types by its faces, diagnostic tagmemes by its ascending edges, predicate-types by the sides of its base, and the total set of clauses by the base itself. But the set of clauses before differentiation must be represented by the apex, the base merely indicating the relative post-analysis placing of the four predicate-types.

and prepositions, categories not unknown to Varro. Besides, this matrix combines a spoiling of *display* (by a limiting of the dimensions) with a spoiling of *discovery* (by a limiting of the criteria of relevance). Nor is it always realised that a matrix can include naturally empty (i.e. unfillable) cells. If an aspect system is set up in terms of duration vs. momentaneity, with the full temporal implication of those terms, in a language where the basic temporal key is the speaker's present, the crossing of this system with a normal past/present tense system must give an empty cell:[19]

	durative	momentary
past	√	√
present	√	Ø

But this kind of emptiness is easily confused with accidental emptiness; and any empty cell may be regarded by the analyst as a challenge to his ingenuity.[20]

Pike's interesting schematization of Ixil clauses (1962, 234f.), initially according to the cross-plotting of ⟨predicate type⟩ and ⟨absence of object × variety of 'topic'⟩, permits an ultimate reduction to a completely filled Varronian type of matrix. On the way, however, it is shown how the ampler dimensions allow a single (clause-type) entry in each row and column (a fact which links up with Longacre's notion (1964, 18) of dual formal difference in contrasting structures). But Pike insists that 'one cell per row per column' is the significant factor, and not the adventitious 'pattern' (diagonal or other) which may be achieved by manipulation of the matrix. For instance, an intersecting of four terms in one dimension with four terms in another produces from identical data the patterned

---

[19] See chapter 6, (p. 121); also K.L.McKay, *Bull. Instit. Class. Stud.* 12 (1965), 5. This is an inescapable deduction from the nature of our universe; apparent contrary cases rest on different grammatical systems or misunderstanding as to the contextual application of particular phrases.

[20] So Pike was right to be scornful of Trager who, having interpreted a gap in his description of a phonology as just such a challenge, returned to the data and 'discovered' a silent feature (cf. *Word* 8 (1952), 108 and fn. 8).

	a	b	c	d
1	√			
2		√		
3			√	
4				√

or the patternless

	a	b	c	d
1	√			
3			√	
4				√
2		√		

And the same applies to set-theory Venn diagrams and the like.[21]

Reverting to the nature and implications of 'pattern' as used in Hockett's second sense, one is aware here of a unifying concept common to all grammars which formulate structure and are not content with mere classified inventories of items. These grammars are sometimes written off (as by those who favour spotlighting speakers' tacit competence, ignoring the physical limitations of individual structures, and identifying the multiple relations of co-occurrent elements by search in depth) as 'taxonomic', a term as easily applied to classifying phonologies — where syntagmatic potentialities are so vast and so defeating to generalization — as it is hard to justify as a predication of an even slightly structure-conscious grammar. 'Phrase-structure grammar', slanted a term as it is, is a fairer appellation; but at least for Pike-Longacre tagmemics and Hallidayan scale-and-category analysis (and Hallidayan deep, and maximally delicate, realization-statement of related systemic properties in relevant structures), the best general title must be 'hierarchic grammar'. In grammars of this type, whether the formulae are expressed exponentially or symbolically, and

[21]   E. g. Mulder's patterned diagram (1965, 25; fig. 7) can be made symmetrical, and the incidence of the Dutch archiphonemes /D, Z/ be symmetrically placed within the set of all apical phonemes, merely by transposing the ellipses ⟨-d-tz-s-n⟩ and ⟨-d-t-z-sn⟩.

whether they look like lineal mathematical expressions or dynamic flow charts, a type-two pattern can be said to exist: without internal responsion, the formula permits the 'cutting-out' (and 'tacking-in' to discourse) of acceptable structures. And if terms from dressmaking have been employed in that last sentence it is because these patterns have in common with those of dressmaking the power of 're-superimposition' on the material.[22]

In transformational theory 're-superimposition' has little place (and possibly less place even than pattern of Hockett's first type — which is paradoxical in view of their general interrelation). True, unless every sentence in a language is unique some application of this sort of pattern is undeniably present, in the form of recurrence of rules. And the whole point of implanting exponential values into the grammar, or grammatical characteristics into the attendant lexicon, or into the grammar itself by the use of L(exical)-rules or C(ollocation)-rules (cf. Matthews, 1965), is to recognize repetitive pattern in the transformations, individually or in batteries. But the pursuit of explicitness has the effect of involving transformationalists in a search for an ever increasing number of distinctions between rules and an increasingly complex system of ordering of these more numerous rules — which ultimately, at least in theory and for the purposes of this exercise, writes off grammatical identity of utterances as an uninteresting linguistic fact (though presumably it remains an interesting social event). To put it otherwise, for them high pattern-incidence equals shallowness. Moreover, such physical

---

[22] It is in this sense that McIntosh fixes the grammatical term 'pattern' as a model for the equivalent lexical term 'range' (1961), although the latter has points of contact with Wittgenstein's use of 'family' and rests on a Firthian idea of collocational limitations. Note the very similar usage in the remark "by COLLIGATION I understand the relationship between classes forming a pattern and by COLLOCATION that between individual elements satisfying such a pattern" (Matthews, 1961, 196 fn. 3). Such a grammatical pattern may itself be produced by a transformation (Quirk, 1965, 214). For Longacre (1964, 13 ff.) this type of patterning is linguistics' central concern; and he even characterizes Chomskian grammar as 'linguistic patterns presented obliquely', although admitting that pattern reflection is 'not a focal concern' of a rules-model. See below, footnote 24. (It may be noted that Hockett uses 'pattern' to mean 'arrangement of phonological units' at *Language* 41 [1965], 195).

pattern (configuration, subconfiguration) as is visible in 'Phrase-markers' is specifically devalued as a statement of deep relations;[23] and this whole theory has been expressly dissociated from pattern-seeking.[24] (To be sure, the earlier reference to dressmaking may turn the reader's mind at this point to knitting patterns. These claim, indeed to convey 'tacit competence': the one at present in my wife's workbag purports to formulate the intuitive achievement of the Aran Islanders. Moreover, they offer a series of productive rules which are readily rewritten into a currently recognizable grammatical form (e.g. 'Pattern → row 1⌒row 2⌒... row n; row 1 → K3⌒P6⌒K3⌒... etc.'); and the rules show some context-sensitivity (e.g. as applying only in the context ⟨non-decreased section of right front⟩ etc.). But transformations are rare — apart from the purely physical reversal of the work between rows — and any ordering of rules is merely additive and does not at each stage change the existing material. Therefore this analogy holds for generative, but not for transformational, grammar).

Transformational morphophonemics, however, is quite another matter. Its presentation by ordered rules in cyclic sequence (cf. Chomsky, 1967, 115 ff.) diverges curiously from its phonological base.[25] The latter is clearly patterned, and is presented after the matrix fashion (see Halle, 1959, 32 ff.; 44 ff.; 1962, 59; 1964, 324 ff. — indeed the 1959 work is *The sound pattern of Russian* (cf. the promised *The sound pattern of English*) a Sapir-reminiscent title). Chomsky's general definition of the distinctive-feature inventory

---

[23] So Chomsky (1964, 941-943); Chomsky-Halle (1965, 98, 114 — esp. "the syntactic component generates a 'surface structure' which consists of a string of formatives ... and a Phrase-marker ... of this string").

[24] So Thorne (1965, 75); but his scorn of pattern-discovery is not echoed by Chomsky-Halle (1965, 103) who accept it as an aim, merely insisting on its being based on 'assumptions' which have been properly tested for 'adequacy'.

[25] This base is the essentially universal Jakobson-Fant-Halle theory of binary oppositions of distinctive features. See now Chomsky-Halle (1965, 120 ff.). It serves as the organized phonetic 'alphabet', providing the items upon which the phonological rules work directly, with no necessary interposition of tradi-traditional phonemes, on the path from systematic phonemics to systematic phonetics. Halle (1959, 34 f.) sees 'hierarchy' ensuing when 'matrix' is mapped on to branching diagrams.

('universal phonetic alphabet') makes of it a super-overall-pattern (1964, 945); but the presentation is a highly idiosyncratic matrix, or pair of matrices. Although the mathematician's matrix is no more than a rectangular assembly of numbers (however the ordering is motivated), the linguist normally writes in a rationale, in the form of co-ordinated dimensions. One thinks of the 'rhyme-tables' employed for syllable-description in classical Chinese phonology (cf. G. B. Downer, *TPhS* 1963, 132 ff.), where the gridding is of ⟨initial consonants⟩ × ⟨tones and vowel-grades⟩. Less relevant are uses of matrix presentation for marginally linguistic purposes like code-breaking: one recalls Ventris' 'Work-Notes', gridding the consonant × vowel values for the signs of the Linear B script. But the transformationalists (accustomed to saying 'sentence' when they mean 'utterance', and 'context' when they mean 'environment') apply the term 'matrix' to a (horizontal) succession of (vertical) check-lists, the succession being externally determined as the sequence of segments in particular sentences. (The two matrices — 'classificatory' and 'phonetic' — differ merely in representing the stages before and after the phonological rules have realized the 'categories' (assigned to segments) into features (comprising phones). Halle actually equates features and categories (1964, 332); and he and Chomsky have differed as to whether empty cells are permissible at least in the prior matrix (Halle, ibid; Chomsky, 1964, 85; cf. Halle, 1959, 30; and see also Robert D. Wilson, *Journal of Linguistics* 2, 1966, 200). Hence, there is no difference of substance, for our purposes, between the matrices). This unique use of segment-succession as a dimension is, not surprisingly, ignored by Halle when he gets down to business (e.g. 1959, 45); and the atopological 'ingredients' of the phonic language need no such misleading rectangular format (indeed, unused format). In other words, these transformational matrices represent a mésalliance of unpatterned Chomskian grammar and incidentally patterned Hallean phonology.

It has been our purpose to locate and identify the types of patterning inherent in some general linguistic theories; it has not seemed worth while offering a judgement on relative efficiency. The conditions of equal and consistent interpretation and application are lacking. Let us now turn to history, where a value judgement might be approached. It may be counted as common opinion that comparative historical language study proceeds by three stages. Of these, the first is a theoretically and empirically adequate description of each language which is to be used in the subsequent comparative processes; and here, clearly, pattern is to be assessed precisely as the chosen descriptive model allows. Enough has been said on that score. The second stage is internal reconstruction,[26] the unilingual comparison, most commonly within grammatical paradigms, which yields the phonological elements (again commonly of the sequences which form the paradigmatic terms, now in their pre-morphophonemic shape) restored to a more honest and fit-for-interlingual-citation condition, as one might say. So far we have found nothing new.

But at the third stage, comparative reconstruction, pattern appears in a new guise, a kind of power-tool capable of fashioning an artefact (for that, surprisingly enough, is what each finding of historical linguistics really is, commonly susceptible to nothing more than personal, and even aesthetic, critical reaction). Indo-European offers several sectors which are instructive in this respect. Of the two discussed below, the first permits a partial 're-super-imposition' of a type 2 pattern in PIE, the second rather allows a reduction to a type 1 matrix — but a cost of special pleading and 'appeal to type 3' which may seem to an unprejudiced judge to be exorbitant. The following remarks are offered merely demonstratively: the reader must decide which approaches, and which results, to praise or blame.

Nothing could be more chaotic than the apparent distribution of secondary nasal elements in the morphophonemics of the PIE verb, if reconstruction is hampered by being limited to the Greek and Latin reflexes (which are no longer morphophonemic, except vestigially and spasmodically, in Latin: cf. the various stems of, respectively, *iungō*, *pingō* and *rumpō*). We find stem extensions in

[26] On which see H. M. Hoenigswald (1944; and 1965, 34 ff., with the references there cited, fn. 16); one may ignore Kuryłowicz's recent laxer use of the term.

$-n^e/_o$- $(-n̥^e/_o$-), $-nā/ă$-, and $-nū/ŭ$- $(-nu̯$-?), we find infixation of $-n$- (after a semivowel), and we find an idiosyncratic Greek combination (in ἀνδάνω etc. as against ἁμαρτάνω etc.) of infix $-n$- and affix $-n̥^e/_o$- — cf. Armenian *lkʻanem* — (a combination which has all the signs of a polysyllabic prosody) — such is the harvest. Kuryłowicz's solution of the problem posed by Hittite *harnikzi*, *harninkanzi*[27] replaces the $-n$- infix-form by the alternating $-né-/-n$-. But it is only the advent of the Sanskrit comparanda that puts any sense into this mélange of what were originally present stem formants. One arranges the removal of excrescences — block additions, probably as in *math-nắti*, *stigh-nóti* (cf. Greek extension of *nū/ŭ* to ὄρ-νυμι, δείκ-νυμι etc.) — and of productive suffixal variation, as in *aśnắti/aśnóti*; and of analogical extension to other root shapes, as to *anákti*; and of the VIIIth conjugational class, which in all probability wholly derives from a false analysis of *tanóti* (originally *$tn̥$-né-u-ti*, cf. *tanú-*, *tenuis*; then as if *tan-óti*). Then, at last, two major insights become possible. First, that a form like *yuñjánti* is derivable equally from *$i̯u$-n-g-énti* and from *$i̯ung$-ónti*, and thus the latter, thematic, declension (as if from *TRnT-é/o*-) may well have evolved from morphological misunderstanding in the zero grade of the athematic *Tr-né/n-T*- (passing from VIIth to VIth class, in Sanskrit terms). Secondly, that *TRnH-énti* (third plural zero grade form of *TRnéH-ti*) may by a similar meta-derivation give rise, with the disappearance of the laryngeal as such, to a new thematic type *TRn-é/o*- (hence the Greek and Latin $-n^e/_o$- forms).[28] Now the PIE statement can be reduced to a simple 'resuperimpositive' pattern-formula (let us, ironically, express it as a context-sensitive T-rule):

[27] 1957, 221. De Saussure saw that the vowel, when present, belongs to the preceding nasal: cf. now Cowgill (1963, 252).

[28] This is a much abridged account of a complex problem: Watkins (1965, 184) has a similar idea of $-nH\bar{o}$ > $-n\bar{o}$ etc. in Latin, though I do not share his idea of a regular phonetic $a > i$ shift. Cf. Puhvel (1960), and Cowgill's review of that work (1963). Puhvel's division of $-ne-H$- verbs into $-ne-A$- and $-ne-O$- types is vulnerable by the general considerations of chapter 5 below. Cardona (1961) reasonably corrects the notion that the κάμνω type is immediately formed with a suffix $-nā$, and replaces this with $-n^e/_o$; but, as is clear from the discussion above, it comes to the same thing in the end.

$$T\left[R \Rightarrow R\begin{Bmatrix}né\\n\end{Bmatrix}\right]\begin{Bmatrix}u\\T\\H\end{Bmatrix}.$$

The Greek and Latin shapelessness can be taken back either to suggestive confusion (evidenced by Sanskrit) or to vestigial simplicity (evidenced by Hittite), but then further to clear patterning in PIE — although the rule is subject to lexical limitation, and roots like *bhug, *bhidh do not obey it. It seems Lehmann is justified, at least in part of the field, in his view that 'the forms we reconstruct will have to be symmetrical, as are, for example, Benveniste's PIE roots' (1954, 103).

But this eminently satisfying result of pattern application suffers a setback if one considers the formation of infinitives in IE ('infinitive' here being a blanket term for the form-scatter of nominalizations or semi-nominalizations of verbal roots which may then be grammatically fragmented in attested languages into different but linked classes; 'infinitives', 'supines', 'gerunds' and so forth). Latin gives an indication of the messiness supposedly concomitant with lengthy evolution: its relevant forms (ignoring the *-tūrum* problem) are:

-ī	< ? Ø⌒*ei* or *ai*
rī	< ? *s*⌒*ei* or *ai*
-re(-se)	< ? *s*⌒*i*
-tum(-tū)	< ? *tu*⌒*m* or:

— with an *-i-er* form of uncertain origin, and sporadic nuisances like *fi-erī*. Sanskrit is a little tidier, if only by its reduction of infinitives, in the normal syntactical scope of that term, to the single form *-tum*; but some noun-formants (e.g. *-van-*) linger on the fringe of relevance, and the *tu̯* base is visible in the 'gerund' *-tvā* and 'gerundive' *-tavya*. The *-ya* formant cuts no ice (for PIE) in this sector, nor do the Vedic variants *-yā* (gd.), *tu̯a-*, *-enya-*, *-āyya-* (gdv.; cf. Skt. *-anīya*). The full range of infinitive possibilities (with differing placing on the clines ⟨frequent → rare⟩ and ⟨verbals → nominals⟩) in Vedic is, however, more striking and more defeating. This range, and that of Hittite (using the forms

TABLE 1

IE infinitive formations: Formula =⌒(e)Xy; (e)X = noun-stem-form-ant; y = case (or adverb) ending (Ø, i, ei, m)

PIE values for *X*		Reflexes in			
Simple	Complex	Hittite	Vedic	Greek	Latin
Ø		—	dr̥ś-é	(?-s-ai) (?eîp-ai)	-ī(?agᵉ/₀+¹)
i		—	dr̥ś-áye	—	(?-i + er)
s		—	áy-ase	?lū-sai ?the-s	-is-se (age)-re etc. (amā)-rī etc.
	sei̯	—	?róhi-ṣyai	—	—
	ser/n	-eš-šar (n) -eš-na-aš(g)	ne-ṣáni	-ein (?theinai)	
(u̯)	u̯er/n(t)	-war -wan -uu̯arᵃ -wanzi	?dā-váne	—	—
(m)	?mer/n(t)	-manzi	?dá̆-mane	domen domenai	—
	tei̯	—	vi-táye i-tyai	—	—
	teu̯	—	é-tave é-tavā u -tvā -tum	?-téo-	-tum
	ter/n	adatar i-tar adanna	dhar-tári	—	(iter, *itinis) -ndu-
	dh(e)i̯	—	śucá-dhyai	-sthai? -thi	—
?n		—	-ane -áni (rare, doubtful)	lu-thēnai leluk-enai phere-n	—

ᵃ genitive = -uu̯aš; therefore *X* = u̯?

judged to be relevant in the discussions of Ose, 1944, and Kammenhuber, 1954-55), is included in Table 1.

Clearly, some structural sense emerges from this picture. PIE
offers a limited range of nominalizing suffixes (X) and these in
turn attract a limited range of what may reasonably be called
case-markers (y). But the gaps are manifest (or, if this were made
into a generative formula-pattern, the depth — i.e. the complexity
of progress by ordered rules — is curiously variable): e.g. note
the absence of '$X = t$'. Apophony is *ad libitum*; and the relations of co-selection between variant X and y forms are haphazard.
Presumably the responsion, the geometrical satisfaction, if any,
will have to be sought in 'pre-IE' or the like.

Now, what of Greek in particular?[29] It stares out at once from
the graphic evidence that the values of y are reduced to Ø and
ai, and that the latter appears to serve as a phonologically and
morphologically 'frozen' (infinitive) class-marker — Benveniste's
'post-position' or Meillet's 'élément accessoire'. Secondly, where
X is complex (i.e. disyllabic) there is no ablaut, the guṇa grade
being generalized except in the PIE zero grade formant *dhį̄*;
nobody is likely to disinter the unnecessary speculations involving
-mnai, *-snai*. Thirdly, the values of X are drastically cut. Thus
Greek has already actualized the PIE possibilities in the direction of
greater cohesion and compactness; and Table 2 (which is a morph-
matrix) shows, with the usual reservations, the sort of minimum
formal evidence which may be adduced.

At this point we may exercise our ingenuity, in four phases, on
this already more tractable material.

PHASE 1. — For ⁀*ųenai* the only direct testimony is Cyprian
towenai (*toena* in an inscription which omits digamma regularly), and
this has long been suspect, for several good reasons. There is no sign
of, say, *ϑεϝεναι anywhere; Umbrian *purdouitu* and Skt. *dhūrv-áṇe*
seem to show that *ų* represents in those languages a final consonant
of a multisyllabic root; and *ų* operates elsewhere as a glide in
Cyprian. Now Cowgill (1964, esp. 354), in a paper where the

---

[29] One can afford to ignore exploded etymologies, like *$eid^e/_os + thai$*, and
dialectal vagaries such as Rhodian and Epicharmian *-mein*, Cretan *-me:n*.

TABLE 2
Greek infinitives

X	$y = \varnothing$	$y = ai$
$X = \varnothing$	—	?lūs-ai ?eîp-ai
$X = s$	—	?lū-sai ?kale-sai
$X = n$	phere-n (Locr.)	lu-thē-nai di-do-nai
$X = sen$	pherein[a] ekee (Myc.)[b]	?theinai ?dounai
$X = ɥen$	—	?theinai ?to-we-na-i (Cypr.)
$X = men$	domen	domenai
$X = dhị$	—	?lue-sthai

[a] Normal result of -esen in Attic, etc.
[b] *seg'he+sen > ekhe-en, spelt e-ke-e.

dubious matters lie in another quarter, cogently establishes the glide value of $ɥ$ in this dialectal and morphophonological environment, and restores to the problem the simpler choice between reconstructing δο‿εναι or δο‿ϲεναι — simpler, however paradoxical it may sound, because the sole testimony for -ϝεναι now vanishes. Benveniste's rightness in calling this business of *towenai* 'le vieux et vain débat', and wrongness in seeing -ϝ-εναι and -ϝεναι as different stages of history, are both demonstrated.[30] But if "the most economical solution ... is to suppose that proto-Greek had only two active infinitive formants (outside the s-aorist)" (Cowgill, 1964, 357), it is better to set up 'South Greek' -*sen*, alongside -*men* elsewhere, rather than -*en*, -*men*. An evolution of -*sen* to -*en* is very credible, the reverse less so; and Cowgill eventually opts so, (cf. his well-argued fn. 65 with the discussion preceding it), seeing

[30] Cowgill dismisses the evidence of all cognate forms which show a $ɥ$ element, on the grounds that the labial arises from *a*) special suffixes, like *dā-ván-*, gathā-Av. *vídvanōi* (*εἰδϝεναι is not found); *b*) special histories (PIE -ō > Balt. Slav. -*oɥ* > *ɥo/aɥ*); *c*) special root-forms (Italic *dŏɥ-*).

difficulty only in the clearly early infinitive of εἰμί. Here the root *es* plus the infinitive-marker *-sen(ai)* must result in the dialectal variants *ἐccεν(αι) and *ἐcεν(αι) and the troublesome εἶναι (and W. Ionic and Chian εἶν) then poses a phonological riddle. Let us, however, invoke a procedure of historical morphological development which may be called 'dovetailing', where identity of the final element of a root and the initial element of a suffix (for instance) allows a phonological overlap. (Indeed, this structural possibility may prompt a deliberate choice between competing derivative forms — a matter which is ventilated in what follows.) With this

tool — that is, in this case, $*e\begin{vmatrix}s\\s\end{vmatrix}enai > {}*esenai$, giving the inherited single *-s-* needed to explain εἶναι — the last obstacle is cleared; and we may remove a whole rank ($X = yen$) from the Greek matrix, and fill all the cells of the '$X = sen$' rank (for Myc. *ekee*, Att. φέρειν display *-sen*).

PHASE 2. — The forms εἶπαι, χεῦαι need not detain us. Whatever the detailed history of this aorist formation it is clear that its paradigmatic formal associates are homalized, and the apparent suffix *-ai* is no argument against a general adoption of *-sai* in this tense and voice. More crucial is the precise analysis of λῦcαι, δεῖξαι, καλέcαι and the rest. The *s*-aorist is notably abnormal in IE (e.g. it is, as has often been pointed out, the sole athematic formation which lacks a properly ablauting predesinential syllable). Watkins (1962), following Meillet's clues, sees a middle voice origin for this late and intrusive formant — which makes relevant the dual role of λῦcαι etc. as active infinitive and middle imperative. Now it may be that 'dovetailing' is present here also. It is this process, allied both to haplology and to 'enhanced graphic recognition' (cf. Hitt. *har-ni-in-kan-zi*, discussed above), which selects the morphemes *medic* and *care* (and cashes in on the potential metanalysis *medi + care*) for the United States social scheme 'medicare'[31]

---

[31] Of course one must establish this process within the *grammatical* history of each language: cf. Eng. $eigh\begin{vmatrix}t\\t\end{vmatrix}y > eighty$ (not *eightty* as *nine-ty*, etc.);

(cf. *service* + *center* > *servicenter*); or which may explain the awkward form *senātus* (*senaH-* (or *seneA-*)+*-ā-tus*?), and which probably accounts for our hesitation over Lat. *minuō* (have we *mei/mi* plus block-addition *-nu-* or verbalization of original noun *minu-s*? Probably both). It is possible to see in λῦσαι the powerful *-sa-* marker plus a locative *-i*: but this formation would sit on the Greek 'pattern' like a carbuncle. One might split the form into λῦc-αι ($X = \emptyset$); but εἶπαι cannot be counted on for help, and compactness is lost. To posit $^{*}lu\begin{array}{|c|} \hline sa \\ \hline sa \\ \hline \end{array}i$ is at once to preserve the permeating tendency of *-sa* in this tense-paradigm (only the subjunctive remains unscathed) and to ensure the cell-filler (*sai*) of the intersection, in the matrix, of '$X - s$', '$y = ai$'. The rank '$X = \emptyset$' can now be omitted.

PHASE 3. — As the double use of λῦcαι shows, imperatives in IE languages may draw on infinitive forms (or infinitives may extend their functional range). Hence we can invoke the imperatives in -θι (ἴθι, φάθι, and, by a dissimilatory process, the λύθητι type) to fill the '$y = \emptyset$' cell in the '$X = dh\underline{i}$' rank. For *-dhi#* will readily give -θι; and *-dhiV* will equally have the reflex *-dh\underline{i}V* > ?-cθV. The latter shift ($dh\underline{i}$ > cθ) is not impossible in Greek where, if *d\underline{i}* results in ζ but also cδ, then an assibilated aspirated apical (if it lacks a special orthographic sign, not to be drawn from an exhausted Semitic repertoire, and so cannot receive graphic notation of its overlapping articulations) might reasonably appear as cθ. But it is unlikely, because *dh\underline{i}* should give *th\underline{i}* and fall in with *t\underline{i}*; and analogy (the effect of the -cθε 2 pl. finite forms, where a 'dh' appears in PIE) must be invoked to clinch the matter; usually *dh\underline{i}* > c, cc, ττ in Greek, as in μέcοc etc. Thus we might perhaps fill the '$X = dhi$' rank, and decrease our gaps yet further.

PHASE 4. — We are left with an apparent emptiness in cell '$y = \emptyset$' in rank '$X = s$': has Greek a relevant morph in -(*e*)*s*? One thinks

---

Skt *áṃha*$\begin{array}{|c|} \hline s \\ \hline s \\ \hline \end{array}u$ > *áṃhasu*. It has affinity with Homeric 'hyphaeresis', and with haplology.

at once of the imperatives θές, ἔς, δός and σχές. Most attempts to explain these away are ludicrous,[32] and here is a perfectly acceptable candidate for the empty cell.

It must be noted, however, that Szemerényi, building on Brugmann's hints, has put forward a very adequate alternative account of these -s imperatives (*Egyetemes Philologiai Közlöny*, 70 [1947], 102-103): namely, a shortened vocalism supervening (perhaps for marking peremptoriness?) on an injunctive *θής etc. (The absence of *στάς goes hand in hand with the employment of forms which are indistinguishable from the injunctive as 'root aorist' in that verb.[33] Hence evolves impv. στῆθι to indicative ἔστης.) Then *θής etc. were displaced as indicatives by the ἔθηκας etc. formation, specialized in imperatival function, and acted as models for a limited extension into thematic forms (σχές — cf. ἐνίσπες). This is a watertight and satisfying evolution.

On the one hand, by the successive phases of applied ingenuity, the complexity and absence of cohesion in the multidimensional pseudo-pattern of PIE infinitive markers has been transformed into a maximally compact Greek scheme,[34] a fully realized and economic matrix as in Table 3 (p. 41).

On the other hand, alternative accounts are neither lacking nor incredible, as has been seen. And the general question arises: is it necessary and justified that we reconstruct this degree of compactness, especially as the progress would then appear to be

---

[32] Brugmann subsequently abandoned his first wild attempt ($< θέ, + τι$ infinitive). Meyer and others have no phonological corroboration for their derivation from *θεθι, although *θετι is not impossible. Schwyzer's notion, $< θέ, + c$ from the indicative, is incredible.

[33] It does not matter what status is assigned to the IE 'injunctive' forms. If theirs is a separate PIE functional category, the θές type is a vestige like the φέρετε imperative; and then the baneful effect of the formally parallel root aorist indicative has been halted in τιθέναι, ἱέναι and διδόναι. If we have in the injunctive merely one special employment of (augmentless) preterital forms, these verbs are unusual in that they have retained the 'modal' and not the indicative function of these particular items.

[34] Mel'chuk (1963, 121) approves 'compactness of description' (*kompaktnost' opisanija*) as an ideal in grammar; but this reflects the relation of the overall 'size' of the grammar (symbols plus rules) to the number of items in the describable totality. There is no spatial aspect involved.

TABLE 3

	$y = \emptyset$	$y = $ ai
$X = $ s	θές, cχές	λῦcαι
$X = $ n	φέρεν	λυθῆναι διδόναι
$X = $ sen	φέρειν δίδουν	θεῖναι δοῦναι
$X = $ men	δόμεν	δόμεναι
$X = $ dhi̯	ἴθι	λύεσθαι

(Guṇa AND zero grades for X are demonstrable, except for ⁀edhi̯, where no inescapable -εθι presents itself, and perhaps ⁀en, where Arc. ἐξίεν, W.Ion. εἶν probably reflect ⁀sen).

bidirectional, from luxuriant formlessness in PIE *both* to full economy in Greek *and* to less mappable vestiges in other IE languages? Probably it is not justified; a matrix does not demand maximum cell-filling or balanced gaps, although one pauses to ask for a calculus of acceptability — that is, below what degree of emptiness does it cease to be a matrix?

Again, the Greek row '$X = n$' is a special development; such a value for X is uncertain for PIE, to put it mildly; and, quite apart from the general credibility of the solutions offered, the multiple origin and dialectal disparity of -*n* and -*nai* in Greek further undermine the power and value of pattern reconstruction.[35] In other words, even more dubious, in a more practical way, is the status of the 'common-Greek' data-source which allows the apparent full matrix patterning in our analysis. The result has depended, in fact, on adducing at least three contemporary états de langue; to rely even on Attic dialect alone would be to introduce some gaps (e.g. at -*en*, -*men* and -*menai*), and any other single

[35] As was hinted above, one can feasibly elicit -*(e)n(ai)* from -*(e)sen(ai)*. East Greek institutionalized -*nai* (λυθῆναι etc.) may well derive from, for instance, γνῶναι < *γνω-εναι < *γνω-cεναι to the model of *θε-cεναι (> θεῖναι). And for West Greek (thematic) -*n*, one may cite, exempli gratia, Günther's (1913, 377 ff.) suggestion — itself of the short-range type of pattern process we call analogy — ϝοικέετε: ϝοικέεν (< *ϝοικει̯-esen):: φέρετε: φέρεν.

dialect would present a worse case. This is to say that recourse has been had to what Hockett calls 'overall pattern', in his third application of the term pattern, an application familiar enough to phoneticians and phonologists.[36] Nevertheless, such a citation of data must mean that the analysis is, at worst, that of a pseudo-language, and, at best, that of a highly homomorphous totalité de langue which possibly represents a sort of variorum inventory within the tacit competence of a native speaker,[37] but which, equally possibly, is merely a convenient historical supposition on the part of scholars puzzled by dialectal likenesses which do not seem to be idiosyncratic innovations (so Coleman, 1963, speaks of like selection from a common Greek 'stock' of features).

And the moral of all this? That ingenuity expended on a search for pattern, of whatever kind, in the comparative stage of historical linguistics at least, is an expression of a personal aesthetic. It may lead to productive analysis. If it produces credible as well as elegant results, it has justified itself. If it does not, no surprise should be felt. If this means that historians do not always follow the same rules, that does not matter. Housman is famous for deriding the textual scholars who clung to the 'authority' of a

[36] The concept was set out by Trager and Smith in 1951, and applied historically by Stockwell (1964, 663 ff.); it separates total inventories (of phonemes etc.) from interacting subsets. Allen (1959, 248) describes how the articulatory relationship between Greek long and short mid vowels may have been conditioned by the shape of the joint triangulated display of the long and short subsystems. He calls this joint display the 'overall pattern' — a usage which, though macro-systemic, is free from the unrealities of the more traditional application, even when that application is only by features and not phonemes. Nonetheless, a 'variorum inventory' as spoken of above may be a valid part of a total grammar (see above, and footnote 14).

[37] The words for 'six', 'seven' and 'ten' in European and Syrian Romānī show three 'comparative reflexes' of voiceless spirants ($š/š$, s/s, $š/s$). The overall pattern, however, corroborates, in the number of distinct items, the information provided by each language separately (i.e. it predicts that two phonological entities are to be reconstructed at an earlier stage). But the correct number of proto-forms is three; we happen to know that Sanskrit has respectively $ṣ, s, ś$. This shows the predictive weakness of overall pattern. The range of PIE dorsal stops may be two in each series (as the individual languages suggest), or three (as the number of comparative reflexes suggests). That in this case the overall pattern also suggests three — what may be called the s type, the k type, and the qu/p type, to cite the voiceless series — is therefore a valueless circumstance.

single manuscript, and for likening their criticism of his own eclectic approach to denunciation of a sound man's method of walking, one who may indeed be seen "putting forth first one foot and then, with strange inconsistency, the other".

REFERENCES

Allen, W.S. 1959, "Some remarks on the structure of Greek vowel systems", *Word* 15, 240-251.

Bloomfield, Leonard 1935, *Language* (British edn., London).

Cardona, George 1961, review of *Evidence for Laryngeals* (1960), *Language* 37, 413-424.

Chomsky, Noam 1964, "The logical basis of linguistic theory" (For this paper and its various editions see *Journal of Linguistics* 1 (1965), 97 fn. 1, and 138 (entries Chomsky 1964a, 1964b, 1964c).

—— 1965, *Aspects of the theory of syntax* (Cambridge, Mass.).

—— 1967, "Some general properties of phonological rules", *Language* 43, 102-128.

Chomsky, Noam and Halle, Morris 1965, "Some controversial questions in phonological theory", *Journal of Linguistics* 1, 97-138.

Coleman, R.G.G. 1963, "The dialect geography of Ancient Greece", *TPhS*, 58-126.

Collinge, N.E. 1963, "The Greek use of the term 'middle' in linguistic analysis", *Word* 19, 232-241.

—— 1965, "Some linguistic paradoxes", *Journal of Linguistics* 1, 1-12.

Cowgill, Warren C. 1963, review of Puhvel (1960), *Language* 39, 248-270.

—— 1964, "The supposed Cypriote optatives *duwánoi* and *dŏkoi*", *Language* 40, 344-365.

Entwistle, W.J. 1953, *Aspects of Language* (London).

Greenberg, Joseph H. 1963 (ed.), *Universals of Language* (Cambridge, Massachusetts). (Cf. 1966 'Language universals' in *Current trends in linguistics* III, The Hague, 61-112).

Günther, Richard 1913, "Zu den dorischen Infinitivendungen", *Indogermanische Forschungen* 32, 372-385.

Halle, Morris 1959, *The sound pattern of Russian* (The Hague).

—— 1962, "Phonology in a generative grammar", *Word* 18, 54-72 (= Fodor, Katz, *The structure of language*, New York, 334-352).

—— 1964, "On the bases of phonology", in Fodor, Katz, *The structure of language*, New York, 324-333.

Halliday, M.A.K. 1964, "The linguistic study of literary texts", *Proceedings of the 9th International Congress of Linguists*, 302-307.

Haugen, Einar 1962, "On diagramming vowel systems", *Proceedings of the Fourth International Congress of Phonetic Sciences*, 648-654.

Hockett, Charles F. 1958, *A Course in Modern Linguistics* (New York).

Hoenigswald, H.M. 1944, "Internal Reconstruction", *Studies in Linguistics*, 2, 78-87.

Hoenigswald, H. M. 1965, "Phonetic Reconstruction", *Proceedings of the 5th International Congress of Phonetic Sciences*, 25-42.

Householder, Fred W. Jr. 1965, "On some recent claims in phonological theory", *Journal of Linguistics* 1, 13-34.

Jakobson, Roman 1957, "Typological studies and their contribution to historical comparative linguistics", *Proceedings of the Eighth International Congress of Linguists*, 17-25.

—— 1962, *Selected Writings* I (The Hague).

Kammenhuber, Annelies 1954-55, "Studien zur Hethitischen Infinitivsystem", *Mitteilungen des Instituts für Orientforschung* II, 44-77; 245-265; 403-444; III, 31-57; 345-377 (Deutsche Akademie der Wissenschaften, Berlin).

Katz, Jerrold J. and Postal, Paul M. 1964, *An integrated theory of linguistic descriptions* (Cambridge, Massachusetts).

Kuryłowicz, Jerzy 1957, "Le Hittite", *Proceedings of the Eighth International Congress of Linguists*, 216-243.

Lamb, Sydney M. 1966, *Outline of stratificational grammar* (Washington, D.C.).

Lehmann, Winfred P. 1954, review of W. Brandenstein (ed.), *Studien zur indogermanischen Grundsprache*, *Language* 30, 99-104.

—— 1962, *Historical Linguistics* (New York).

Longacre, Robert E. 1964, *Grammar discovery procedures* (The Hague).

Lyons, J. 1963, *Structural Semantics* (Oxford).

McIntosh, A. 1961, "Patterns and ranges", *Language* 37, 325-337.

Malone, Kemp 1962, "On symmetry in phonemic analysis", *Language* 38, 142-146.

Matthews, P. H. 1961, "Transformational Grammar", *Archivum Linguisticum* 13, 196-209.

—— 1965, "The inflectional component of a word-and-paradigm grammar", *Journal of Linguistics* 1, 139-171.

—— 1966, "Latin" in *Word Classes = Lingua* 17, 153-181.

Mel'chuk, I. A. 1963, "O standartnoj forme lingvističeskix opisanij", *Voprosy Jazykoznanija* 1963, 1, 113-123.

Mulder, J. W. F. 1965, "Some operations with sets in language", *Foundations of Language* 1, 14-29.

Ose, Fritz 1944, "Supinum und Infinitiv im Hethitischen", *Mitteilungen der Vorderasiatisch-Aegyptischen Gesellschaft* (47.1), 1-88 (Leipzig).

Pike, Kenneth L. 1962, "Dimensions of grammatical constructions", *Language* 38, 221-244. (Cf. also *Anthropological Linguistics* 5 (1963), 1-23).

—— 1966, "A guide to publications related to tagmemic theory", *Current Trends in Linguistics* III (The Hague), 365-394.

Puhvel, Jaan 1960, *Laryngeals and the Indo-European Verb* (Berkeley and Los Angeles).

Quirk, Randolph 1965, "Descriptive statement and serial relationship", *Language* 41, 205-217.

Robins, R. H. 1957, "Dionysius Thrax and the Western grammatical tradition", *TPhS* 67-106.

Stevick, Robert D. 1963, "The biological model and historical linguistics", *Language* 39, 159-169.

Stockwell, Robert P. 1964, "On the utility of an overall pattern in historical English phonology", *Proceedings of the 9th International Congress of Linguists*, 663-671.

Strang, Barbara 1962, *Modern English Structure* (London).

Thorne, J.P. 1965, review of Postal's *Constituent structure*, *Journal of Linguistics* 1, 73-76.

Watkins, Calvert 1962, *IE origins of the Celtic Verb*, I: *the sigmatic aorist* (The Dublin Institute for Advanced Studies).

—— 1965, "Evidence in Italic", *Evidence for Laryngeals*[2] (The Hague), 181-189.

3. NAMES AND RESISTANCE TO SOUND SHIFTS*

It is a commonplace that names tend to be idiosyncratic in their syntactical and morphological patterning; it is worth noting that they also frequently display an abnormal reflex in relation to the sound shifts of the language or dialect of which they form part. The examples which follow are taken from the classical languages, with all the customary checks and reservations as to graphic-phonic relationship. In sequence on a rising scale of intransigence, the phenomena are these:

1. Deviation from the normal pattern of evolution, because of some special shift; this interference may follow a lexical cue or a phonological one. For the former, cf. the tradition that the Greek lexeme *penth-* induces *Pentheus* from earlier *Tentheus*, without justifying elsewhere a shift [t]>[p] (such popular etymology is common). For the latter, it suffices to mention hypocoristic gemination, rare outside actual names. This type of additional shift may, however, develop a virtual regularity of its own (one may state a Thessalian loss of [-ri-], in environment *V-C*, in names: *A(ri)-stódāmos, La(ri)saíois*). Again, vowel harmony is scarcely a Greek trait; yet in names Attic transforms e.g. *Erkhomenós* to *Orkhomenós, Wheká-dāmos* becomes Attic *Aká-dēmos*, Thessalian and Boeotian *Weké-dāmos*.

2. Deviation from the synchronic (description-)pattern, as if names 'contract out' of the regular phonology of their language. So Latin [#ŋn-] appears (apart from loanwords and loannames, and the unique *gnārus*, on which in any case see Cicero, *Orator*

---

* First published in *Proceedings of the Eighth International Congress of Onomastic Sciences* (The Hague, 1966), 94-95.

47, 158) only in *Gnaeus, Gnīpho, Gnātia* — and if this were a mere graphism, the abbreviation *Cn.* would be doubly odd. This anomaly can also be expressed as an exception to a diachronic shift ([#ŋn-] >[#n-]); but the possibility of catering decriptively for these cases by a separate entry in a polysystemic analysis of the language may justify excusing them from liability to the historical change, so to speak, thus mitigating their resistance to shift as such. Where instances are individual, like *Poseidā́n* occurring in a Gk. *-tei-* dialect (Argolic), we infer a loan (and here the displacement of the presumed native form). In these cases there is no homalizing of the names to the normal phonotactic pattern, or to uniformity with other co-instances of the same lexeme, as when Phocian has *Histió* against regular *hest-*, or Lesbian *Dāmokrétō* against regular *-krit-*.

Is there then a degree of 'sacrosanctity' attaching to names, especially loan-names, inhibiting conformity to normal evolution? Not, of course, if there is no general synchronic nonconformity involved (so Attic admits *Hermês* in that form), nor if no diachronic shift is still operative which could amend the situation (as Attic leaves alone the morphophonologically odd *Pán*). Here there is nothing to resist; and yet only the deduction from comparative evidence that these names have succumbed to some non-Attic shift somewhere encourages us, possibly unduly, to read them as non-Attic themselves (respectively Ionic and Arcadian). Arcadian *Brókhus* (< *mrg'hw-*) fits here: is it an Aeolic loan or a Mycenaean vestige? Where, however, an amending shift is still, or becomes, valid, an ambivalent attitude is visible: a shift felt as highly 'national' affects even loan-names—so Laconian changes (Arcadian) *Posoidā́n* to *Pohoidā́n*, Thessalian Attic ending *-dôn* in this name to *-doun —*, whereas an 'imported' shift is resisted in respect of names, as if these enshrine local speech identity — so in Rhodian (-)*xeinos* in names alone survives the incursion of Attic (-)*xenos*.

3. a. Simple resistance to shift. A name becomes a stereotype, insulated from 'faits de langue'. So in Latin we have the ethnic *Poenus* (despite adjectival *Pūnicus*); likewise, in Greek personal names with final element '-horse', the inherited non-aspiration of

the composition form -*ippos* (*A'lkippos Leúkippos* etc.) resists the usual Greek innovation (*híppos*).

b. Tendency to resist even congeneric analogy. This prevents, for instance, a levelling between pairs like *Poenus* and *Pūnicus* or *Falerii* and *Faliscī* (cf. *Firenze* and *Fiorentini*) with functional relation; and inhibits attraction by formal similarity, as the common name-suffix -*icius* does not disturb *Minucius*. Only if the affecting form is very frequent, as well as assisted by vowel harmony, does the affected form succumb — so *séptimus* produces *Septímius* (against expected *Septúmius*) but rare *póstimus* fails with *Postúmius* (see Coleman, *TPhS*, 1962, 88-92); the fact that *Póstumus* arises suggests that the analogy of *Postumius* and the vocalic attraction are here reinforced by popular etymology (cf. the spelling *posthumus*); the name then holds the epithet, as a technical term, in the -*u*-form.

It would seem that names are characterized by a strong tendency to independence and nonconformity, in relation equally to shift patterns, to particular shifts, and even to 'organized resistance' to shifts. And there remain, and historical phonologists should not be surprised at, isolated phenomena like the predominant spelling *Themisthoklês* on Athenian ostraka, which represents a pronunciation previously unguessed at.

4. PREHISTORY VIA LANGUAGE: SOME GUIDELINES

If descriptive linguistics has recently shifted its centre of interest from taxonomy to competence and from elements of language to mental processes of native speakers, it has had some shade of a precedent in historical linguistics. There, shunting has long been practised between the reconstruction of linguistic forms and the reconstruction of the prehistory, and linguistically relevant ambience, of the users of those forms. Descriptivists consort happily now with mathematicians, psychologists and philosophers; historians have always turned to — and have recently increased their yield from — archaeologists, anthropologists and ecologists.

Yet even in so well-cultivated a field as Indo-European our ignorance of 'the Indo-Europeans' remains profound. What we know, we know with gross uncertainty as to time and place. Hence we are ever in the debt both of the many who constantly increase our factual resources and of the few who intermittently lay bare our theoretical poverty or disingenuousness. The procession of known contributors of the first sort, and the mass and solidity of their findings, can be seen and felt in the discussions and bibliographies which abound on the subject. There is no need to rehearse them here. But on the side of theory the probings towards a methodology are rarer; one can quickly number those who have sought a rationale which will make sure sense of the facts. This area of study — call it, with Pisani, 'linguistic palaeontology' (a term first appearing in Meyer-Lübke, 1900) or what you will — has been marked by a distaste for rigour. There have attempts at regulating what is necessarily a semantic and almost entirely a lexical discipline, which aims at furnishing the proto-situation with flora and fauna, social institutions and implements. But the attempts have tended to be subjective and to rest on undefined axioms. The lexical level is the most shifting in language (notwithstanding notions of 'lexical core') and the least identifying,[1] and more codification is needed. Rules, preferably in some such form as Boolean expressions, are to be prized as nuggets; and a formulation of the ground logic is immensely superior to the intuitive thumb.

When Pedersen reviews the progress of nineteenth century scholarship in this field (1962, 319-339), he displays the data and awards marks for relevance sensibly enough (*in parvo*). As to rules however, he is content to state one and imply another. These are worth testing for strength. The former declares that nothing can be inferred from the non-occurrence of a context-word;[2] that is, if there is no PIE word for 'tiger', this fact does not rule out the tiger as a proto-item. The reason given is that a word must be lost when its users move to an area where its referent is absent (a principle accepted as the norm also by Thieme, 1953, 545). This ignores the frequent maintenance and re-application of a word to a fresh referent, like the American robin. Indeed, given the validity of the notion of 'cultural slot' discussed below, this frequency is a regularity. A study of the 'salmon' word, or several tree names, disproves Pedersen's point; and cousin to this re-application is the

---

[1]   Hence e.g. Troubetzkoy's reaction, in the posthumous paper, 1939, 81 ff., was to deny all PIE cultural identity and genetic connexion, and to rely on comparatively late areal contacts to explain shared items. This extremism, shown also by Pisani, Altheim and the school of Marr, is unjustified in the face of detailed sound congruence of most of the cited equations with the systematic findings of comparative phonology, operating historically on morphologically located comparanda. But Indo-Europeanists invite this kind of suspicion. Another source of distortion is to approach the problem with sociological prejudices.

[2]   Some terms here used need glossing. A 'context-word' — the reason for this name is given in what follows above — is a lexical element in a relevant language used in palaeontological reconstruction; the situational referent is called an 'item'. 'Commonalty' means an item's original existence within the common experience of the ancestors of the speakers of all the IE languages (to use this field as a paradigm), at a time accessible to historical linguistics. 'Proto-situation' is the total contextual ambience within which that experience was shared; and 'proto-item' is a convenient shorthand expression for 'item in proto-situation' (and *not* 'item reconstructed by comparison of items').

usage which fathers 'Spanish burgundy' or 'New Zealand cheddar'. There is, however, a more crucial consideration. If no trace is to be found of interlingual formal cognateness in a context-word series, the item concerned is not ascribable to the proto-situation. This deserves stronger emphasis, as a positive inference: the proto-situation is to be denied the item. The loss of a common word for 'tiger' may be a reflex of a total ecological shift of the as yet undifferentiated Indo-Europeans; but because the loss is total the shift sets up a barrier beyond which linguistic search cannot penetrate. If archaeology succeeds here, it is on its own; linguistics has merely the duty of presenting its own prima facie case, positive and negative. What is beyond the barrier is irrelevant to our discipline;[3] and PIE is indifferently 'post-tiger IE' and 'post-non-tiger IE', to put it quaintly. The rule is useless.

Pedersen's implicit rule is: if a cognate context-word is limited to languages which are neighbours during the historical period, it cannot be more than 'dialectal' in PIE, and its item is not a proto-item. This axiom tacitly accepts historical contiguity as firm PIE dialectal-areal relationship, which is like putting one's weight on an ice floe.[4] The most that is being said is that anything short of cognateness of word plus near-identity of referent, across all the IE stocks, imposes greater or less doubt on the candidacy of the item for 'proto' status. Which is true but trite.

Among the more recent, but still traditional, handlings of the problem is that of Thieme, whose concession to theory is to outline what he calls the "least objectionable methods" for situational reconstruction (1953, 543-548). These reduce to a search for word-item relations which betray shift, in so far as they are positive. An identical relation in several languages, with cognate forms and contextual identity of the item, characterizes the item as 'original'.

---

[3] As Meillet said (1948, 323), "la linguistique n'a pas le moyen de remplacer l'histoire". Therefore Crossland (1957, 17) is right to define the Indo-European homeland as "the region which the Indo-Europeans occupied immediately before their dispersal".

[4] Pedersen also invokes peripheral retention, to cope with non-contiguous likeness; but note what is said by, and on, Crossland.

Any other item as referent is held to be a replacement, either as a comparable cultural item or (to take a type-instance) as an element in the name of an artefact of equivalent function to some predecessor but of new material. And a replacement signals the unacceptability for 'proto' status of the context within which its users live and speak. This is all very sound; but the use made of it is purely negative, aimed at answering, negatively and by elimination, the question "where did the speakers of the language presumed by the PIE complex of systems live"? Not, one may note, the question "what PIE situational description can be offered as a datum to archaeologists and anthropologists"? Thieme rejects, as *Urheimat*, areas in which occur items of short-range dissemination with clearly non-IE names (e.g. Gk. *kuparissos*, Lat. *cupressus*); and he excludes Greece (546) because of the geographical impossibility of originality there of what is optimistically regarded as both a known and a critical word-item linkage, the 'beech' word and the beech tree.[5] A satisfactory methodology should promote reconstruction of contextual positives.

Somewhat more delicate awareness of principles — at least of the shortcomings of previously recommended methods — appears in Crossland's treatment (1957, esp. 21 f.). He characterizes as a rare luxury a reconstruction which rests on full-range cognateness of words combining with full-range identity of referents. Other lifelines are viewed with healthy suspicion. The prima facie case for according most weight to those languages which have early records or display minimal change of form is not to be trusted too far. Too much (as critics of lexicostatistics have shown) can interfere with rate of change, accelerating and decelerating. It is admitted that like phenomena in peripheral languages may show retention of features original to a now dispersed mother-tongue; but the historical positioning of the evidential languages does not need to reflect the order of movement from the centre, and tells us nothing (and even obscures what is to be told) about interim placings and 'areal' effects. Peripheral languages certainly keep clean

[5]   See e.g. Friedrich, 1966, 3. The phonetics of the 'beech' word puzzle honest historians.

of 'post-proto' innovations assignable to their genetic group;[6] but the shifts we can see in them may, as such, have involved more than one peripheral language, depending on contiguity at the relevant time. Hence emerges a body of pseudo-evidence, applicable only to some transitory sub-group.

At the third American conference on Indo-European (held in Philadelphia, April 1966) the general topic was indeed 'The Indo-Europeans'. Yet only one paper out of twenty-seven consciously concerned itself with the procedures and regulations of linguistic enquiry. The archaeologists produced theoretical situations and an actual culture ('Kurgan') to fit Indo-Europeanists' needs (and to supply a third millennium link with Caucasian Kartvelian); comparative studies of law, folklore and religion assisted orthodox comparative philology to delineate a credible PIE world. But the linguists mostly restricted their purview to corners of the field and avoided explicit justification of their predications. All the more welcome, therefore, is the set of postulates enunciated by Wyatt in his contribution (1966). These do much to control and fructify deduction; that they do not do more is a shortcoming partly arising from their being tailored to a particular problem (the Indo-Europeanization of Greece) and partly from a reluctance to appreciate the complexities of even the most basic theorems of this discipline. It is asserted, by way of general appendage to the axioms below, that if an IE name is attached to a cultural innovation the IE 'invaders' cannot have preceded that innovation in the area (but came with it or found it on arrival). Ignoring the imprecision of the term 'innovation',[7] this pronouncement seems to state that a word does not survive anywhere if it precedes its

[6] This point, if now practically a cliché, is crucial to the genealogical model. For some logical implications, see Collinge, 1965, 8-10. It must be understood that an innovation is non-IE because the language concerned is marginal, and not the other way about, in the final analysis; marginal status is assigned when a language (or group) is, isogloss-wise, in a pronounced minority.

[7] If the 'invaders' found the item in the new area, the term is relevant to IE studies, but is grossly different in its application from its use in the other case. If they brought the item with them, it is not for that reason, in any sense relevant to IE, an innovation. It could be a non-PIE item and/or word; but those possibilities need separate proof, in respect of an earlier period.

referent in arrival. Now the early Virginian and New England settlers preserved the word *horse* from their pre-colonial experience, and it abides; yet the animal itself was a delayed addition to their American scene. It is neither likely nor material that the inventory and contexts of the language in the mother country should determine word survival in fringe areas. What IS relevant is that a complex time relation subsists between the loss of an object and the loss of its name, and that a culturally central object needs a comparatively long absence before forgetfulness strikes its name from the language. These factors discourage reliance on simple axioms unless they are reduced to, but no further than, minimal deductive complexity. If the data are surprising, one should search for obscure features of historical interference, and not use pseudo-axioms to deny them.

Wyatt's three major postulates are:

(1) A borrowed word, other than a technical term, is not borrowed unless the thing designated is known to speakers of the source language and speakers of the borrowing language.[8]

This would appear to disallow the existence of any loan which crosses a major cultural barrier of time or space. Yet Greek or Latin loans denote modern technological objects or processes unknown to the Greeks and Romans.[9] It is tempting to sweep

[8]   Although it need not have been previously known to speakers of the borrowing language (in these postulates Wyatt's wording has been somewhat abridged). Hope's researches lead him to suggest (1964, 56ff.) that it will not have been previously known to them, on the grounds that real synonymity between old and new (borrowed) words is practically non-existent. However, 'noa' borrowings defeat this ruling. Of course, the facile use of the term 'loan' should not obscure the need for a systematic categorization of the phenomena, which present a continuum (best stated in terms of E. Haugen's cline, 1958, 777) ranging from *code-switching* through *interference* to *integration*, and involving the relationship of L_2 REPLICAS to L_1 MODELS and L_2 NORMS). As Haugen says, "detection ... is not always so easy as one might think, especially in the case of dead languages".

[9]   Or one may cite individual loans whose regular new meaning corresponds to no such equivalent in the source language. Italian *tartuffola*, if the source of Germ. *Kartoffel*, yet retaining only the sense of 'truffle', is a case in point (the 'potato' sense attaching comparatively late to the intruding *patata* in Italian itself).

them all into the bag of exceptions labelled 'technical terms'; but if this may account for *phoneme* or *vector*, it is scarcely fair for *consul* (in the modern sense) or *vacuum*, and arguably wrong for *motor* or *cinema*. At the very least we need a criterion of 'technicality'; not everything in a technological context is 'technical'.

(2) A neologism — which may be a calque — probably denotes an object not previously known.

But that 'probably' hardly hedges against the frequent re-fashioning of terms for perfectly well-known things, under pressure of prudery or social ranking or mere improvement of designation. Refashioning does not always produce a neologism, but it often has: so *mortician, beautician*.[10]

(3) An inherited word, if maintained in the usage of an 'intruder', denotes an object or concept known to that intruder which may or may not have been present in the experience of the earlier inhabitants of the intruded area (once again, the guiding thought is of the Balkan peninsula). That is, such an inherited term, if applied in a new environment, denotes something introduced by, or both known to and found there by, the intruder.

This is a strong and reasonable axiom. One must, of course, remember the reservations outlined above, and one should exclude the converse: it is not safe to conclude, if an object is known by a non-inherited word, that the speakers were unaware of that object originally. It merely becomes difficult to define that 'originally', a. negative evidence at once sharpens and erodes positive evidence. The crucial thing, however, is to read 'object' (or 'concept') here as importing "item filling the equivalent cultural slot". Cognate words (or even one word in one language) may signify objects of wide physical divergence but like cultural function; *corn* may be wheat or maize or barley, and the word really means 'staple farinaceous crop'. Slot-naming is to be recommended to linguistic prehistorians. It is doubtful if, for their purposes, the 'beech' word

---

[10]   A calque certainly suggests that the referent was previously absent; but speakers may look abroad for a start-point when merely changing nomenclature, as well as when initiating it: Eng. *littlest room* probably derives at least in part from Fr. *petit endroit*.

affords any more secure contextual sense than 'prevalent bushy-topped tree'[11] — a consideration which converts sense-transfers into quite a different kind of evidence. This is not a matter of genus and species but of umbrella terms allowing gross deviations between the physical exponents of shared cultural items. An *Urlexikon* may be — in part, must be — a function-lexicon or a cultural-slot lexicon. So we are in another world from lexicostatistics, where such deviation would be a strong argument for the deletion of the term from the 'core' or retention-lists. It is a fault to confuse the two branches of study, to fail to relate a word used as a palaeontological clue to the distribution of all items associated with it, to ask "what is the word for α in L_1"? instead of "does *a* occur in L_1, and if so does it apply to α"?[12] Imprecision may indeed be expected to exist in order to reinforce, in its negative way, explicit and exact semantic positives in certain cultural sectors. For instance, the kinship system of PIE as described by Delbrück (patriarchal, patrilocal, patrilineal) has been equated (Friedrich, 1966) with the 'Omaha' type and terminology as defined and illustrated by Lounsbury in particular. Here critical relationships are terminologically distinguished in respect of generation, sex and consanguineal or affinal status; but there is a major diagnostic in the imprecise over-riding of generations (and other distinctions) in, say, the wife's family where, from the point of view of the group centred on the husband's father, they are trivial.[13]

---

[11] To quote a defining term one recalls employing in army fire orders. A pellucid etymology may supply the missing precision — if, for instance, the beech really is 'the shining (tree)', as Krogmann thinks (1956, 23; but he sees the birch as 'the white tree', confusingly enough). But this ingenuous approach is not conspicuously successful; anyone who believes that such descriptive names are always applied accurately, and to the most suitable objects, will go far astray. One thinks of *wildebeest* or *blackbeetle*.

[12] Cf. the fault of those, castigated by Ellis (1966, 138[11]), who ask the wrong question in comparative reconstruction generally: i.e. seek "the word in each language for ..." instead of words of potentially related meaning that can be related by phonological correspondence. Note also Hamp's remark (1967, 89) about names assigned to objects "after fairly specific cultural roles ... rather than from their physical taxonomy and characteristics".

[13] Even within the patrilocalized group terms may, by lack of differentiation, equate the socially equal (as sibling terms may include some kinds of cousins),

This kind of balancing of the precise and the imprecise in proto-terminology reflects a complex sociological calculus unlikely to be paralleled in the concrete and objective sectors of the proto-situation; and variations of the item-term equation between languages in an evolving group rests here on adjustments and relaxations of behavioural constraints (whatever the economic basis of those adjustments), rather than on simple changes in the phenomenal items of the outer situation and the effect of these changes on the exponence of cultural slot-fillers. We can choose whether to treat relations like plants and family ties like metals, or not. We must at least recognize that while reflex variety in the terminology of a sector like kinship indicates the social unimportance of what is so reflected, in the sector of natural resources it indicates absence or inaccessibility of the original exponent.[14] But in any case the slot, or semantic space, system will nullify the damage at present done by the compulsion which many feel to pretend that clear equations occur where, in fact, they not only do not but cannot. Impossibility is sometimes mistaken for inefficiency on the part of earlier scholars, despite obvious barriers such as the non-congruence of semantic boundaries in even genetically close languages. To anticipate the simple notation used below, in L_1 a may convey $\alpha_{1,2}$, where b does $\beta_{1,2}$; but in L_2 a may convey $\alpha_1\beta_1$, b stand for $\beta_2\gamma_1$, and so forth.

---

and these terms are then not identifying but classificatory. Friedrich (1966, 25) sees *au̯ios*, in particular, as denoting 'a set of older men in the mother's patrigroup'; and *nep-* is no doubt best glossed as 'blood-linked once-removed child (in other patrilocality)' — or even more broadly, if we wish to avoid, in the deductive process, imposing a delimited kinship structure on the proto-situation.

[14] Basically, the slot system operates alike in either type of sector. 'Husband's father' is the same sort of item as 'chief staple crop'. Even the relative placing of undivided semantic space (where widely inclusive reference occurs) rests on frequency of experience: minor plants, and relations outside the patrilocality, are each simply less often met or made use of.

The contribution of each sector is separate; but they combine. Archaeologists can be asked to look for sign of a 'small-house' culture because we have added the inferences from our sociological sector (as to relative size, number and placing of dwellings) to those from the term- and item-variety inherent in the *dem-*, *u̯oik̑-* etc. words.

Which, though elementary enough, has usually been ignored as a tiresome obstacle in the black and white world of linguistic prehistory.

Even the 'onomastic logic', if it may be so called, inherent in useful postulates like Wyatt's should yield precedence to a sort of 'existential logic' at the basis of this study. The elements of the palaeontologist's system of linguistic enquiry need to be presented, the more baldly the better, if only to separate the rigorous ground patterns from the capricious, or at least from the supervening. This we may proceed to do. In the formulae which follow, let it be understood that the compared languages are denoted by $L_{1234\to}$ and their evidential forms are respectively represented by the successive columns (the heading being often implicit). The cultural items are signalled by $\alpha\beta\gamma\delta\to$ and the context-words by $abcd\to$. Now certain theorems are statable.

But first, two words of warning. The cultural items may be concrete or abstract, and no harm done. But they may also divide into the epiphenomenal and the fundamental. On the one hand, a particular plant or animal or, say, the sea does not have to be part of the total situation of L_3 or L_9; on the other hand, 'mother' or 'staple drink' is inescapable. Not everything that is fundamental is helpful — again unlike the position in lexicostatistics — for we gain no ground by deducing that all Indo-Europeans have always had noses. Nor are fundamentals to be confused with the items of precise definition, nor the epiphenomenal with the imprecise, which were mentioned above in the theory of cultural slots. The present distinction is natural; and the relevant point is one of inferential procedure. In dealing with epiphenomenals, the absence of a context-word entry in a column affects (in part) the reconstruction of the proto-situation; in the case of fundamentals, such anomalies control the reconstruction of the geographical or sociological shifting of the relevant speakers, or 'stock'. Secondly, the term CONTEXT-WORD is chosen to convey combined cognateness of form and of meaning. Formal non-cognateness (where the words are unrelated as phonological or morphological structures) can reflect mere coincidence in situation; referential non-cognateness (where the meanings just will not tie together) precludes all identifying of what seem to be the proto-items.[15]

With so much said, this presentation is possible:

Languages $\quad$ L_1 $_2$ $\quad$ $_3$ $\quad$ $_4$ $\quad$ ...

Formula 1
(word-item parity)
$$\left. \frac{\alpha \quad \alpha \quad \alpha \quad \alpha \quad ...}{a \quad a \quad a \quad a \quad ...} \right\} = 100$$

Formula 2
(word-item
non-parity)
$$\left. \frac{\alpha \quad \beta \quad \gamma \quad \delta \quad ...}{a \quad b \quad c \quad d \quad ...} \right\} = 201$$

$$\left. \frac{\alpha \quad \alpha \quad \alpha \quad \alpha \quad ...}{a \quad b \quad c \quad d \quad ...} \right\} = 202$$

$$\left. \frac{\alpha \quad \beta \quad \gamma \quad \delta \quad ...}{a \quad a \quad a \quad a \quad ...} \right\} = 203$$

Formula 3
(word-item
part parity)
$$\left. \frac{\alpha \quad \alpha \quad \alpha \quad \alpha \quad ...}{a \quad a \quad a \quad b \quad ...} \right\} = 301$$

$$\left. \frac{\alpha \quad \alpha \quad \alpha \quad \alpha \quad \alpha \quad \alpha \quad ...}{a \quad a \quad a \quad b \quad b \quad b \quad ...} \right\} = 301A$$

$$\left. \frac{\alpha \quad \alpha \quad \alpha \quad \beta \quad ...}{a \quad a \quad a \quad a \quad ...} \right\} = 302$$

$$\left. \frac{\alpha \quad \alpha \quad \alpha \quad \beta \quad \beta \quad \beta \quad ...}{a \quad a \quad a \quad a \quad a \quad a \quad ...} \right\} = 302A$$

$$\left. \frac{\alpha \quad \alpha \quad \alpha \quad \varnothing \quad ...}{a \quad a \quad a \quad \varnothing \quad ...} \right\} = 303$$

[15] Always allowing for conditioned shifts, which can be neutralized for

These formulae cover all the basic relationships constituted by the interlingual item-word equations. All other patterns are either extensions, like

$$\left.\frac{\alpha \quad \alpha \quad \alpha \quad \alpha \quad \alpha \quad ...}{a \quad a \quad a \quad b \quad c \quad ...}\right\} = 301 \text{ ext.}$$

or combinations (see below). Within the formulae, the preponderance of one type of item-word correspondence is indicated as economically as is convenient, with the obvious practical reservation that the more equations of correspondences there are the more deviant correspondences, or zero entries, they can outweigh.[16] Some patterns are false and inadmissible: by itself

$$\left.\frac{\alpha \quad \alpha \quad \alpha \quad \alpha \quad ...}{a \quad a \quad a \quad \emptyset \quad ...}\right\}$$

---

academic enquiry. Once Gk. *oxúā*, *oxéā* is for our purpose restored from its usurped meaning of 'beech' to its earlier meaning of 'ash', *phāgós*, *phēgós* may be handled as if it filled its original slot.

[16] Most researchers rely, if somewhat spasmodically, on the quantitative axiom: that cognateness of terms, and linkage between terms and items, gains strength in direct proportion to the number of 'stocks' which offer evidential support. Certainly, a count of twelve out of twelve witnesses cuts out the suspicions and complications attaching to situations where only a couple of neighbours or only a couple of distant languages are in accord; besides, deviant entries in the formula examples are less troublesome and more transparent the greater the number of congruent entries. But let us evoke this pattern (type 302, of those here codified):

$$\frac{\alpha \quad \alpha \quad \alpha \quad \beta \quad ...}{a \quad a \quad a \quad a \quad ...}$$

with the exponents: α = 'rough country', β = 'shrub'; $a = bush$; L_{1-3} = various examples of 'colonial' English (cf. American, South African, Australian), L_4 = British English. We should rightly arrive at the result that α is, provisionally, a proto-item (i.e. there is a proto-item here, and it is semantically close to α); but the greater claim of β, and the fact that L_4 alone is 'unshifted', would be obscured by the quantitative principle.

cannot stand, item α in L_4 being unjustified.[17] There is no sense in citing

$$\frac{\alpha \quad \alpha \quad \alpha \quad \beta \quad (\gamma \ \text{etc.}}{a \quad a \quad a \quad b \quad (c \ \text{etc.}} \Bigg\}$$

unless β etc. are types of α, or b etc. are types of a; and then distinction is otiose.

These theorems follow:

IF 100, THEN commonalty can be assigned to α and it becomes a candidate for the status of proto-item. This is the optimum case implied by Pedersen and cited as a rarity by Crossland. Shifts of the languages compared, and interruptions in the application of a, remain possible, but do not affect the status of α. If, however, the equations are limited to a minority of columns, there remains the possibility that a is a loanword and α a loan-item.[18]

IF 201, THEN the cultural items have no significant lexical relationship: moreover, interlingual and intralingual comparison are indistinguishable.

IF 202, THEN no commonalty of a particular α can be stated; it is to be denied, except for the implication of a fundamental 'cultural slot'.

IF 203, THEN a denotes an item of the proto-situation, but one of which the precise definition is inaccessible.

IF 301, THEN commonalty can provisionally be assigned to α, with the reservation attaching to 100 above. Moreover, L_4 will have suffered either inclusion within a new speech province,[19] or a physical shift of its speakers to an area to which α, originally absent, has later been brought. This general condition, however, may leave

---

[17]   Unless this pattern is established indirectly; see footnote 20.

[18]   Like the 'wine' word. Of course, a word may have entered undifferentiated PIE as a loan, and have been thence inherited by all the IE languages. Until we attain to a really working knowledge of the successive historical stages inside PIE itself, such a nicety remains academic.

[19]   That is, became subject to the vocabulary dominance of a non-IE language, or of another IE language which happens to have lost and replaced some context-words. This need not involve physical movement of the speakers of the affected language.

no trace. If only L_1 is unshifted, the pattern will be

$$\frac{\alpha \quad \alpha \quad \alpha \quad \alpha \quad \alpha \quad \dots \qquad\qquad \dots \varnothing}{a \quad b \quad b \quad c \quad d \quad \dots \qquad\qquad \dots \varnothing} \quad \text{(cf. 202)} \pm \quad —$$

or the like (and see footnote 16). The converse axiom, that the history here outlined must produce pattern 301, is not admissible.

IF 301A, THEN the proto-language suffered an early split. Either one group (L_{1-3} or L_{4-6}), having known α, entered a new speech province or shifted to a new area where α was later brought, and/or the other group found a new word for α (then α is a proto-item); or one of these groups shifted to an area where α was later brought or was found on arrival, while the other group remained in the original area to which α was not indigenous but later brought (then α is a late proto-item); or L_{1-6} moved as two groups to two areas where α was either later brought or found on arrival (then α is not a proto-item). This formula presents a limiting case of the usefulness of 301.

IF 302, THEN commonalty can be assigned to α. Moreover, L_4 will have suffered physical shift of its speakers to an area outside the original homeland (or, if α is fundamental, to a new social calculus). This crossing of an ecological frontier is subject to the same difficulties of recognition as the shift in 301 (see footnote 16). Note that 301 and 302 commonly co-occur. L_4 may use word b for item α because word a has been transferred to the non-proto but now (as slot-filler) more important item β; or it may have transferred word a to item β because item α, common to the situations of both old and new habitat, has come to be more conveniently denoted by a name drawn from the new speech province. In either case, the formula which is consequential (as between 301 and 302) is to be disregarded; if no priority can be established, both theorems remain provisionally relevant.

IF 302A, THEN the proto-language suffered an early dialectal split. Either L_{1-3} or L_{4-6} or L_{1-6} shifted to a new area where, respectively, α replaced β, or β replaced α, or α and β replaced an unknown proto-item.

IF 303, THEN commonalty can be assigned to α. Moreover L_4 will have shifted to an area where α is not present.[20]

These formulae and theorems are restrictive and exhaustive. Consideration will soon show all others to be secondary.[21] For instance.

$$\begin{array}{cccccc} \alpha & \alpha & \beta & \beta & \beta & \beta & \dots \\ \hline a & a & a & a & b & b & \dots \end{array}$$

[20] Except where this apparent formula is in reality a disguised form of the pattern (by itself inadmissible and unhelpful):

$$\begin{array}{cccc} \alpha & \alpha & \alpha & \alpha & \dots \\ \hline a & a & a & \emptyset & \dots \end{array}$$

which is to be replaced — because, despite the documentary absence of a context-word, α IS present for L_4 — by a 100 formula based on closely related items:

$$\begin{array}{c} \alpha_2 \dots \alpha_2 \dots \\ \hline a_2 \dots a_2 \dots \end{array}$$

Wyatt (1966) sensibly allows for just such a hypothetical case, where the relevant presence of words for plough-parts nullifies the apparent absence of a word for 'plough' itself (see next footnote).

[21] As well as establishing items via other, related, items, one may plot words so as to refer to semantic constellations of items. This device has the advantage of giving clues to students of other disciplines — so Friedrich (1966, 19), as an anthropologist, welcomes the cluster 'husband'-'master'-'powerful one' as evidence for viripotestality in PIE marriage. The formalization will be:

$$\begin{array}{cccc} \alpha_3 & \emptyset & \alpha_3 & \emptyset & \dots \\ \alpha_2 & \alpha_2 & \emptyset & \alpha_2 & \dots \\ \alpha_1 & \alpha_1 & \alpha_1 & \emptyset & \dots \\ \hline a & a & a & a & \dots \end{array}$$

or the like. But formulae of this type are essentially superimpositions of (incomplete) examples of 100. Likewise one may meet word clustering (a_1, a_2 etc.) which could have a single referent (α) in each case — although it is somewhat overconfident to judge that a "semantic slot may have been signalled by two proto-allomorphs" (Friedrich, 1966, 13). These formulae could conceivably give way in certain equations to a de-synonymizing; the result

$$\begin{array}{cccc} \alpha & \alpha & \alpha & \alpha & \dots \\ \hline a_1 & a_1 & a_2 & a_2 & \dots \end{array}$$

and so forth represents a special kind of type 301A, with divergent movement between the languages but proto status for α.

derives from a combination of 302A and 301A; that is, from

$$\frac{\alpha \quad \alpha \quad \beta \quad \beta \quad \dots}{a \quad a \quad a \quad a \quad \dots} \text{ plus } \frac{\beta \quad \beta \quad \beta \quad \beta \quad \dots}{a \quad a \quad b \quad b \quad \dots}$$

and nothing else. Any attempt to cite a basic pattern including both $\frac{\alpha}{a}$ and $\frac{\beta}{b}$ is without meaning, for the reason given above. And the apparent formula

$$\frac{\alpha \quad \beta \quad \beta \quad \dots}{a \quad a \quad b \quad \dots}$$

is merely the combination under discussion shorn of that plurality of like reflexes which permits the combinatory deduction — namely that there is a high probability of the commonalty of β as a proto-item, of the shifting of L_1 and L_2 ecologically, and of the shifting of L_5 and L_6 in terms of linguistic dominance (speech province).

If examples will clarify these formulations, they are to be extracted with ease from the relevant literature. PIE *māter-*, pursued through the evidence, is a case of extended 302 applied to a fundamental item; the variant words in the IE languages for 'fire' and 'water' —protagonists in the fight over marginalità — offer a luminous example of 301A; and the extremes of 100 and 202 are illustrated by the equations for the item 'husband's father' as against 'wife's father' (or 100 and 203 by those of the term *sué $\acute{k}$uros* as against *bhendh-*). But examples have been deliberately shunned in this codification. This is no theoretical model, commended as an adequate explanation of the data. It is a strict statement of the rudest elements of a methodology, to the rules of which data-handling must conform and which the data themselves must not mould. Linguistic prehistory owes itself more than ordinary rigour. It does not, however, owe itself the neogrammarian rigidity which sees dialects as linguistically and physically watertight. Hence the need to face all, but only, the equipollent deductions which follow from these formulae. Elimination is possible only when all the relevant data are formulated, and a statistical assessment is made of the assorted results of the applied theorems.[22]

REFERENCES

Collinge, N.E. 1965, "Some linguistic paradoxes", *Journal of Linguistics* 1, 1-12.

Crossland, R.A. 1957, "Indo-European origins: the linguistic evidence", *Past and Present* 12, 16-46.

Ellis, J. O. 1966, *Towards a general comparative linguistics* (= *Janua Linguarum* 52) (The Hague, Mouton & Co.).

Friedrich, P. 1966, "Proto-Indo-European kinship", *Ethnology* 5, 1-36.

Hamp, E.P. 1967, "On the notions of 'stone' and 'mountain' in Indo-European", *Journal of Linguistics* 3, 83-90.

Haugen, E. 1958, "Language contact". *Proceedings of the Eighth International Congress of Linguists*, 771-785.

Hope, T.E. 1964, "The process of neologism reconsidered with reference to lexical borrowing in Romance", *Transactions of the Philological Society*, 46-84.

Krogmann, W. 1955, "Das Buchenargument" (*Kuhn's*) *Zeitschrift für vergleichende Sprachforschung*, 72, 1-29.

—— 1956, *Ibid.* 73, 1-26.

Meillet, A. 1945, *Linguistique historique et linguistique générale* I (Paris).

Meyer-Lübke, W. 1900, *Einführung in das Studium der romanischen Sprachwissenschaft*.

Pedersen, H. 1962, *The discovery of language* (translated by J. W. Spargo, 1931; reprinted in Bloomington 1962) (= *Sprogvidenskaben i det Nittende Aarhundrede: Metoder og resultater*) (Copenhagen 1924).

Thieme, P. 1953, "Die Heimat der indogermanischen Gemeinsprache", *Aka-*

---

[22]   Pattern prediction may be applied to items. The patrilocal configurations

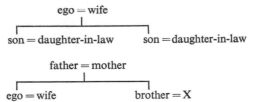

and

lead to expectation of contrasting terms for all the relations cited (or, alternatively, the 'Omaha' system might suggest that brother's wife would have the same term as son's wife). In fact, in PIE 'brother's wife' seems neither to have a special name (hence Troubetzkoy's attempt to push *neu-istā* into the gap) nor to be denoted by the *snusos* word. But all this kind of speculation is relevant rather to chapter 2.

demie der Wissenschaften und der Literatur in Mainz, *Abhandlungen der Geistes- und Sozialwissenschaftlichen Klasse*, 1953.11, 535-613 (Wiesbaden).

Troubetzkoy, N.S. 1939, "Gedanken über das Indogermanenproblem", *Acta Linguistica* 1, 81-89.

Wyatt, W.F. Jr. 1966, "The Indo-Europeanization of Greece", *Preprints of papers given at the conference of 'Indo-European and the Indo-Europeans'* (Philadelphia).

5. THE INDO-EUROPEAN LARYNGEAL

The clearest feature of the Indo-European supposititious laryngeal phoneme is its instability. All speech sounds find some positions untenable, in time, in some languages, and some sounds find all positions untenable in some languages; perhaps some sounds find some positions untenable in all languages, although that is more doubtful. But within the IE speech-field, to which it was originally assigned as an item theoretically predicted from the patterns of historical evolution, the laryngeal has found all positions untenable in all the languages, except for one group where it appears to have maintained some strongholds, probably at the cost of considerable modification of its own nature.[1] So widespread an operational failure points to a fundamental unsuitability. H was the wrong sort of sound, at any rate for the IE phonemic team. Besides, its use in IE as a morpheme-constituent (or, more correctly, the employment, for the purpose of distinguishing morphs, of its phonological polarity characteristic of likeness/unlikeness to other segmental units) is notably sparse. It is once a regular but late, and elsewhere a rare, noun and adjective stem formant; it is one element in the complex optative mood marker; it is probably, but not certainly, a person marker in one active perfect verb form. Nothing more, except speculatively:[2] probably never a lexical

[1] The Anatolian reflex is usually taken to be some sort of oral fricative, with or without a spirant component; this allows the cuneiform signs to convey more or less the same sounds in Hittite etc. as in Akkadian, where a voiceless (post) velar fricative is denoted. See Crossland (1951, 92 fn. 2).

[2] It is possibly a component of some neuter plural morphemes, but these may all derive from the -aH feminine singular formant. If it seems preferable to regard this morpheme as attaching to an IE neuter collective (to follow Sturtevant rather than Schmidt), the point remains that the plural function is secondary. H may enter into the long-vowel instrumentals of o-stems, and their

instrument of derivation. Which means that its unsuitability correlates with its infrequency; and this leads us to Zipf's formula, that what is phonemically rare must be, in proportion, phonetically complex.[3] Or, in case we seem, as Zipf has seemed to some, to assert the complexity simply because we see the infrequency, it may be preferable to concentrate on the infrequency and to connect this with the phonetic idiosyncrasies which have been credited to this phonemic item. These latter include the power to voice contiguous consonants, to aspirate them, to 'colour' vowels, to lengthen them, and yet to stand apart from all close homorganic relation to the oral or buccal items which make up the solid core of the IE phonemic inventory — and this is a conservative estimate of the peculiarity of H, omitting several more questionable attributes. It is precisely because of such nonconformity that items like Proto-Indo-European [þ], which has been posited[4] after /k/, /k̂/ must be assigned the briefest of lives; or, better, must be rejected as insufficiently likely PIE reconstructions, in favour of more integrated sounds (or more subtle group-evolutions of established phonemes).

Now H cannot be rejected entirely. That move would consign again to chaos the dozens of apparent cognates in the compared languages which have, via H, been so satisfactorily equated at an earlier stage of formal history; it would also jettison the increased morphological neatness of revised PIE. Nor is its distribution in

---

analogical creations; and it has been in neuter dual forms (Kuiper, *Die Sprache* 7, 1961, 19f.). But it is surely analogy (to *curāre* or *nouāre* etc.), rather than regular use of a fresh laryngeal formant, which produces the *laudāre* type. There are difficulties attendant on the equation of the *-Hm* segment of the *ego* word and the 1.s verbal endings (see Collinge, 1959, 230); and the derivation of thematic *-ō* from *-oH* remains a pure guess.

[3]   See Zipf (1929; 1935, 49ff.), Martinet (1955, 132f.), Joos (1936, 207ff.). Martinet (1955, 85f.) shows how even a phonetically isolated phoneme like /l/, in many languages, may be to some small degree 'integrated' and so saved from loss, by (e.g.) gemination. This may possibly be relevant to the Hittite opposition of *h* and *hh*, where maintenance and perhaps gemination go hand in hand; not that this gemination belongs to PIE, despite Gamkrelidze's belief that sometimes *hh* < *HH* (1960, 48f.).

[4]   On this see the articles listed by Polomé, fn. 73 (adding V. Georgiev, *Proceedings of the Ninth International Congress of Linguistics*, 739).

any way incredible, except in the dispensable fancies of etymologists of the wilder sort. But *H* must be recognized as very largely 'obtrusive' (in Hockett's sense) in PIE in respect of its constituent distinctive features; though it must not, of course, be made out to be so bizarre as not to have credibly existed long enough to win its currently presumed status in the proto-forms of those languages which it helps to tie together. The symptoms must combine for the diagnosis to be meaningful. Mere underemployment is neither unparalleled nor solely explicable by component oddity; and non-integration does not of itself ensure instability.[5] Nevertheless a laryngealist's first duty must be to discountenance any attempt to give *H*, phonologically, a good name. Martinet's matrix of interlocking articulations (and the same would be true of any similar arrangement of co-occurrent alternants taken from a series of distinctive feature binarisms, à la Jakobson-Fant-Halle) is nothing more than a device for imposing on PIE *H* the very characteristics which its history shows it conspicuously lacks, such as thoroughgoing voice/voicelessness (like the oral stops) or the regularity of labial co-articulation (like the velar dorsals). A president does not create popular confidence in his favourite general by appointing him out of hand to all the orders of courage and chivalry of which he is obviously devoid.

It is not quite the same, nor so vicious a fault which makes objectionable those essays in patterning which build up a close-knit family of laryngeals themselves, by means of a matrix of features special to such a phoneme-type. (Indeed, Watkins, 1960c, 237, seems to think them poorer substitutes for total integration; they

---

[5] Cf. Allen's remark (1958, fn. 75) about "the long tail of meagrely employed consonants" in Abaza, whose average frequency, with one exception, is around 0.3% of all consonant occurrences. None the less, they are well integrated; this reservation must be borne in mind when Allen remarks (1965, 122) "the typological relevance to IE of the N.W. Caucasian languages is all the greater in view of ... the existence of palatalized and labialized series of dorsal consonants, and of a series of pharyngal fricatives, voiced and voiceless, plain and labialized, with effects of opening and backing on adjacent vocoidal sounds". And Greenberg (1950, 168) has cautionary words, from Semitic, on the problem of stability. It is a pity there is as yet no general calculus of complexity and conditions of tolerance for linguistic units.

may be a subtler danger). Adrados's six-H system meshes a binary sub-system (palatal or labial component) with a ternary (one of three attendant vowel-colorations). In so far as this scheme rests on H, the absence of $*/ki̯/$, $/ti̯/$, $/pi̯/$ in PIE is not a drawback, as Adrados seems to feel. It is a positive recommendation (of non-integration), as is the absence in his scheme of a plain H (again unlike $/k/$, $/t/$, $/p/$). Overall PIE phoneme-symmetry is not claimed, and this scheme is a trifle better for that reason, in view of what was said above, than Puhvel's eight-H theory. This latter multiplies three binary subsystems (plus or minus a-coloration $\times$ plus or minus co-articulatory feature $\times$ plus or minus voice).[6] But the trouble with these schemes is that they more insidiously destroy the essential isolation of H in IE, and make its morphological laziness harder to believe. An interlocking family of PIE phonemes of this kind is insulated from the ravages which time and usage may be expected to wreak upon a single, exotic and generally inadequate ugly duckling of a speech-sound. The patterning of $k\ t\ p$; $g\ d\ b$; $gh\ dh\ bh$; $\eta\ n\ m$ long preserved them: H fell.

Apart from those who have never accepted any part of the laryngeal theory (and this essay is not addressed to them), several scholars insist on a fully or partly vocalic H (or retain the old $ə$). Weighty reasons for accepting a consonantal value for H have, however, always been available.[7] Cuny (1912, 101 ff.) put forward a celebrated argument, based on the apparent reflexes of RH in the environment $T - T$ (to put it in Kuryłowiczian terms), which showed that the vocalism must reside in the R and not in the H if the vocalic length (or its reflex) is to be explained at all. This demonstration is not to be faulted on the grounds that in PIE

[6]   See Adrados (1961, *passim*), Puhvel (1960a, 11 f. and 1960b, 171; the tally is given as six at 1965, 92, because Anatolian offers a partial conflation of E and E^y). The co-articulatory feature, for Puhvel, is realized as palatalization if the laryngeal is e-colouring, and labialization if it is a-colouring. Cowgill's comment (*ad. loc.*, 172; also *Language* 39, 1963, 266 fn. 56) that "E^y would be hard to fit into the PIE phonologic system" is presumably meant to be adverse; if anything, it rescues this concept.

[7]   See Martinet (1957a, *passim*), Collinge (1953, 79). It is essential to realize that consonantal H, in zero grade consonant clusters, can help to induce a forced vocalism (see next footnote).

sequences of this type "we do not know which of the two vocalizable elements ... was in fact vocalized".[8] For one thing, to call H a vocalizable element is a *petitio principii*; for another, precisely this kind of 'phonetic speculation' applied to phoneme-sequences — and not merely the stating of such PIE sequences — is the business of comparative reconstruction when it relates its findings to constructs, when it shunts forward, in fact. Again, from comparison we DO know whereabouts the vocalism was carried in such a sequence, as well as drawing encouragement from the theoretical factor that, in forms like $*\#plH\text{-}C$, to assume '$H = C$' permits a valid Sievers-Edgerton formula ($\#tit$) to produce $*pl\overset{\circ}{H}\text{-}C$; while '$H = V$', if seen in $*pl\overset{\circ}{H}\text{-}C$, invokes the invalid $*\#tyut$. Moreover, to ask for 'phonemic evidence' that /H/ contrasts with /ə/ is to hold to the incorrect notion that /ə/ is part of PIE at all. It is equally strange news to be told that a 'central tenet' of laryngealism is that [ə], [:] (and [h]) are allophones of /H/; or even that "[ə] is the reflex of a laryngeal consonant between consonants". The only sensible use of 'ə' is as a shorthand symbol for saying, or taking as said, something like "here must stand a vocalism, phonemicized in the evidential language(s) but not necessarily so in PIE, within what is etymologically and morphologically a PIE zero-grade syllable, to the evolution of which syllable a laryngeal sound has at some stage contributed". It should figure as a datum-label, not as a starred reconstruction. Nor is [:] a PIE allophone, although it may develop into one in later (e.g. post-Anatolian) IE. It is a phoneme or prosody in individual attested languages under comparison, and as such it helps towards the establishment of the PIE distribution of consonantal H. To assign historically attested [:] to PIE /H/ is like assigning French [p] to Latin /p/. Description

---

[8] The references hereabouts are to Wyatt (1964, *passim* but esp. 141, 151 f.). He states Cuny's argument fairly and clearly. For other comments on this article, see below, fn. 35. But one must decisively reject the renewed plea for vocalic ə, or H, as adequate signs for PIE segmental entities (cf. Puhvel, 1960a, 6). They insensibly import a sort of laryngeal vocoid into contexts where only 'peak position' and vocalic impulse are arguable. Likewise 'schwa secundum' tends to deceive people into seeing a 'reduced grade' of PIE ablaut. (See also Collinge, 1956, 127; and footnote 41 below.)

and history — and different languages — must be co-used, not confused. Indeed the chaos to which '$\underset{.}{H}$' leads is so overwhelming that in what follows '$H = C$' will be presumed as dogma.

Some articulatory basis must, then, be sought which explains an evolutionary phenomenon: namely that this unstable PIE item H, if immediately preceded by a vocalic peak to which it acted as syllable-coda, was always replaced (in the languages where it WAS replaced) by extension of the phonetic domain of the vocalic element. This is not to be confused with mere maintenance of a segment's duration despite the loss of the segment itself, for that principle was irregularly applied, as we teach ourselves by contrasting such various developments of e.g. proto-Greek /ksenwons/ as /ksenos/, /kse:nos/, /kseno:s/, /kse:no:s/ according to dialect (Thessalian, Coan, Attic, East Ionic, *exempli gratia*). Here must rather be a feature which is stable in its relating of duration to environment but which tends in IE evolution towards an unstable consonantal exponence, though not identically in all IE languages. That is, $C + H + V = [C] + [\ ] + [V] > [C\text{-}]\text{-}[\rightarrow][V]$, the new consonantal length being as phonologically insignificant as in MnE *beňt/beňd*; or $V + H + C = [V] + [\ ] + [C] > [V\text{-}]\text{-}[\rightarrow]\ [C]$, i.e. $> /V:C/$, where, however, the 'vowel length' (or /:/) IS significant in that environment and therefore maintained. Now these are not PIE forms, but late IE replacement-tendencies in structures.[9] In these shifts the empty [ ] represents the phoneme-long feature which is H, which may very likely be no more than an interruption of the sound track (otherwise consisting of breath, voice and oral/nasal modulations) by an occlusion and release which themselves have so small a degree of integration with the oral occlusions of IE for their occurrence to be felt as a mere hiatus, to be filled by phonetic extension of neighbouring phonemes.[10] Phonetic overlap

---

[9] They are simply extreme cases of the undeniable practical overlap of articulatory features (as shown up by Truby, 1964) and of phonemic features (see Collinge, 1965, 3f.).

[10] This view is quite different from the notion of Marstrander (*Norsk Tidsskrift for Sprogvidenskap* 3, 1929, 290-296) and Petersen (1932, 199f.) that, if not H, at least Hitt. *h* (as Kronasser later thought) is a mere hiatus-filler (or even — as Petersen, 1934 — a mere vowel-precursor).

happens all the time, as we shall see: the oddity in these sequences is the occlusive phoneme gap which transforms overlap into extension.

Laryngealists tend to divide themselves into 'phoneticians' and 'algebraists'. The fault of the former class is to attach plausible, simple phonetic features to laryngeals (one major feature regularly requiring one corresponding laryngeal: hence many laryngeals) in order to push the variety of reflex-types back, as a problem, into proto-IE. Benveniste (1962, 10) is right to call this procedure an obstacle to progress. Sapir and then Sturtevant took it practically as far as it would go without ever commending it to the world in general, though sporadic adventurous followers are not lacking. But the algebraists are not right either. The extreme form of their approach leads to an arid and incredible wilderness of tortured etymons and metathesized root-structures. Whatever our historical limitations and however non-phonetic our 'published' reconstructions, the elements we work with must rest on, and have their development consonant with, real articulatory behaviour of possible phonetic entities.[11] Therefore it is crucial that we accept the obvious, given behaviour of even a theoretical item — for the behaviour is not theoretical, but is the factual source of the hypothesis which sets up the item. A laryngeal in PIE means an infrabuccal closure. Where precisely the occlusion took place might well be environmentally determined, and a complexity in the nature of the closure (and the possible combination with oral closures, and regular co-occurrence with nasal closure) must be countenanced. Indeed, that is the clear inference from our argument so far. A diagnosis (as by Puhvel, 1960a, 11 f.) of H as a series of oral fricatives is less likely than the traditional American view of some Hs as (velar) spirants. A prosodic feature of glottalization is possible; but an even partly prosodic PIE, arrived at via phonemic interpretation of graphic evidence (as Hoenigswald's famous 'Principal Step' made

---

[11] Relevant here is Kurath's article (1961); see, however, the proviso as to 'workshop' forms in Collinge (1956, 120). The distinction between valid phonetic speculations and invalid phonetic regulations resolves a debate which began with Pott and Scherer last century and still intermittently rages.

it clear that our procedure must be) is unmappable. Nor should mapping it be attempted; for there, to be sure, hindrance WOULD lie, in the absence of a general calculus of the probabilities of evolution from prosody to phoneme and vice versa. We had better stick to a phonemic H, but one which is in its nature wildly unlike all other IE phonemes.

One possible component of such an infrabuccal closure as has been suggested is a noticeable expiration or injection of air.[12] Here and there speakers of later IE languages may hear this as aspiration (simple glottal fricative- or mere 'breathiness') and subsequently exploit it phonemically. De Saussure, Kuryłowicz, Sturtevant, Lehmann and Burrow have all seen in H an origin of the voiceless aspirates of Indo-Iranian — to cite Burrow's famous example, '$*roteH_2$' (whence Lat. *rota*) produces an Indian adjectival form $*rotH+o-$ ('wheeled', 'chariot'); and the Sanskrit reflex, pat on cue, is *rathá-*. Now, as many have pointed out,[13] despite common acceptance of $*pHtér-$ there is no form $*phitár-$. But consideration of other cases may show why not. Lehmann's interesting demonstration (1952, 82f.) of the lateness of the period at which voiceless aspirates became unitary Indian phonemes (the clue being their failure to participate in secondary palatalization) does not really touch the IE problem: Sanskrit is equally likely/unlikely, therefore, to accept *ph-*. More crucial is the distribution of these Indian voiceless aspirates within roots, as apparently favouring final position (as Hoenigswald has shown: see below). Relevant, too, is the acoustic difference of relative voice onset time between *p-V* and *b-V*, etc. (see Lisker, Abramson, *Proceedings of the Fifth Congress of Phonetic Sciences*, 390), the former producing automatic aspiration [*phV*], which must affect /ph/ vis-à-vis /bh/ somehow. It is difficult to deduce anything very much from the comparanda; Greek has σπαίρω along with σφαῖρα, where Sanskrit

---

[12] In this connexion, and together with much of what follows, one may with profit consult Catford's remarks on glottalic stops (1939, 4), especially on vocal cord movement in place of full glottal closure, and on laryngeal components in general (1964).

[13] E.g. Mayrhofer (1955, col. 900). Messing (1947, 184f.) disputes the shift IE gH > Hitt. *kk*.

offers *sphuráti*. Where both show an aspirate, as in *sphyá-*, cφήν, other languages do not hint at one (Lat. *spīna*, Toch. *ṣpin*, OE *spitu*). Sometimes it is a matter of sound-play, as with *kákhati*, καγχάζω, *cachinnō*. A composite and partly inherited origin of these aspirates seems likely, taking into account Jakobson's typological findings, which should assign to **kh* etc. at least as much PIE frequency as **b*, if no more. SOME voiceless aspirates do not derive from voiceless $C+H$, and some CH sequences do not give voiceless Ch; but some do, and voiced aspirates or their ultimate reflexes arise likewise (*mahás-*, *ahám* < **megH-$^e/_o$s*, **egH-$^e/_o$m*). Objection has been raised (by Wyatt, 1964, 150) to the absence of aspirate in Sanskrit *kakudmant*, Latin *cacū-men* and in Sanskrit *kekara*, Latin *caecus*. Now it is pointless to bring in *khidáti* and *caedo* (where Greek has cχίζω), or any Skt. (or Middle Indic) *kh* which correlates with PIE **(s)C-*[14] (e.g. *kháñjati* ~ cκάζω, *phála-* ~ Pers. *supár*, *khan-* or *khā* ~? Gk. cκάπτω, cκάλλω etc. — cf. *phárvara-* ~ cπείρω), where some $s > h$ process akin to Greek **teksnā* > τέχνᾱ, or **sųios* > Cor. ϝhιόc, may be lurking. If the *a*-quality of the vowels in *kakúd-* and *cacū-* indicates a preceding H, then these words, and *pitár-* etc., reveal that before the onset of the vowel postconsonantal H is lost (like intervocalic H) without trace of aspiration. In these cases the sequence CHV is close-knit, with no intervening lexical or morphological juncture. A morphemic boundary might split the sequence thus: $-C+HV$; then a similar loss of aspiration would be natural. So **-C+Ha* as 1st. sing. active perfect ending is to be seen in *non*-aspirated forms. Kuryłowicz (1935a, 254) corrects the theorists on this, for Sanskrit shows the unaspirated reflexes and the Greek evidence (post-Homeric πέπομφα etc.) does not help to prove the '$CH > Ch$' case.[15] The deduction of Kuryłowicz is that we have a multiplicity of laryngeals, and that the one which appears in perfect **Ha* (or **Ae*) is just not the aspirating type. This is unnecessary (it might be a matter of analogical deaspiration — so Crossland, 1958, 82f.), and dangerous: one loses confidence in an

---

[14] See also Polomé (1965, fn. 120).
[15] This false derivation, of Sapir and Sturtevant, was long ago refuted by R. G. Kent, *Language* 17 (1941), 189-193.

approach which, unable to solve problems of evidence with the
laryngeals available, simply invents more to fill the bill. The crucial
point is the structure. The relevant sequence has, once again, such
a structure as to preclude the phonological appreciation of the
breath feature. Thus we have e.g. *veda*, οἶδα, with *-da* from *-d+
Ha*. The second singular perfect forms of Sanskrit and Greek
are probably to be ignored, the Greek forms coming quite possibly
from *-sta* (Cowgill, 1965, 173) and the Sanskrit forms from *-ta*,
by Bartholomae's Law (Kuryłowicz, 1956, 381).[16] If *H* was never
in these forms, and unless we deduce too much from Gk. 3.s. -ε,
there is a plain hint (if no more) that the *-a* of the first person also
is itself original (i.e. the sequence is not *-H^e/_o*- or *-A^e/_o*- but *-Ha*),
fact which will be relevant presently.

Now to consider some lexical equivalents. Hittite *palhis*, and
perhaps Latin *palam*, point to *pal-H-*, Latin *plānus* to *pl-aH-*;
Old Irish *lethan* to *pl-e/ot-*; and Greek πλατύς to *pl-t+u-*.[17]
These are built of root plus alternating suffixes *t* and *H*, which are
quite separate but may combine: so *pl_etH+_eno-* appears to give
πλάθανος (unless this is from πλαθ+ιō cf. πλάτανος without *H*),
and *pltH+u* gives Sanskrit *pṛthu-*. In these cases (unless πλάτανος
is otherwise felt) there is a major morphological juncture AFTER
the laryngeal — thus, for the first time, we find a structure really
analogous to that of *rathá-*, *mahás-*. From another root, *pṛtH+*

---

[16] Hitt. *-ti* (<*t'*+*i*), Lat. *-ti* (<*ta*+*i*?), may have had a stage involving
-t+H (the Hitt. form is, after all, not *-ʒi*). The relevance of 2 sing. mediopassive *-thās* (?-θης) is disputed.

[17] It is misleading of Cowgill (1960a, 135; 1965, 172) to cite the place-name
Πλάταια as if it were the regular feminine to πλατύς (instead of πλατεῖα).
Admittedly, this vocalism would demand *pltH + eu + ia*, and would damage
my present argument. But place names are awkward creatures in phonological
and morphological reconstruction (see chapter 3); and a glance at the site of
Plataea in Boeotia makes a direct derivation from πλατύς ('flat', 'expansive')
unlikely. It cannot even signify 'the only relatively flat spot in a hilly terrain',
because there IS a flat plain immediately to the north and north-west. In any
case, for Cowgill's derivation the accent is wrong. More likely the origin is
πλάτᾱ ('oarblade', or some such equation; names so derived abound in the
Greek world, like Zancle), probably involving an extremely early process,
^ˌᾱ> ^ˌαια, as in Homeric Ἱστίαια (where the only *H* occurs after the original
stem-vowel).

eno- gives παρθένος and **prtH+uko-* gives *pṛthuka-* (cf. Arm. *ortʿ*), whereas πόρταξ is affected by the *H*-less πόρτις, itself parallel to the *t*-less πόρις. Indeed, Arm. *ortʿ* may also be *H*-less (see Winter, 1966, 205). Confusion is not unknown; *prathamá-* goes its own way. But the general process and conditioning is reasonably clear in these sequences of *CH+V*: namely, a consonant may be aspirated by the breath feature of an immediately following prevocalic laryngeal, PROVIDED THAT H IS SUNDERED FROM THE VOWEL BY A MORPHEMIC BOUNDARY.[18] Just so, the new Sanskrit thematic formation **ti-stH+eti* results in *tiṣṭhati* (with *sth* thence generalized throughout the verb, as conversely *st* is generalized in the Greek equivalent, spreading from the full-grade cτᾱ forms, where *H* is not post-consonantal). Now we can see why root-final position is so characteristic of Indian voiceless aspirates, not merely as a feature of frequency of lexical types but (as in *prath-*, *krath-*, etc., of *CCeC-C* pattern?) as a reflection of favourite — Benveniste would say permissible — IE root forms (see Hoenigswald 1960, 14 f.; 1965, 93 f.). The upshot is that a laryngeal has rightly been identified as the aspirating element in many, but not all, examples of *Ch* in IE languages: that structural (and not systemic) considerations explain curious apparent gaps in the reflexes; that only one *H* is needed still; and, further, that the sub-buccal occlusion which *H* represents holds some of the air-stream at a differential pressure from the outside air in a closed cavity (see Catford, 1939). This in turn indicates a lower and an upper point of constriction forming

---

[18] But three considerations give pause to the theory that morpheme boundary inhibits phonological shift: (1) a boundary may cut clean through a sequence which nevertheless suffers shift — cf. Lat. *uel + se > uelle* (despite the visible part-relation of *uel + se* to *uel + im* etc.); (2) morphological and phonological frontiers may be at variance — cf. Eng. *foolish*, which is morphologically *fool + ish* but phonologically *foo-lish* (see *Journal of Linguistics* 2 [1966], 207); (3) scholars differ as to whether the inhibition causes time-lag or articulation-lag, so to put it: when Attic Gk. *t(h)y* passes to ττ (? = [tʃ]) in some words where a morpheme boundary interferes, is this the reflex of the sequence's being too slow in forming a close-knit cluster (so as to miss the earlier assibilation of that cluster in this dialect but still to catch the general Gk. affrication) or of its being held back on the articulatory shift-path [tʼ > tʃ > ʃ > s]? See chapter 7, fn. 6.

the limits of that cavity, for example at glottis and pharynx respectively. Whether the two constrictions are entirely simultaneous or overlap, and, in the latter case, in which order they are applied and released, are questions to which fresh inspection of the evidence may provide an answer.

Co-articulation with an oral closure is perfectly possible, indeed likely; the velic regularly occludes nasal articulation in connection with *H*. Palatal constriction, but scarcely total closure, is acceptable for the '*H*ʲ' of limited occurrence which Diver has proposed. Acceptable, too, at least sporadically, is the well-known labialized type *H*ᵘ, *A*ʷ, etc.). But only one type of supra-glottal constriction will, combining with a glottal occlusion, ensure a complete closing of the overall mouth and throat cavity. That is a full bilabial closure, a 'p', not a 'w', feature. The overlapping exponence of speech-sounds in sequence, which Truby (1964) has put beyond doubt by his observation of speech-acts through several simultaneous experimental media, will mean that sequences of bilabial stop + *H* (or vice versa) — as long as no morphemic juncture intervenes — will either be released as 'popping' sounds or else the complete closure, which might place a misleading pause in the speech sequence, will be offset by a replacement. This replacement may be, and often is, vibration of the vocal cords instead of glottal occlusion, some air being admitted into the cavity but as much interference as possible being applied. Then, if the bilabial stop is voiceless, voicing of it must ensue, but only as long as its own release is inhibited until a point during the articulation of *H*. (Although $pH > b$ is a possibility, the reverse order, Hp, will hardly show this effect, for a preceding vowel would usurp the place of *H*, as we saw; and a preceding consonant would force elision of *H*, as also in *pHC*. Therefore *pHV* [$> bV$] remains the sole susceptible sequence).

At first sight the phenomena are not encouraging. *Pắjrá-* etc. (not **bắjra-*), if relevant at all, may be affected by the similar superficial appearance of other forms from the **pag* root; and *pitár-* (which is not only not **phitár-* but is not **bitár-* either) is still of obscure etymology and is possibly a *Lallwort* built up to fit in the pattern of the 'mother', 'daughter' and 'brother' words (Avestan having *dugədar*- but *ptar*-, *pit*- not occurring until Old Persian).[19] But the group summarized by πῶλος, *πάϝις (παῦς, παῖς), *putrá*- etc. probably reflect *pH^u_a- (to use a Martinet construct for convenience) in varying grades and environments. These forms demand some *H* (cf. the vowel length in πῶλος) and a mere '*pau* : *pu*' base is inadequate. Moreover, *πάϝις would seem to rest on *pH^u_a- plus reinserted vocalism (*$pH_e{}^u_a$-). Hence a sequence of close-knit *pHV- occurs, yet shows no voicing of the labial stop. Therefore,

---

[19] In view of what is said below of the crucial nature of a following labial item, the non-voicing of apparent *pH in the 'father' word may need no further excuse. Nevertheless, it is worth reiterating the possibility that the 'daughter' word affected the 'father' word in PIE — as the Avestan evidence seems to suggest — since the reverse process has been supposed (as by L. Deroy, in *Innsbrucker Beiträge zur Kulturwissenschaft*, Sonderheft 15, (1962) 160, = 'Deroy, 1961', in Polomé's list). The Skt. forms *duhitár*- and *pitár*- show at least that, if there is cross-influence, the other kinship words do not come into it. Certainly, Deroy's idea assists those who want to have both (non-aspirating) *A* in the Greek θυγάτηρ and laryngeal-prompted aspiration in *duhitár*- (Winter, 1965, 112, goes so far as to posit an 'extended' *$dhugH + A$-, the *A* borrowed from *pitár*-); but with a plurality of laryngeals to play with, their problem is inconsiderable. However, for the purposes of this present argument the direction of influence would preferably be 'daughter' → 'father' (where the cause of effects like voicing or aspiration must be the environmental position, not the nature, of *H*). Now if *duhitár*- etc. rest on *$dhugH$-, a similarly based Greek form should result in *τυχατηρ. One could claim that the base was aniṭ *$dhug$-; but then we should expect Gk. *θυκτηρ. One could say 'Grassmann's Law' has operated in inverted sequence; but the appeal to e.g. λύθητι (from λυ-θη-θι) is useless, as overall morphological conservatism (as in φάθι) as well as late local paradigmatic levelling (the influence of λυθήτω) are factors here, whereas θυγάτηρ stands alone. Moreover, even so, the result would be *θυκάτηρ, unless this dissimilation is seen as preceding the devoicing of aspirates in Greek history (as if *dhugH > dhugh > dhug > thug*); whereas the reverse is normal, and very early dissimilation is only true of those Greek words which are of 'Aegean' or 'Pelasgian' stock and follow an altogether different shift path (e.g. *$bhergh$- > *$bergh$- > πέργ-αμα etc.) The Greek reflex, simply because of the syllabic structure, must nevertheless derive from *$dhugH$-; the absence of the aspiration (in face of the favourable placing of the morphemic boundary) can only be attributed to a fundamental Greek incompatibility of aspiration and voice. That is to say, what is already aspirated is, at a very early stage of pre-Greek, devoiced; what is voiced but not yet aspirated resists aspiration — hence voiced *$CH + V$* > voiced *$C + V$*, *H* leaving no trace beyond the *a*-colouring of *V* (see below). But one cannot disguise the consequent weakening this 'solution' produces in the general theory outlined above.

both *a fortiori* and *ex argumento*, a sequence $*p+HV$-, with a morphemic boundary before the H, will equally reject such voicing. What then of $*pH+V$-? This is harder to find. But the expectation is that it will show the same effect as does intra-root, non-junctured $*pHV$- (for the articulatory processes are quite dissimilar to those involved in the aspiration problem). Now a voicing H has been sought without the limitation as to the type of affected consonant which has just been argued. Greek ὄγδοϝοϲ has been cited ($*ok̑teH^u_a$- > $*ok̑tH_e{}^u_a+o$-), but the analogy of ἕβδομοϲ, rather than the reverse influence, cannot be ruled out; and, for ἕβδομοϲ itself, βδ < πτ is paralleled in κρύβδην ~ κρύπτω (κρυφ+ι̯ō ~ κρύφα).[20]

Otherwise we are left with the notorious *píbati*. Now this form shows a fine intransigence towards other explanation.[21] It is not a mere Indian speciality (cf. Old Irish *ibid*, Latin *bibit*); nor is it a lone lexical item or unique morpheme, but is embedded firmly in the form-scatter of the verbal root *pā* (and its Latin relation to *pōtus*, *pō-culum* etc. is less obvious but as close). The contiguity of *p* and *H* is corroborated by the morphologically identical *tíṣṭhati*; i.e. $*Ci-(s)CH+eti$. Why has this sequence alone produced voicing?

It may well be because Semitic 'ain' is breathed and sub-buccal (and also provided a sign which the Greeks saw fit to use as the vehicle for their *o*-vowel), that scholars have been prompted to

---

[20] The favourable phoneme sequence for this shift may be present in the word for 'seventy'; cf. Szemerényi, *Studies in the Indo-European Numerals*, 6ff.

[21] Messing (1947, 185f.) sees here the result of a dissimilation (curiously isolated!); and Machek (see his comments on Martinet 1957a, *ad loc.*) suggests that the intensifying initial reduplication caused an internal 'weakening' of-p($>b$). Manu Leumann (*Museum Helveticum* 14 [1957], 76) seems to misconceive the origin of *píbāmi* in relation to 'low-class' *píbati*, and falsely sunders the *p* and *H* by undervaluing the new thematic declension, despite *tíṣṭhati*; he insists on a late *pō*/*pī* ablaut in this root, despite the heavy use of analogy to which he must then resort; and he reiterates Schulze's $*pōi/pəi$ on the basis of Skt. causative *pāyáyati*, despite *gā:gāyáyati*, *chā:chāyáyati* etc., which suggests that the -*i*- (-*y*-) is no more original than the *p* of *sthāpáyati*, etc. These are panic-stricken writings. (Of itself, absence of Latin $*pibit$ might be explained away, as if $*$-pH- > $*$-ph- > -b-, for *ph* appears in loans as *b* — cf. *bulla*, *basēlus*, *bālaena* — and $*$-bh- > $*$-ph- > -b- is seen in *orbus*, *nebula*, etc.)

assume an *o*-colouring *H* so readily. And equally readily have they attached voice to it, and a power of voicing too. Yet the semi-traditional 'H_3' theory is unsafe. Sturtevant demonstrated how feasible, though not necessarily right, it is to dispense with 'non-apophonic *o*-vocalism'; and Martinet's development of an old idea of Henry Sweet's into a full-blown theory centring round a basically *a*-colouring labiolaryngeal still avoids 'H_3' as such. Even to be content with a shift variety like 'e $+$ A $> \bar{a}$ but o $+$ A $> \bar{o}$'[22] is to do without 'H_3'. The relation of *a*-vocalism to *H* will appear when we have considered the full sub-buccal nature of the occlusion which is *H*. As for the co-articulatory features of labialization and palatization, these cannot well be denied as sporadic components (on their phonological status, see fn. 36). And the relevant sporadic component, in our analysis of the process which has produced *píbati*, must be the ʷ which attends this *H*. For this sequence is in fact of $*pH^u + V$-; and any tendency towards an early release of the [p] is clearly inhibited by the forthcoming labiality of the close of the cluster. Elsewhere, if a 'stepping-out' of the cluster is possible (that is, $*pH_e{}^u$-, as it seems to occur in $*pH_e{}^u{}_a$-*is*) no voicing would ensue, as the labial stop may be released close to the onset of *H* and long before ʷ; hence *πάϝιc, etc., and one would expect *ὄκτοϝοc. But this escape hatch is barred in the case of *píbati* by the morphological structure, as seen in *tíṣṭh-ati*; and voicing of the prelaryngeal stop is enforced. (Of course, the Sanskrit patterning, as discussed above, here prompts the further question: why not *pibhati? To which Winter (1965, 108f.) offers a possible (non-Jakobson) solution: that in PIE itself the voiced stop resulting from this clustering had to fall into the /b/ phoneme, the /'bh'/ phoneme being neutral, or even negative, as to the voice-feature. But *gH* gives $(gh >)h$ in Skt. not *g*, and only negativity would ensure such a PIE redistribution, not mere neutrality; more likely, the breath-feature of *H*, in this labial structure, is masked). At all events, an anomalous and apparently unique phenomenon is the result of the

---

[22] So Cowgill (1960b, 350). On this view, the alternation type φᾱμί/φωνή rests on *e*/*o*A, parallel to ῥήγνυμι/ἔρρωγα (on *e*/*o*E, presumably). But *a*/*o*H may be safer; see fn. 35.

phonetic structure in the case of *píbati* etc.;[23] it is explainable, but in terms partly phonetic, partly morphological, and wholly idiosyncratic to the relevant environment. The 'colour' of the laryngeal is entirely immaterial; and to split *H* into one variety which causes this voicing unaided, and other unhappy varieties without this power, is misguided and misguiding.

The question as to whether *H* is itself voiced — or, as commonly put, whether one of the *H*s is voiced — is usually hopelessly entangled with the last problem. Martinet is in error (and not alone so) in supposing[24] that only a phoneme's distinctive voice can cause voicing in contiguous sounds, and that any laryngeal with this property must justify the supposition of its own voiceless counterpart as an equipollent PIE phoneme. Nor need a voicing effect depend on vocal cord movement as an original component of any individual segment; that movement may be induced by secondary physiological reactions attendant on the co-articulation of overlapping elements in the sequence. Therefore nothing of this proves the presence or absence of voice as an essential feature of *H*.

An argument which might lead to a decision derives from the rules of Hittite orthography. It is possible to hold, as does Gamkrelidze (1961, 211 ff.), that double writing of stops indicates not merely voicelessness but also voiceless aspiration; and that consonants of

---

[23] Anomalous also because its voicing has not spread to e.g. *apāt* (cf. *asthāt* with spread of aspiration); but homalizing of paradigms is a very idiosyncratic matter, even when the same feature is under comparison (cf. the variant spread of Latin nasal infix in *iungere, pingere, fundere*). One should note, however, that if the articulations of the [p] and '[H]' overlap as far as is suggested above the production of the labial stop must initially inhibit a pharyngal closure, especially when voicing ensues (cf. Yanagihara and Hyde, *Studia Phonologica* [Kyoto], 4 (1965-66), 79 on this late closing — or for [b] the late and weak closing — of the 'velopharyngeal space'). Hence in the 'bibo' word, and any others of like structure, no shift of $HV > a$ is to be expected.

[24] See Martinet (1957a, 44). So also Lehmann (1952, 107), Winter (1965, 158). The devoicing power of [s] in many Latin environments (*rēx, apsente*, etc.) rests on no distinctive feature opposing /s/ to */z/. Cf. also the voicing power of (only voiced) /m/ in *segmentum*. (Yet the voice-feature need influence contiguous phonemes no more than, say, Gk. -κμ- is affected: i.e. ἀκμή etc. are regular, and the shift -κμ- > -γμ- always permits ultimate tracing to a start-point in a verb like λέγω where γ is etymological).

this class are equally the ultimate reflexes of (a) PIE voiceless stops alone, and (b) PIE voiceless or VOICED stops plus H. It seems inconceivable that the equation $*gH > kh = kh < k$ (whatever the actual phonetic nature of what is thus written as -kk- or -gg-) can admit of any maintenance of voice in the PIE laryngeal. Still, differences of features between PIE vowels (duration, aperture etc.) are often obscured at even the earliest attested and comparable stages of IE languages; and one cannot securely assign to, say, PIE /t/ a central allophone on the basis of reflex-comparisons. So it is hardly feasible to establish, on the mere basis of Hittite writing, whether in these sequences the H is a particular one chosen from a multiplicity, or the only one PIE offered, and whether its phonetic nature was changed in pre-Anatolian or not.[25]

If anything, the balance of probability is very slightly in favour of a voiced H in PIE, without a voiceless partner, if the Greek evidence is to be fairly weighted (cf. Cowgill, 1965, fn. 1). A well-known connexion was made by Rosén (1957; 1961) between Greek — ἀζω verbs and —ᾱ nouns, the latter displaying the PIE 'late-blooming laryngeal', as Householder has called it, in its non-ablauting version (with -aH throughout, basically). The discussion of this grammatical relationship was soured by side-issues and personalities. To ignore all that is marginal and merely imaginative, the hub of the matter is really the brigading together of e.g. δικάζω (δίκᾱ), ἐλπίζω (ἐλπιδ-) and ἀρπάζω (ἀρπαγ-), although the late emergence of -αδ- stems is an awkwardness. The morphological argument is extremely strong.[26] It does not matter that we prove that $H\underset{\sim}{i}$

---

[25] It can scarcely be thought that -hh- means a reflex of H with the value of velar stop plus aspirate release.

[26] The phonological argument, however, is weak. $H\underset{\sim}{i} > \zeta$ has never been proved (see esp. Cowgill 1965, 163 ff.); and although $Hs > \xi$ is less objectionable — because the feature of voice can be indifferently present or absent in the original cluster, where the stridency of s masks it — it is for this very reason useless as a diagnostic of voiced or voicing H. Rosén also quotes (1957, 366) inscriptional Ναhϲιοϲ and relates *Ναhϲοϲ to νῆϲοϲ; but general acceptance of a local name-pronunciation hardly clinches a common-Greek shift of $Hs > ks$. Frequent extrusion of d from H is urged, without necessity and with a wildness of hypothesis bereft of firm evidence; e.g. "Latin tendō < tennō < *tṇ-nXō- (i.e., tn + nH + ō)", ignoring the unlikelihood of such a two-stage

develops as do $d\underset{.}{i}$ and $g\underset{.}{i}$, for once grouped with them in this morphological consortium $H\underset{.}{i}$ will be at the mercy of co-paradigmatic analogy. So, for instance, in the Attic aorists ἐδίκασα, ἤλπισα and ἥρπασα the -c- develops regularly from none but the -ds-sequence (ἤλπισα) and yet the majority follow suit, despite occasional blacksliders like ἐστήριξα (no doubt the ἔδειξα type makes the -ξα ending attractive). In West Greek there is no need at all to insist that -Hs- becomes -ξ- (as well as do -gs- and -gᵘs-), and that then this larger block influences -ds-. What is crucial is the mere fact that (in all Greek) -H$\underset{.}{i}$ chooses to align itself with -d$\underset{.}{i}$- and -g$\underset{.}{i}$- in verbs, and not with -t(h)$\underset{.}{i}$- and -k(h)$\underset{.}{i}$-. Otherwise one might indeed object that it is not H but $\underset{.}{i}$ which is voiced and which voices ($H\underset{.}{i} > \zeta$). This objection fails. The reflexes of $t\underset{.}{i}$ etc. (voiceless (c)c or (τ)τ, the differences arising from the dorsal/ apical distinction, from dialect choice, and from the position of the sequence in relation to the morphological structure), and of $p\underset{.}{i}$ also if voiceless πτ is its outcome, show that a voiceless stop is more powerful in such a sequence than the voiced semivowel. Therefore, if in $H\underset{.}{i}$ the laryngeal is voiceless it is less strongly so than k, t or p. If we are to deal in yes-or-no terms, it must count as voiced.[27] The verb-types in -$t\underset{.}{i}\bar{o}$ etc. are not absent; but a cognate pair, of noun in -$\bar{a}$ and verb in -άττω, is absent. And the well-established inventory of -ττω verbs (φυλάττω, ἐρέττω etc.), although it could have accommodated a voiceless -$H\underset{.}{i}\bar{o}$, simply has not done so. True, Thessalian has ἐμφανίσσω (Att. ἐμφανίζω),

---

effect, especially when the first stage produces an apparently stable form; ignoring, too, the probable analogical pressure on earlier and straightforward *tennō* of lexically similar *-hendō*, *pandō*, whose own *-nd-* is respectably achieved; cf. the reverse effect of *distennite* on *dispennite*, which is what Nonius seems to read at Plautus, *Mil.* 1407. Likewise the statement '**-CeHiō/-CHiō > -άζω/ -ίζω*' will convince few.

On the priority of -άζω verbs to -αδ- nouns see E. Schwyzer, *Acta Jutlandica* 9 (1937), 63 ff. He derives -άω from -άζω, where Rosén sees a difference between -$\bar{o}$ and -$i\bar{o}$ formations.

[27] Differential cavity pressure was mentioned above. This, when sublaryngeal versus buccal, has been cited (e.g. by Lisker, *Word* 19 [1963], 377) as a prerequisite for voicing: at least then we have favourable conditions for voiced PIE *H*. (The fortis-lenis distinction Lisker relates to another 'mode' of description; it is, as usually by laryngealists, ignored here.)

and Attic has ἁρμόττω and (in prose) cφάττω (elsewhere ἁρμόζω and cφάζω), and so forth; but these are rarities on a par with the curious Attic avoidance of *πτηττω (and Attic δεcπόζω shows the reverse process). True also, one could believe that the verbal formants -άω and -άζω, one of which has always been an isolate either in PIE or in Greek, answer to nothing more than the presence of devoicing/non devoicing H (before i) respectively; this would explain why -άζω verbs occur before the relevant -αδ- nouns. Then a negative argument — the failure of -ττω verbs to pull voiceless -Hio into line — would undermine the morphological point just made in respect of the -cω forms. But a shift $Hi > \emptyset$ is neither proved nor likely, and the -άω verbs remain a mystery, although they may simply arise from forms without -i-. Thus it looks as if it is not possible to deny a voiced Greek reflex of a PIE laryngeal; but this consideration is open to the same weaknesses, as a PIE statement, as the Hittite suggestion of an inherited voiceless H; and it cancels out, and is itself cancelled out by, that possibility. A multiplicity of laryngeals may provide a solution. But as no other evidence has yet pointed to such a multiplicity, it is more likely that one environment's supervening effect was generalized in each case. Evidence in particular languages for the absence of a significant dimension of voice in inherited H (as Winter finds in Armenian, 1965, 107) should be recognized as such, and not related to an unproved 'loss' of voicedness, nor used to establish basic voicelessness of H.

A laryngeal enthusiast who has been following closely may now be moved to cry out for attention to the two major indications of laryngeal multiplicity (and corresponding reduction of PIE basic vowels) — the variety of graphic reflexes in Hittite, and the morphological patterning of Greek $e/a/o$ vowels. Now another clear fact in laryngeal spotting is that the evidence of Hittite is precious little help. One does not undervalue the perspicacity of Kuryłowicz (and Cuny) in identifying Hittite h and PIE H. Some of the equations are unexceptionable (*tar-aḫ-ḫu-un* ~ Skt. *tiráti, tīrṇá-*; *pa-aḫ-ḫa-aš-mi* ~ Skt. *páti*, Lat. *pāsco*; *la-aḫ-ḫa* ~ Gk. λᾱός); and not a few of those which seem to be at variance with the theory are easily weeded out as false etymologies. The trouble with Hittite is the combined obfuscatory power of (a) a largely opaque orthography, and (b) an unknowable range of permissible semantic slip. We cannot be sure either what sounds are co-present or whether, in a language long separated from the majority of IE, the words containing the sounds are really the right ones to be looking at. The controversies over the meaning, and hence the congeners, of the verb *weh-* are a solemn warning (see Polomé, 1952b, 451f.); it is obvious that a standard of semantic closeness which will please everybody is not easily to be had hereabouts. Even if a non-laryngeal source for *h* is unlikely in every contested case, nevertheless a laryngeal history is often very tenuously adduced, by disputable comparisons. As soon as an oral (dorsal) articulation is the outcome of *H* (and the value of written *h*), the sign *h* may very possibly be employed in a historically misleading fashion, especially in a post-merger phonemic orthography.[28] Cautionary examples are rife: just try taking every Laconian β straight back to PIE *b* and see what happens.

Let us ask one or two questions. Is the variation *aḫ-ḫa/ḫa-ḫa* (*i-ya-aḫ-ḫa-ri/e-eš-ḫa-ḫa-ri*) in any way significant? If we add to these digraphs singly written *h*, have we three speech-sounds, two or one? And how many phonemes? Kuryłowicz has given a convincing explanation (1958, 220; based on Kronasser, 1956) of inter alia, the apparent conjugational oddity *ḫar-ap-zi*, *ḫar-ap-pa-an-zi*, as being a merely graphic distortion of regular *harpzi*, *harpanzi*, which is induced by the desire to link the two forms of one lexeme visibly in the script by making them identical in respect of the first two, and not merely the first, cuneiform sign. But this undermines even the limited confidence previously felt in 'spelling rules'. Does *ehh* ever reflect *$*e + H$*? If the apparent germination

---

[28] The direct equation of the outset of *Ahhiyawa* and 'Αχαιϝοί is no longer seriously contested, although the phonetic equivalence of the middle, and the form-identity of the endings, of the name are still uncertain. It may be that Lat. *lacus* (orig. 'trough'?) answers to *la-aḫ-ḫu-uš* ('basin'?) — see Couvreur 1935, 192f. Szemerényi (*Bulletin of the London School of Oriental and African Studies* 27 [1964], 159A) has drawn attention to the Luwian use of *h* where Hittite itself has a velar stop (*nahhuwa* ~ Hitt. *na-ak-ki-e-eš*).

in *te-iḫ-ḫi* derives from two contiguous laryngeals, and that in *ne-iḫ-ḫi* from *nei-H, Hittite really only offers *eh*,[29] *ah* and *ahh* for *H* after a vowel. How do these assort themselves? Not, at any rate, as the outcome of three laryngeals, in view of *na-aḫ-mi*, *na-aḫ-ḫu-un*. Two laryngeals, then? For the existence of *ú-e-iḫ-zi*, *ú-e-ḫu-un* alongside the *nahmi* forms seems to demand the distinction: that is, intervocalic non-variation/variation of the graphic form of *h* would seem to go hand in hand with vowel difference before it.[30] But the obscurity of the root **(H)u̯eH*, which several scholars would relate to Latin *uārus*, and the possibility of vowel harmonizing (*asanzi, atanzi, nahhanzi* may show it) of wide paradigmatic spread, rob these compared conjugations of most of their force. It is quite possible to set up two laryngeals (by asserting, for instance, that nouns like *mehur* and *pahhur* are otherwise identical — so Winter, 1965, 195); but there seems to be no way of telling whether to combine *ah* with *ahh* (against *eh*) or *eh* with *ah* (against *ahh*). The first way leads to two phonemes of laryngeal origin, with differing powers of vowel-coloration, not merely the allomorphones of the one but also its free variants (cf. *la-ḫa-a-wa-i*, *la-aḫ-ḫu-u-wa-i*) including the regular, single, exponent of the other. This is a curious result within one stage of one language. The second way gives two laryngeal reflexes as Hittite phonemes, with differing glottality and with restriction of the range of vowels which

---

[29] That **-ehh-* is non-existent is roundly stated by Crossland (1951, 108) and Polomé (1965, fn. 160): Sturtevant (1951, 50) prefers to derive *-ehh-* from **-ei-H*. Now *-ah-* is infrequent; and Cowgill has suggested that *-eh-* in *-ehu-* may be a graphism (for [-ɛ-u-], whereas *-eu-* denotes [-ɛu-]), *h* operating somewhat as in German. (This notion leaves *h* as the visible reflex of *H* ('*E*', scarcely '*O*', as Winter 1965, 196f.) in e.g. *sehur* (cf. *sēmen*, etc.), and absence of glide may be historically directly linked with faucal occlusion; but it allows non-*H* origins for *-ehu-*, as in (**pewate-* >) *pehute-*. Then, even if we allow the 'metathesizing' form *pahhur*, the opposed reflexes in the wider range of comparanda reduce themselves to *hh* (the post-*a* allophone, perhaps arising from a velarized dissimilation from pharyngal occlusion) and Ø; but etymologies involving Ø are usually suspect in their uncontrolled application — see fn. 32.

[30] See Crossland (1958, 81) who makes out a strong case for dispensing with all but two laryngeals, visible in Hittite. (Note that *wahzi* and *wahhuzi* occur in non-native texts). The same authority was earlier (1951, 107) prepared to see analogical vowel homalizing in *nahmi*.

may precede in one case; but with a unwelcome intra-paradigm phonemic opposition between *nah-* and *nahh-* (one cannot, this time, excuse it as phonemic neutralization in the very forms which serve as a theoretical base for its assertion). In the absence of a clear indication of the purpose of the dittography of *h*, arguments from elsewhere are unhelpful. The morphological imbalance *eh – eh*, *ah – ahh* may be no more mysterious, and no less a matter of unilingual form-history, than e.g. *ia:–ia:* alongside *ia:–iaØ* in Greek (gen.) coφίας ἡδείας, (nom.) coφία ἡδεῖα.[31] Why not experiment with one laryngeal? The phonemic status of *h* is then secure, as it must be; and an original allomorphonic variety would have to be admitted in only one class of environments (i.e. after *a*). Or, perhaps, it was only there graphically noted (Hendriksen at least thought of allographic variation here). In Sanskrit mere phonetic variants of PIE /n/ are not specially marked in writing in some environments, so that one has, in the succession *m* ... *V/C*, no indication of any shifting of /n/ along the dental-alveolar axis as between *manu* and *manda-*, etc. (the use of anusvāra for homorganic nasal preceding a consonant is a reflection of the phonological irrelevance of any distinction between nasal phones in that position, of course). But the different signs in *kurvanti, karṇa* show a native phonetic awareness which leads (unlike the difference apprehended between *n* and *ñ*) to a phonemic opposition, when ultimately extended even beyond the 'long prosodic domain' of *..r...C* and *...r...V* successions. So that Hittite may here be showing the separate vowel phonemes /e/ and /a/ in skewed co-occurrence with one/both of two exponents of a single phoneme derived from *$*H$, these latter variants being environmentally induced in the post-*a* position (the stimulus is no longer necessarily perceptible), and possibly passing later into phonemic opposition elsewhere. Such skewness is not too difficult to show within these localized, part-paradigm, pseudo-comparisons: for a generally similar example, there is the unbalanced Latin co-occurrence of *u* and *i*, with Ø/Ø and Ø/: respectively (which do not continue distinct PIE phonemes), in the parallel

---

[31]   This example is, however, morphologemic, not lexemic. For the distinction, see chapter 2, p. 25.

sectors *lŭ-erem*, *lŭ-ēbam* but *fĭ-erem*, *fĭ-ēbam*. If it is all mere graphism, we may note the British English pairings *parallels*, *paralleled* as against *travels*, *travelled* where the stimulus IS still visible.

The arguments which have employed negative evidence in Hittite (zero reflexes being supposed to be really present and corroborative of some PIE H) have led to results as suspect as the process. The undeniable fact that Hittite *h* and *hh* sometimes turn up where the heavenly twins 'H_1' (or 'H_3') and 'H_2' are looked for, and sometimes do not, is erected into a hypothesis of at least four laryngeals. A second pair ('H_5' or 'h_1', and 'H_4' or the like) is added, their distinguishing characteristic being simply that they vanish between PIE and proto-Anatolian. Kuryłowicz (1935a, 254 cf. Polomé, 1965, 15) makes the most of this device by adding other non-powers: after H_4 is devised, H_2 is credited with not aspirating a preceding consonant and not colouring /o/. Those must be right who express unease when absence of evidence leads to depth of theory; but voices of doubt rarely become a powerful chorus, because 'laryngeal problems' usually offer a wealth of alternative explanations. More revealing is the absence of unison on the positive side. It is interesting to compare the divergent relating of Hittite Ø/h/hh to types of H by successive theorists.[32]

Recently, with a few notable exceptions, it is the conservative faction which has been the more vocal and effective. Have they been even cautious enough? The Hittite sequence *eh* is frequent; the reverse, *he*, is hard to find. As *wahanzi* can occur in the same paradigm as *úehzi* — a common pattern — and *wassanzi* alternates with *wessanzi*, no weight attaches to *hesanzi* (alongside *hassanzi* and sing. *has(z)i*), as Polomé shows (1965, fn. 131). For *hegur* (*ḫe-gur* or *ḫe-kur*) there is no clear etymon (cf. Pedersen, 1938, 183f.), and what IS offered does not help to establish *e*-colouring (cf. Puhvel, 1965, 88). The allegedly parallel lexical forms adduced

---

[32] See, for example, the digest by K. Ammer, *Wissenschaftliche Zeitschrift der Martin-Luther-Universität, Halle-Wittenberg* 7.1, 136. Sturtevant's rule 'IH *erC* > Hitt. *arC*' makes little difference, except that his own assignment of *xe-* and *γe-* may need re-thinking.

to account for *henkan* (*ḫe-en-kan*, *ḫi-in-ga-an* etc.), namely Irish *ec* (cf. *écen*?) and Welsh *angheu* (cf. *anghen*), do not provably need any more complex origin than $*\eta k(u)(en)$- (alongside guṇa $*nek(u)$-; in any case Benveniste (1935, 155) relies on this word (I $\partial_2 én$-k-, II $\partial_2 n$-$ék$), and its cognates which shown *ank*- like reduplicated ἀνάγκη, if there is an initial laryngeal, to establish the occurrence of the *a*-colouring variety. If not a lot remains of these *he* occurrences, the preponderance of Hittite words beginning with *ha*-becomes overwhelming and suggestive. Some words clearly began with a prevocalic laryngeal and show *o* in the cognate forms elsewhere (ὄρνις, ὄϊς etc.). But no laws of formation prevent their being cases of 'spoiled metaphony' ($^e/_o$ replaced by $^\emptyset/_o$), followed by the shifts $Ho > o$ outside Hittite, $Ho > ha$ within it. Even this general Anatolian $o > a$ shift removes a mere handful of items from consideration; Szemerényi, 1967, 93, cites only five. Apart from a few cases of special interference,[33] Hittite proclaims that prevocalic *H* turns its vowel into *a*. Historically, this doctrine involves adjustments of analogy (see page 94) or etymology. Either the alternating absence and presence of *H* as C_3 explains the divergence of e.g. γένος ($*g^len + ^e/_o s$; for the possibility of an aniṭ form see Cowgill, 1965, 148) from e.g. κρέας ($*kreuH$- $+ _e s$ or restored guṇa $^e/_o s$); or the morphemic boundary in $*g^l enH + ^e/_o s$ precludes the pharyngalization of the post-*H* vowel, while in $*kreuH_e s$ the prosodic nature of the vocalism $_e$ obscures the boundary; or else we can use the escape hatch offered by Benveniste, 1935, 32f. ($*κρέ$-$αρ$). In articulatory terms we should conclude that the infra-buccal closures which produce the exponent of *H* have as their final component a constriction of the pharynx, which affects the ensuing vowel as one might predict: maximal pharyngal contraction correlates directly with the frequency raising of the first formant (F1), and so with the production of a low central (flat, compact) vocoid. This simplicity of acoustic-articulatory relation

[33] E.g. *li-ik-zi*, *li-in-ga-zi* ('swears oath') formally parallels *ḫi-ik-zi*, *ḫi-in-ga-zi*, and the lexical connexion ('oath' ~ 'self-destruction sanction', or the like?) is at least as close as is that with νέκταρ which is sometimes stated as a cognate. Therefore a pressure of conformity, upon the form of an earlier $*hank$- is not impossible.

is nowhere else afforded by a pattern of basic *i-a-u* triangulation.[34] One need not suppose a total transfer of articulation features to the vowel, at least not regularly (for the 'loss' of *H* was explained before); so *hanti* etc. are the expected Hittite forms. Nor is the pharyngal effect coterminous with the whole duration of *H*; the presence of *eh* and rarity of *he* in Hittite argues for *a*-colouring as being only a post-laryngeal feature, and other evidence points the same way.[35] Perhaps failure to realize this led Martinet (1957a,

[34] For a statement, and a radiographic display, of this articulatory relation, see Fant, 1965, 126, 128 and 129 fig. 8, and Truby, 1965, 351-353. It is true that [ə] also correlates with narrowness of the pharyngal gap, but this feature in [a] is the dominant factor of its discrimination from front vowels. In view of the Greek transfer of the Sem. *ain* sign to *o*-value, and the interplay of *a/o* in the reflexes of *$^*\eta$, *$^*r$ etc., it is just conceivable that constriction of the upper larynx is part of *H*; cf. Catford, 1964, 33f., who attaches 'ainish' quality to that constriction. (The same writer, 1964, 34f., links vertical displacement of the larynx directly with raising and lowering of the first formant (and lowered larynx, as a feature of a stop, is said to be heard as a 'muffled' or 'centralized' quality of the following vowel — which is surely true only of a vowel which has a naturally high F1 to start with, like [a]). This may hint that one component of *H* is a raising of the larynx, and so of F1).

[35] Before *h* Hittite *e/a* alternation remains possible; after *h* is a different matter (see above). From what has been said it is reasonable to expect *ha*- as the general reflex of *$^*HV$-, and nothing points to *H* being lost at the time of its pharyngalizing effect. This makes all the more curious objections like Wyatt's (1964, 149) to the absence of c.g. *$^*henti$ (or, presumably, *$^*anti$) in place of *hanti*; especially curious, since Wyatt here dislikes the co-presence of *h* and *a* in a form cited to corroborate '*H_2e*', but on the next page equally dislikes the absence in Sanskrit and Latin of *H* reflex before *a* (*kakúd-*, *cacūmen*; but on this presumed connexion — see Kuryłowicz, 1956, 192). To be sure, laryngealists tend to be inconsistent, but Wyatt merely inverts the inconsistency. This whole thesis in favour of returning to PIE vocalic /ə/ (plus /h/) rests on a fundamental anxiety to see PIE fitted out with a neatly patterned vowel-system — which is an over-optimistic aim in what can only be a skeleto-phonemic statement — and he tilts above all at '/H_2e/ > [a]', which is probably the second strongest point in all laryngealism. But he does very well to show up *H* as rather a morphophoneme than a phoneme, as being derived from morphological-cum-phonetic speculations (as is any finding of internal reconstruction). This fact makes the grammatical underemployment of *H* as a morpheme constituent all the more of a problem in relation to its phonological description.

Wyatt must be right, too, in his suspicions over the removal of /a/ and independent /o/ from PIE. The number of PIE vowels is not argued out in this present discussion, because it need not be tied to the number of *H*s (except that, in seeking base + process explanations for complicated IE reflexes, the

42) to deny to some laryngeals (that is, to set up a multiplicity of laryngeals in order to deny to some of them) this feature of pharyngal 'darkening' ('effet d'assombrir'). There must be all the difference in the world — corroborated by the relative IE frequencies of e/o/a (long and short) — between the environments where PIE *H apparently preceded the syllabic and those where *H followed. That is why 'A' is a tiresome symbol, for it not only suggests too much (like 'ə'), but posits a pharyngalization by H in all directions.

Anyone who has tried to give a sensible comparative account of IE zero-grade syllable behaviour knows what hard cases present themselves. Examples like χάτις (along with χῆρος, χωρίς) or ἐρράγην — in which Cowgill (1965, 150) sees 'a new super-zero grade' — (along with ῥήγνυμι, ἔρρωγα) or ἔπτακον (along with πτήσσω, πτωχός) — merely to cite some famous forms — make hazardous any manipulations with unaffected 'restored guṇa vowel' or 'anaptyctic vowel which then falls together with an allophone of a frequent vowel phoneme'. These processes should produce Greek ε or ι, as in reduplication (πίπτω, πέπτωκα) or in euphonic insertion (as in π-ί-τνω, or π-ί-Hνω, πίνω, etc.). Equally difficult is any Greek explanation which simultaneously hopes to cope also with e.g. θετός, δοτός. Again, Latin *satus* and the like

simultaneous reduction of number of vowels and number of laryngeals is a theoretic luxury we cannot afford). That is, although the PIE phonological system may have had a maximal consonantal component and a minimal vowel component, these facts must be separately proved. Typologically, even ten Hs scarcely compensate for the reduction to one PIE vowel. In any case, the metaphonic relation of o to e might restrict its free occurrence, and a may be less rare and able to be explained away than has been thought (see Szemerényi, 1964, esp. 8 and 25ff.), and simply more susceptible to analogical shifts in non-initial, less lexically fixed, syllables. This imbalance of frequency of vowel types need not depend on H. But a one-vowel system is not typologically impossible (see Allen, 1965; also the comments in fn. 41 on Szemerényi, 1967). Pulleyblank (1965) rehabilitates a as a basic PIE vowel; but gives cold comfort to this present thesis by supposing at most a two-vowel system (ə/a-, the choice of these two depending on the greater viability and typological strength of aperture contrast than of front-back distinctions). His approval of Allen and Kuipers and their Caucasian findings perhaps indicates a supporter of multiple H; but at least Pulleyblank sees a as original (though also as a morpheme marking 'introvert' meaning as against 'extrovert' ə, following Aert Kuipers's ideas on Kabardian) and o as possibly nothing but shifted a.

are much more awkward than is usually admitted. It is not possible to import an *a*-colouring into *sēuī* (or into the **dheH* root, to cater for *facio*). Yet once a vocalism has been introduced into a basically vowelless syllable-slot — and that despite some inconvenience in the case of **dhH+k-iō*, for which **dh(H)-ō* or **didh(H)- ō* might have served (cf. *dō, sistō, serō*) — it is allowed, against paradigmatic levelling, to assume *a*-colour. Hence **CRHeC* > ῥαγῆναι etc. All of which is cogent indication of a laryngeal's pharyngalizing offset.

That the Greek triad τίθημι, ἵcτᾱμι and δίδωμι are a team devoted to thoroughgoing and incorrigible vowel-analogy, so that we learn nothing about 'colour' or number of laryngeals from θετόc, δοτόc etc., has been accepted doctrine since Brugmann's days, or de Saussure's. Possibly the latter's notation '*A*' and '*Q*' imply a basic but unmentioned '*E*' and give a three-*H* status, to speak anachronistically, to this theory of PIE vocalism (for the permutation of a_1, $a_2 = e$, *o*, with *A* and *Q* gives an unbalanced frequency of *ē/ō/ā*). But it was the variety of the IE guṇa grade, and not the Greek triple zero reflex, which took de Saussure on that path. So Couvreur and others have since then rejected this evidence (but now see Winter, 1965, 201). And where ρω, νω, νη etc. are clearly analogically affected reflexes of * r̄* (in form-scatters including guṇa -*roH, -neH* etc.), ρᾱ, νᾱ etc. are merely the long equivalents of ρα < *r̥*, themselves echoing the vocalic colour of other co-paradigmatic forms. Forms like κλῆcιc, τρῆcιc would naturally affect κλητόc and τρητόc; and although 'guṇa restoration' (or even just the euphonically motivated choice of adding a suffix in guṇa rather than zero grade) is not to everyone's liking in coping with τρητόc, θνᾱτόc, γνωτόc, a single *H* would lengthen, and analogy would then colour, the vocalism however it came into being.

But what of, say, ἔπορον, ἔμολον etc.? Have we here what Kuiper (1947, 199) termed 'laryngeal Umlaut'? Now a direct transsyllabic phonetic effect by '*H₃*' can be ruled out, unless *H* is put back into the melting pot and brought out afresh in the form of an extensive prosody. No evidence supports that idea, and the different vocalism of *tīrṇá-* and *pūrṇá-* argues against it. The Greek forms which are often held to show such Umlaut are the aorists of the type ἔμολον and the sigmatics ἐκόρεσα (unless this has the wrong sort of *H* — cf. *crēscō*) and ἐστόρεσα (cf. Lehmann 1952, 93 f.). But the Greek variation in the reflex of 'ṛ' (not always homalized in the dialects, by any means) allows a choice even outside Aeolic and Arcado-Cyprian; and the choice may here be influenced, perhaps at the cost of remodelling, by the analogical pressures outlined by Kuryłowicz (1956, 206 ff.) and made quite explicit by Cowgill (1960a, 101; 1965, 147 f.). That is, for the first type, a replacement of βλώσκω, *ἔμαλον and πέπρωται, *ἔπαρον etc. by -*o*- forms has been induced by the κμᾱτός, ἔκαμον correspondence. If, as Kuryłowicz suggests, ἐγενόμην, γένεσις and γνητός are analogical also, one looks desperately for *ToRo* types to answer to γενε-, and he offers ὀμόσαι and (Aeolic) ἐστόροται. This allows for, but hardly explains, a shift *ἐστάροσα > *ἐστόροσα > (curiously) ἐστόρεσα; a better start-point might be *ἐστάρασα, in view of the general IE post-laryngeal vocalism we are arguing. Or else (Cowgill, 1960, 114) guṇa forms like *stera*- (< *'sterO*-') are analogically shifted first to *stero*- and then to στορε- (as Ruipérez proposed, *Emerita* 18 [1950], 386 ff., but deriving the aorist shift from that in the future). Or again (to cite Cowgill's later ruminations, 1965, 158) *stero*- was assimilated to *stere*-, then remodelled to στορε- (alongside στρω-) like γενε- (alongside γνη-). But ἐκάλεσα, with no analogical reflex in the root (*κελε-), seems to argue for *σταρα or *σταρο-. One might offer a quite independent analysis, for example, of ἔπορον as being parallel to πόρος with basic *o*-metaphony and no root-final *H* (any more than γένος need have one: see above, p. 90): so τόρος beside τιτρώσκω. Sturtevant's rejection of non-apophonic *o* seems to have bemused scholars into refusing to admit even apophonic *o*; this is an act of panic unnecessary even if no *e*-vocalism of the root remains visible — in *that* case they rush in terror back to non-apophonic *o* (cf. Cowgill, 1965, 145 fn. 2) — whereas it IS visible alongside πορ- (in πείρω, περάω etc.) and alongside τορ- (in τέρετρον, etc.).

The one obtrusive phenomenon, in fact, within the total range of IE vowel colouring, is the predominance of *a* in syllables which are not, for one reason or another, to be regarded as continuations of the

PIE full grade. Kuryłowicz (1965, 175-195) gives scores of comparative examples of apparent guṇa and non-guṇa a; of the latter, however, he well points out that its permeation of all structures of roots does not enforce (indeed, helps to preclude) its being the total and sole marker of the zero grade. Therefore a is both excessively frequent and yet largely derivative. In initial syllables o cannot be divorced from a basic e/o metaphony (not unless our comparative examples were much more numerous and e positively excluded in all cognates), and is in any case less frequent than a so placed. There are those who prefer a word-initial laryngeal to cope with a-vocalism at a word's onset (Meillet, *Introduction*, 166-168, sees this as the only place where PIE /a/ is well established; see also Cowgill, 1965, 145, who equates the #o- problem with the #a- problem); and, for all the lexical and structural objections possible in individual cases, this procedure is often convincing. Moreover, the range of reflexes of laryngeal-linked 'schwa primum' (especially if Sanskrit, with its overloaded /a/, is disregarded as being a special case, in its divergence to /i/) is revealingly limited, by those who are satisfied with this superficial historical statement, to a general a, even in pre-Slavic — whereas the range for the vocalic elements attaching to zero grade liquids and nasals extends over all the main vowels (*un-*, *cord-*, *ἀν-*, *ueniō*, *dešimt*). The point need not be pressed any further. A pharyngal component within (and with its release operating as the last act of) a complex, and environmentally varying, infra-buccal constriction, plus overlapping oral closures of greater or less completeness — such is demanded as the essential explanatory link between the historical comparanda.

As for the labialized laryngeal(s) of Sweet and Martinet, and the palatalized laryngeal(s) of Diver (and Puhvel),[36] the presence of

---

[36] See Martinet (1953), Diver (1959). Risch (*Corolla Linguistica* 1955, 189-198) has a good argument for H^i in Hitt. *da-it-ti*, *ti-(ya-)an-zi* and like forms. General IE hesitation over *TR*, *sC-*, k^u etc. make one feel that, considering the smaller evidential support for H^u and H^i, these constructs need more frequency and more clear co-functioning (in reflexes) of their components before they are promoted, in phonemic terms, to any status beyond 'favoured sequences'. One feels too suspicious of the very existence of 'long diphthongs' in PIE to place much weight on the argument that co-functioning of components is the possible producer of '*ēi*' and '*ōu*' (see Cowgill, 1965, 178 on these Schulzean

PIE k^u, g^u, $g^u h$ must be as much a positive disincentive to setting up the former (as these would increase the 'integration' which would rob H of its instability in all positions), as the absence of PIE k^i etc. is an encouragement to believing in the latter. If the occurrence of these theoretical creations is really explanatory of some awkward phenomena, and is restricted to sporadic environments, all the better. The argument offered above for the hard case of *píbati*, and the support given by *$\pi\acute{\alpha}$ϝιϲ etc. for H_a^u, inevitably make up for the failures of Martinet's too generalized case.[37] His sponsoring of labial and pharyngal components is therefore quite welcome, and would be thoroughly welcome if these components were not implicated with each other (as Adrados implicitly perceives, and deserves a good mark therefor). Diver's case is even better, as long as it remains limited, at least in theory; though individual etymologies will not please all. The non-universality of this compounding, and its affinity with the fronted timbre which any H might get by associating with front vowels, may explain, and be illustrated by, the palatalisation which connects with 'E' in Tocharian (Winter, 1965, 201 ff.). And actually there is nothing in theory to gainsay — and much to commend — *occasional* co-occurrence of components. Hence Cowgill's creation "$*A^{wy}$", however ironically intended, is at least theoretically acceptable.[38]

---

forms). But in this direction a multiplicity of laryngeal phonemes is not out of the question.

[37] Lat. *octō* and *octāuus*, if so explained, fall foul of Szemerényi's demonstration of $\bar{o}u > \bar{a}u$ (and subsequent emergence of -*ău*-) as a Latin shift (*KZ* 70, 1951, 51 ff.). *Flāuī* is nullified by the Greek evidence (Collinge, 1959, 231 f.). The complex *lahhuwai*-, λούω, *rewotoro*-, *lauō*, *loganam*, etc. remains mysterious (?*leH^u, ?loH^u, ?*$leH^u u$, ?*$leuH^u$: see Winter (1960a, 37 fn. 9; 1965, 108), Cowgill (1965, 158 f.). A shift 'H > ϝ' in Cypr. *towenai* is mythical (Cowgill, 1964, 354 ff.). I say nothing of Adrados's fantasies in equating -*neH*- and -*neu*-verbs, as if all from -*neH^u*-, and arbitrarily differentiating their syllabic behaviour in what are clearly morphologically identical reflexes.

[38] For H^i, note Kuiper's (1955) Vedic Sandhi rule: '-*iH#C*- → -*i:#C*-, but -*iH#V*- → -*iy#V*-' (cf. Allen, 1962, 35). For 'A^{wy}' see Cowgill (1960a, 146 f.; 1965, 178), Puhvel (1960b, 169). If only Greek palatalization could be shown to reflect a PIE tendency, one might relevantly cite what seems to be an overall palatalization of labiovelars: both the regular reflexes, τ before front vowels and π before back vowels, suggest $k^u > \acute{k}^u$ (cf. also (τ)τίτανοϲ, Skt. *śvitna*-, from *$\acute{k}u$-*itn*-).

As Puhvel has said (1960a, 11), "laryngeals of maximum articulatory complexity stand the best chance of being subjected to identification, while such phonemes as a glottal stop and /h/ ... are worst off in this regard, due to their paucity of distinctive components". More to the point, such phonetic complexity, plus short-range environmental effects and plus morphological interference, will alone explain the evidential problems of compared IE morphemes where H is suspected. Again, the impalpability of H is a function of its own instability, and this in turn rests on the complexity we have asserted. Furthermore, we must predicate isolation, and 'asystemicness', of H; theories of multiple H rest on insufficiently widespread constant vowel colouring or non-application of the structural effects just described. Hammerich (1948b) may have urged a single PIE laryngeal, as Couvreur once (1935, 33 ff.) implied such an isolate at a late stage of PIE, for want of confidence in any real differentiating power in the evidence (even in vowel 'colours'). Scardigli (1958, 73 ff.) may, more negatively still, not only decline to set up a multiplicity, but even divest his solitary H of all effects other than that of producing the Hittite phoneme conveyed by some $h(h)$ spellings. Szemerényi (1967) may reduce this sector of PIE consonantism to a single glottal fricative as a counterbalance to the multiplicity, separately 'proved', of PIE vowels, and to give minimal exponence to a typological requirement.[39] It were better that they transform their sensible but unhappy doubts into a cheerful creed: that the whole character of PIE H, far from being an invitation to irresponsible multiplication of its entity, is actually a lucid argument for its essential singularity.[40] And hence the title of this essay.[41]

[39] For other unitarians, see Szemerényi, 1967, 90, fn. 79.

[40] Watkins (1960, 234) ventilates the notion that different placing in root structures may reflect different laryngeals in PIE. If this means phonemically different laryngeals, polysystemicness is here being developed even beyond Firthian bounds, and the concept of phoneme loses some of its usefulness, somewhat after the transformationalist manner. If phonetic difference is meant, however, we can come closer to establishing a single PIE /H/.

[41] I am indebted to several people for comments on this thesis, to none more than to Warren Cowgill, whose penetrating remarks have led me to improvements even in the many cases where he prefers a different explanation. He is

above all correct in seeing a major objection to the theme of this intentionally provocative study in the nasal infix verbs, where Greek shows -nā-, apparently reflecting *-neA-. A purely consonantal root form *TRA (rather than *TRaH) permits the infix to be ablauting né/n, the likeliest form (see chapter 2, footnote 26 and Cowgill, *Language* 39, 1963, 252). Non-colouring H must either return us (via TR-n-aH) to a Benvenistean infix of simple shape n, without a proper 'state II' form, or else force an appeal to vowel analogy: that is, (δάμ)νᾰμεν (< *(dm)-n-H-ₑmen) must be held to induce (δάμ)νᾱμι as (δείκ)νῠμεν induces (δείκ)νῡμι. This latter notion accounts for the absence of other than a-colouring in Greek 'ninth-class' verbs; but then what is the pattern for the νυ/νευ > νῠ/νῡ shift itself? In the basic -mi verbs, it is after all the full grade which seems to have affected (in coloration) the zero grade, and we do not get from τίθημι/ *τιθᾰμεν to τιθᾱμι/*τιθᾰμεν, but to τίθημι/τίθεμεν. But possibly -θημι/-θεμεν brings -νῠμι/-νῠμεν into line, and -νᾱμι/-νᾰμεν fits that patterning. Szemerényi's manifesto (1967) appeared after the first writing of this chapter. It staunchly rejects Benveniste's enforcement of CeC in the basic PIE rootshapes, and would be a welcome reinforcement to the one-laryngeal movement were its suggestions on that score, where positive and new, also watertight (e.g. the comparative frequency of Hitt. he- as against ha- is obscured). Jakobsonian universals, statistical and implicational, are trusted despite the constant emergence of contrary cases; and a revelation, that the vowel systems of PIE and the North Western Caucasian languages are essentially not alike, is nullified by the admission that Ubykh could have an identical C:V phoneme ratio with minimal PIE (80:4::20:1 — not 'almost identical' as is grudgingly said, 87). Viability tests are applied to a skeletal system; and odd things are said about semi-vowels. A single PIE 'laryngeal' (= glottal spirant) is deduced from Jakobson's pronouncement that aspirated stops imply freestanding /h/ as a co-occurrent; and /Cʰ/-type phonemes are formed by a process of cohesion (C + h) somewhere in 'pre-IE', while h-lengthened vowels (eh > ē, etc.) come to compete with original long vowels. But 'typology' does not preclude a multiplicity of /h/s, of which some may be pharyngal; and if Mandarin has a dorso-velar spirant in place of /h/, Anatolian has the same sort of 'near miss' — and so might PIE have. A fixed phonetic unity is not demanded by all this; and the different time-depth of e.g. Skt. /gh/ and /kh/ is blandly ignored. To start with ē etc. as well as eh etc. is to avoid accounting for a loss of original length in Anatolian; but as all sign of the length feature has gone in that group this is false economy. Moreover, the idea (92) that e.g. ā alternates with zero ə, which latter then attracts zero H (whence Hə > ə again) — although it rightly rids us of that chimera, vocalic 'Ḥ' — yet loads us afresh with the incubus of 'shwa secundum' after our recent years of freedom. (And why does e.g. *tā, 'steal', have a zero-grade which 'naturally resulted' in *tə-? If the 'nature' in question is that of stress languages, then unstressed vowels are only readily lost or centralized IF ORIGINALLY SHORT — provided the long/short difference is phonologically distinct from stress itself — and the prime relation would be of *tă- to- to *təᴸ. The oddity of having some zero relict of long vowels where short vowels entirely vanish was the very circumstance which prompted the 'sonant coefficient' — or H — theory in the first place).

REFERENCES

The reader's attention is called to the critical bibliographical survey of the laryngeal theory, exhaustive to 1963, compiled by Edgard Polomé as the introductory chapter to the second edition of *Evidence for Laryngeals* (Mouton, The Hague, 1965), 9-78. The following list is therefore limited to works actually cited or implied above; and where items are common to this list and to Polomé's, *his* 'year-number' (e.g. '1957a') is employed.

Adrados, Francisco R. 1961, *Estudios sobre las laringales indoeuropeas* (= *Manuales y anejos de 'Emerita'*, vol. 19) (Madrid).
—— 1964, "A proposito di laringali", *Archivio Glottologico Italiano*, 49, 147-149.
Allen, W. Sidney 1958, "Some problems of palatalization in Greek", *Lingua* 7, 113-133.
—— 1962, *Sandhi* (The Hague).
—— 1965, "On one-vowel systems", *Lingua* 13, 111-124.
Benveniste, Emile 1935, *Origines de la formation des noms en indo-européen*, I (Paris).
—— 1962, *Hittite et indo-européen: études comparatives* (Paris).
Catford, J.C. 1939, "ən ðə klasıfıkeıʃn əv stəp kənsənənts", *Le Maître Phonétique*, 65, 2-5.
—— 1964, "Phonation types: the classification of some laryngeal components of speech production", *In Honour of Daniel Jones* (London), 26-37.
Collinge, N.E. 1953, "Laryngeals in Indo-European ablaut and problems of the zero grade", *Archivum Linguisticum*, 5, 75-87.
—— 1956, "The limitations of historical phonology", *ibidem*, 8, 111-128.
—— 1959, "External sandhi in Indo-European", *Lingua*, 8, 225-232.
—— 1965, "Some linguistic paradoxes", *Journal of Linguistics*, 1, 1-12.
Couvreur, Walter 1935, *De Hettitsche ḫ* (Louvain).
Cowgill, Warren C. 1960a, "Evidence for laryngeals in Greek", *Evidence for Laryngeals*[1] (The Hague), 93-162. (See 1965).
—— 1960b, "Greek *ou* and Armenian *oč*", *Language*, 36, 347-350.
—— 1964, "The supposed Cypriote optatives *duwánoi* and *dókoi*", *Language*, 40, 344-365.
—— 1965, (= '1960a') revised in *Evidence for Laryngeals*[2] (The Hague), 142-180.
Crossland, Ronald A. 1951, "A reconsideration of the Hittite evidence for the existence of 'laryngeals' in primitive Indo-European", *Transactions of the Philological Society*, 88-130.
—— 1958, "Remarks on the Indo-European laryngeals", *Archivum Linguisticum*, 10, 79-99.
Cuny, Albert 1912, "Notes de phonétique historique. Indo-européen et Sémitique", *Revue de Phonétique*, 2, 101-132.
Diver, William 1959, "Palatal quality and vocalic length in Indo-European", *Word*, 15, 110-122.
Fant, C. G. M. 1965, "Formants and cavities", *Proceedings of the Fifth International Congress of Phonetic Sciences* (1964), 120-140.

Gamkrelidze, Thomas V. 1960, "Xettskij jazyk i laringal'naja teorija", *Trudy Instituta Jazykoznanija, Akademia Nauk Gruzhinskoj SSR* 3, 15-112.

—— 1961, "Peredviženie soglasnyx v Xettskom jazyke" ('The consonant shift in Hittite'), *Peredneaziatskij Sbornik* (Moscow), 211-291, 588-592.

Greenberg, Joseph H. 1950, "The patterning of root morphemes in Semitic", *Word* 6, 162-181.

Hammerich, Louis L. 1948b, *Laryngeal before sonant (KDVS/M*, 31, 3) (Copenhagen).

Hoenigswald, H.M. 1960, "Indo-Iranian evidence for laryngeals", *Evidence for Laryngeals*[1], 13-26. (See '1965').

—— 1965, "Indo-Iranian evidence for laryngeals", *Evidence for Laryngeals*[2], 93-99.

Joos, Martin 1936, review of Zipf, 1935, *Language* 12, 196-210.

Kronasser, Heinz 1956, *Vergleichende Laut- und Formenlehre des Hethitischen* (Heidelberg).

Kuiper, F.B.J. 1947, "Traces of laryngeals in Vedic Sanskrit", *India Antiqua* (= *Festschrift Vogel*) (Leyden), 198-212.

—— 1955, *Shortening of final vowels in the Rigveda* (Amsterdam).

Kurath, Hans 1961, "Phonemics and phonics in historical phonology", *American Speech*, 36, 93-100.

Kuryłowicz, Jerzy 1935a, *Etudes Indo-européennes* I (Cracow).

—— 1956, *L'apophonie en Indo-européen* (Wrocław).

—— 1958, "report on 'Le hittite'", *Proceedings of the Eighth International Congress of Linguists*, 1957 (published 1958), 216-243.

Lehmann, Winfred P. 1952, *Proto-Indo-European phonology* (Austin).

Martinet, André 1953, "Non-apophonic *o*-vocalism in Indo-European", *Word* 9, 253-267.

—— 1955, *Économie des changements phonétiques* (Berne).

—— 1957a, "Les 'laryngales' indo-européennes", *Proceedings of the Eighth International Congress of Linguists*, 1957 (published 1958), 36-53.

—— 1957b, "Phonologie et 'Laryngales'", *Phonetica* 1, 7-30.

Mayrhofer, Manfred 1955, review of T. Burrow, *The Sanskrit Language, Deutsche Literaturzeitung*, 76, cols. 898-901.

Messing, Gordon M. 1947, "Selected studies in Indo-European phonology", *Harvard Studies in Classical Philology*, 56/57, 161-232.

Petersen, Walter 1932, "The personal endings of the Hittite verb", *American Journal of Philology*, 53, 193-212.

—— 1934, "The origin of Hittite *ḫ*", *Language* 10, 307-322.

Polomé, Edgard C. 1952b, "On the source of Hittite *ḫ*", *Language* 28, 444-456.

—— 1965, "The laryngeal theory so far", Introduction to *Evidence for Laryngeals*[2], 9-78.

Puhvel, Jaan 1960b, "Hittite evidence for Indo-European laryngeals", *Evidence for Laryngeals*[1], 164-171; (1960a: = *The Present state of Laryngeal Studies*, introduction to that volume, 1-12) (See '1965').

—— 1965, "Evidence in Anatolian", *Evidence for Laryngeals*[2], 79-92.

Pulleyblank, E.G. 1965, "The IE vowel system and quantitative ablaut", *Word* 21, 86-101.

Rosén, Haiim B. 1957, "Laryngalreflexe und das indogermanische 'schwache' Perfektum", *Lingua* 6, 354-373.

—— 1961, "Greek evidence for laryngeals. A rejoinder to Professor Cowgill", *Lingua* 10, 190-210.

Scardigli, Pier Giuseppe 1958, "Osservazioni sulla teoria delle laringali", *Atti e Memorie dell' Academia Toscana di Scienze e Lettere* 22, 73-116.

Sturtevant, Edgar H. 1951, *A comparative grammar of the Hittite language* (revised edition, I, New Haven).

Szemerényi, O.J.L. 1964, "Structuralism and substratum — Indo-Europeans and Semites in the Ancient Near East", *Lingua* 13, 1-29.

—— 1967, "The new look of Indo-European", *Phonetica* 17, 65-99.

Truby, H.M. 1964, "Pleniphonetic transcription in phonetic analysis", *Proceedings of the Ninth International Congress of Linguists*, 101-108.

—— 1965, "The pharynx in motion", *Phonetica* 14, 351-353.

Watkins, Calvert W. 1960b, "Evidence for Laryngeals in Italic", *Evidence for Laryngeals*[1], 187-197.

—— 1960c, "Componential Analysis of Laryngeals", *Ibid.*, 232-238.

—— 1965, "Evidence in Italic", *Evidence for Laryngeals*[2], 181-189.

Winter, Werner 1960a, "Armenian Evidence", *Evidence for Laryngeals*[1], 27-40.

—— 1965, "Armenian Evidence", *Evidence for Laryngeals*[2], 100-115.

Wyatt, William F., Jr. 1964, "Structural linguistics and the laryngeal theory", *Language* 40, 138-152.

Zipf, George K. 1929, "Relative frequency as a determinant of phonetic change", *Harvard Studies in Classical Philology* 40, 1-95.

—— 1935, *The psychobiology of language* (Cambridge, Mass.) (1966[2]).

6. SOME REFLEXIONS ON COMPARATIVE HISTORICAL SYNTAX*

If a comparison of two or more languages, at any level of analysis, has shown with some plausibility their genetic cognateness, there is a prima facie case for a similar historical connexion in their syntax.[1] Naturally, the first prerequisite is a series of unilingual analyses to establish the syntagms and categories of each language at an adequate number of historical stages within that language (the adequate number being in each case determined empirically, according to the rate and thoroughness of change in the structure of each language). Analysts are on the whole well aware of the difficulties which beset this task. It may be worth saying, however, that where there is a sufficient body of historical material to make worthwhile the search for common origins, it rapidly becomes necessary to handle data of which the only direct evidence is graphic, and to handle it in a manner which approximates as nearly as possible to that used with living and spoken idioms. Now any problem arising in syntactical description is magnified

* This chapter first appeared as an article in *Archivum Linguisticum* 12 (1960), 79-101. I am grateful to the editors of that journal for permitting me to reprint it here, with some small corrections.

[1] It would be better to restrict this term to those grammatical statements which are concerned with the syntagmatic or 'horizontal' relations of linguistic elements, and to balance it with 'morphology', which would denote statements concerned only with the paradigmatic or 'vertical' relations (for these terms, cf. W. Haas, *TPhS* 1954, 56). But in practice handbooks of 'syntax' commonly deal with both types of statement, while 'grammar' too often in fact excludes syntagmatic study altogether. (In handling the two types of relations in this article the terms 'contrast' and 'opposition' are distinguished in accordance with the suggestion voiced (or re-voiced) by A. Martinet, *Proc. VIII Cong. Ling.*, 213, except for the stereotyped expression 'contrastive substitution'; and 'system' and 'structure' in accordance with the Firthian ruling, best expressed by R. H. Robins, *TPhS* 1953, 109 fn. 2.)

when a purely epigraphic[2] language is under review. Two points may serve to exemplify this sad fact.

First, the absence of oral and aural experience of the language on the part of the analyst unduly hampers his application of the *langue/parole* distinction. Personal use (or a rightly employed native informant-reactor), which is impossible with this data, would have prevented the all-too-common practice of parading quotations, in support of some argued structure or category, where there has been no consideration of the possibility of even voluntary catachresis (through sarcasm, paradox, the impulse to vivid or impressive speech, or merely the human penchant for making capital out of the apparently unsuitable). Thus Gonda[3] objects to the diagnosis of a functional opposition objective/ subjective to match the opposed indicative/non-indicative IE verbal forms; his ground is that "a statement can be ... objectively incorrect" or "a wish, a desire, an appreciation ... often couched in the words of an objective statement". These considerations are valueless. If there turns out to be substantial evidence, including statistical, for the basically objective nature of indicative utterances, this finding will not be vitiated by an author's application of this category to unlikely or even apparently impossible tasks. It is inadequate to say that by knocking in a screw with a hammer, so to speak, the author is not really invalidating the distinction between a hammer and a screwdriver; he may, for reasons of his own, be exploiting it by choosing to regard a nail as if it were a screw, and one action as if it were another. He is quite free to do this. The very opposition of a durative *valor* to a punctual, for instance, is a challenge to bolder spirits to treat a period as if it were a point, or

---

[2] This seems the most suitable term to use of languages like classical Latin and Greek, Avestan etc., where the written record (itself usually much removed from the original utterance, whether written or spoken) is alone before us. The meaning 'inscriptional' will then be simply a special application of this term. 'Graphic' is better restricted to use in connexion with the structural analysis of written signals as such, along similar lines to, but quite apart from, any spoken idiom (for this study see A. McIntosh, *TPhS* 1956, 26ff.; R. A. Crossland, *Proc. Univ. Durham Phil. Soc.* I, Series B (Arts), 1957, no. 2, 13ff.).

[3] *The Character of the Indo-European Moods*, 2f.

vice versa — hence *tota nocte continenter ierunt* or ἔτη τριάκοντα ᾤκηcε or the like.[4] Nobody would now deny some sort of 'aspect' distinction, answering to the formal ablaut difference, in the Greek present and aorist verb-stems: are we then to be perverse enough to ignore such clear testimony of meaningful opposition as ἡcϑῆναι μὲν γὰρ ἔcτι ταχέωc ... ἥδεcϑαι δ' οὔ or (better because simpler) ἄνευ γὰρ τοῦ γίγνεcϑαι γενέcθαι ἀδύνατον, simply because of the occasional variation of the type κάτειργε κατάπαυcον?[5] Again, the frequency and distribution of questions prefaced by (ἄρα) μή may well justify the scepticism voiced in some quarters for the past two decades against the explanatory formula "expectation of the answer 'no'". But the case against that formula is not established, and indeed must fail, in so far as it rests on naive observations that an affirmative answer is conceivable, or envisaged as conceivable, or even in fact elicited, in this or that context.[6] It is not even unusual to greet an obvious downpour with the cry "don't tell me it's raining again!" or some equivalent structure of a palpably 'leading' kind; to speak so may indeed be to express "an antinomy, a dilemma, an impasse of thought",[7] but it is not to deny the expectation of a negative answer as a formula adequately descriptive of the *valor* of this structure — it is rather at once to enforce that *valor* and to profit by its paradoxical employment.[8]

---

[4] Caesar, *B.G.* I 26, 5; Lysias, xii, 4.

[5] Aristotle, *Nic. Eth.* 1173 a 34; Plato, *Theaet.* 155 c 2; Eurip., *Med.* 1258f.

[6] As by J. D. Denniston, The Greek Particles[2], 47f., with reference to Soph. *El.* 446, Plato, *Lysis* 213 d 1, *Charm.* 174 a 4 respectively. E. Fraenkel is similarly misled at Aesch. *Agam.* 683, as is Wilamowitz, to whom he refers, on two other Aeschylean passages, and likewise *LSJ* s.v. μή C i 1. Kühner-Gerth is nearer the mark (II 524), but should not say that an affirmative answer "geschieht immer wider Erwarten des Fragenden": it is only contrary to his *expressed* attitude. D. Labéy, *Manuel des particules grecques*, § 37, re-affirms the traditional view. The sceptics ought in fact either to show that a negative answer is improbable, or ruled out by the presence of a positive answer, in a significant majority of the contexts of all μή-questions, or else establish this finding in a significant majority of ἄρα μή-questions and then offer quantitative proof that the relation of ἄρα μή to μή differs from that of ἄρα οὐ to οὐ; either attempt is probably doomed to failure.

[7] Denniston, *op. cit.*, 47. The conventional formula would be improved if 'expecting ...' were replaced by 'suggesting ...'.

[8] Edgerton's phrase about "deprecation of a feared condition" sums up the

(In much the same way, the will/wish distinction, however slight in itself, attaching in many contexts to the Greek subjunctive/ optative formal difference may be disrupted for effect: ὥ μοι ἐγώ, μή τίς μοι ὑφαίνηισιν δόλον αὖτε ἀθανάτων (ε 356 f.) is the expression of will in a context demanding a wish — for Odysseus cannot really do more than voice his hopes — and conversely ἧco παρ' αὐτὸν ἰοῦca, θεῶν δ' ἀπόεικε κελεύθου, μηδ' ἔτι coῖcι πόδεccιν ὑποcτρέψειαc Ὄλυμπον (Γ 406 f.) is a brusque order formally couched as a wish — it is true that Helen cannot enforce her will with Aphrodite, but she is prepared to be rude enough to say ἧco and ἀπόεικε; certainly ὑποcτρέψειαc is not a 'polite' optative.[9] To return to these 'leading' questions, both their own nature and the natural reluctance of the addressee to be so led arc allowed for in such special answer-forms as Fr. *si* or NHG *doch* (or Lat. *immo* in, at least, Plaut. *Pseud*. 495), nor, for Greek, is the converse absent, namely où-questions expecting the answer 'yes' and getting in fact a 'no' (cf. οὐκ ἀκηκόατε cύ τε καὶ Cιμμίαc περὶ τῶν τοιούτων ...; οὐδέν γε caφέc, ὥ Cώκρατεc Plato, *Phaedo* 61 d 6). There should be an end to such cowardly translations as "can it be that ...?", which merely try to avoid doing violence to μή-questions in any context.

The second epigraphic difficulty is this: for all the salutary effect of constant warnings about the danger of allowing one's own *Sprachgefühl* too free a rein, especially where the mental and social background of the language under review is highly exotic, it is still too rarely seen that in the interpretative process of relating text to context it is usually hard, and often impossible, to know the situation in which the text was uttered. The linguistic context, which is available, conceals the absence of the situational context, which is not. Thus, although a statistically established durative/

---

position very well (*Buddhist hybrid Sanskrit*, Grammar, 202): the reference is to similar Skt. *mā*-questions.

[9] The slightness of the subjunctive/optative opposition is noticed below; and a "jussive optative" is not unknown in dialects (cf. Arc. ἐξόλοιτυ, Cypr. δόκοι, δυϝάνοι?; see Buck, *Greek Dialects*[2], nos. 16, 23).

punctual opposition in early Latin prohibitions[10] may need here and there to allow for the sort of misuses noted above, there is no point in overdoing the 'exceptions'. *Mane, aliquid fiet, ne abi* (Plaut. *Truc.* 366) could well owe its *ne fac* type of durative prohibition to Diniarchus' fidgeting ("don't keep trying to make off!") and be as much a stage-direction to the producer as the 'business' with the shoes hereabouts in the scene ('cedo soleas' ... 'deme soleas'). If *neque ego te celabo neque tu me* celassis *quod scias* (*Stich.* 149) is normal and momentary, what is there to justify a different treatment of *noli avorsari neque te* occultassis *mihi* (*Trin.* 627)?[11] — especially when these words, except for a peremptory *sta ilico!*, open the scene between speaker (Lysiteles) and hearer (Lesbonicus). Nothing is known of the earlier action in this situation (beyond the remarks of Stasimus, 621 ff., which do not mention 'hiding') and there is nothing to prevent Lesbonicus' having covered his face in mid-verse with a sudden gesture. It is as well to be aware of pitfalls of this kind, although the subjective element is so inescapable in scenic language as to disarm criticism: more shocking is the wilful ignoring of positive and apprehensible contextual facts. It is astonishing that Wackernagel, in discussing the aorist and imperfect forms in Ἀτρεὺς δὲ ϑνήιcκων ἔλιπεν πολύαρνι Θυέcτηι, αὐτὰρ ὁ αὖτε Θυέcτ' Ἀγαμέμνονι λεῖπε φορῆναι (Β 106 f.), should permit himself the observation "da ist ein gleich-

---

[10]   The examples which follow are taken from S. A. Handford's discussion of these structures (*The Latin Subjunctive*, 45 ff.). Handford's view of a durative prohibition oddly restricts it to the sense that it "calls upon someone not to continue doing something which he is already doing" (45); in fact, it must simply call upon someone not to do something over a period or iteratively, whether he has been doing it before or not. And we should not exclude the notion "let your abstention from such-and-such be itself durative", which sounds curious but is the common English "don't ever ..." prohibition; therefore Handford need not list Plaut. *Epid.* 145 as an anomalous momentary use of the *ne facias* type: on the contrary, *meam domum ne inbitas* means "(if you don't fetch the money before sunset) never darken my door again". (Cf. Soph. *Ajax* 1089 καί cοι προφώνω τόνδε μὴ θάπτειν, which means "I forbid you ever to bury him" and not "don't keep burying him").

[11]   Handford, *op. cit.*, 46, takes the latter as durative (presumably in the sense "don't keep hiding ...") and as an exceptional use of the *s*-subjunctive. He is too scrupulous.

artiges Faktum in einem gleichartig gebildeten Satze das eine Mal durch ἔλιπεν das andere Mal durch λεῖπε ausgedrückt".[12] There is, on the contrary, the significant difference that at the time to which the total utterance has prime reference Agamemnon, the last heir, is alive and wielding the sceptre (the previous holders having resigned it or, if mortal, died) and in his case the bequest is still enduring. It would be a sounder instinct to link this imperfect (λεῖπε) with that present of an enduring act which we know from Ἐχίονος παῖς, ὧι κράτος δίδωμι γῆς etc.[13]

However, once these awkwardnesses have been admitted in epigraphic analysis, it is not always essential to distinguish between them. If an economic description of the *valor* of a structure, or a systemic term found in it, leaves some few apparently intractable examples, it is immaterial whether these are resolved by the admission that the analyst cannot know the full context or by his allowing for a feature of *parole* (provided one or other admission is credible). In either case the anomaly is seen to be apparent rather than real, and the basic descriptional framework needs no amending. But occasionally it may arise that the relation which is felt to exist (by native speakers) between grammatical structures and salient situational features is singularly arbitrary and baffling. Greek shows a curious preference for the imperfect, rather than the expected aorist, in apparently non-durative, narrative past references if certain verbs are involved, notably those of instructing, exhorting or advising.[14] Now this is hardly because of a desire to dwell upon the acts of instructing etc., and to present them to the (inner) eye.[15] The terseness of the average order, and the dullness

---

[12] *Vorlesungen über Syntax* I, 183.
[13] Eur. *Bacch*. 213 (and cf. *vv*. 11, 42, 44). See also R. G. Austin *ad* Virg. *Aen*. IV 228. In each of these cases, the speaker implies endurance of the act or its effects to his present time.
[14] See Wackernagel, *op. cit.*, *ibidem* (he really has no explanation); Schwyzer-Debrunner, *Griech. Gramm.* II, 277f. (quoting Blass's wise observation that all the verbs, even πέμπειν, need another's act for their own fulfilment); A. Svensson, *Zum Gebrauch der erzählenden Tempora im Griechischen*.
[15] As Gonda suggests, *op. cit.*, 182 fn. 6. (For the 'eye-witness' aspectual nature of the imperfect, cf. B. L. Gildersleeve, *AJPh* 1902, 250; Gonda, *op. cit.*, 183; L. R. Palmer, *The Latin Language*, 266).

of the usual advice, is not likely to excite the wish to re-live those moments (at least, not more frequently than with verbs of military action and similar exploits). Nor is it to be explained away by "the neutrality of the unmarked term" or any conditioned suspension of opposition. 'Unmarked' in this connexion must remain a subjective notion (it can only refer to *valor*[16] not phonic exponence: even the guṇa/zero ablaut distinction vacillates between aspectstems according to the verb — λειπ- λιπ- but γιγν- γεν-). Admittedly in present time there *is* suspension, because of the extra-linguistic fact that an utterance in the speaker's present time must be within the duration of the action of the verb or within a series of such actions, and momentaneity — which presupposes the ability to see past the moment referred to, so as to be sure that it was only a moment — is necessarily excluded from the present. But there is no such compulsion on the preterital forms. It may be that with πείθειν and κελεύειν and their like the momentary aspect was felt to carry with it a completive sense, and that this in turn was felt to involve successful completion: ἐκέλευσε etc. would convey that the instructor etc. had had his way (cf. ι 339 with its situation), and something like a lexical shift appears. The lexis/grammar frontier is always an ill-defined one; words like *yesterday* have lexical status but grammatical powers of direction. Latin here has recourse to a differentiation via lexical morpheme (per*suadere* as against *suadere*, ex*orare* as against *orare*) or wholly separate lexical item (*impetrare* as against *iubere*, *orare*) for the completive sense. Reference merely to the giving of advice or of an order enforces the Greek imperfect,[17] it is irrelevant whether the advice or order is later seen to be obeyed, but if it is, the aorist of the same verb will then be expected — and so we find ἐλθὼν ἔπειθον αὐτοὺς καὶ οὓς ἔπεισα τούτους ἔχων ἐπορευόμην (Xen. *Cyrop.* 5, 22).

---

[16] As applied by M. S. Ruipérez, *Estructura del sistema de aspectos y tiempos del verbo griego antiguo, passim* (in any case, for him the aorist is the unmarked term, 79).

[17] πέμπειν, if to be so explained, may enter here because of the uncertainty, in the ancient world, of successful arrival. If Blass is right (see above), to ensure another's arrival one needs a different lexical item (ἄγειν or κομίζειν). ὀνομάζειν is idiosyncratic; now see Fraenkel *ad* Aesch. *Agam*. 681.

Fruitful in hypothesis as the epigraphic analyst may be, many problems of this sort will remain ultimately insoluble. But some odd features of general theory also present themselves. This sort of comparability at the grammatical level is deduced, to begin with, from phonological closeness.[18] Sequences of sounds are equated in two or more languages of a cognate group, in the sense that they do not, in part or as a whole, invalidate the presumed chain of development linking each sound in each language with an original starred phoneme; then these sequences are themselves compared as grammatical elements. But in order to make the phonemic reconstruction in the first place, contexts have been chosen because they are impressionistically alike, and to ensure this likeness as far as possible, recourse has been had to grammatical morphemes above all (because there loans are practically non-existent) and a presumed similarity of function has been allowed to seem to guarantee the comparability of the sequences. The argument is therefore circular. It is not necessarily wrong: but it cannot stand without external corroboration. Before we see what this must be, it is perhaps an intriguing observation that historians must thus make all their phonological and all their morphological analyses equally 'morphophonological'. This notion has found less favour outside than inside America; and one linguist has imagined such inter-independent rôles for phonological and grammatical description as to admit of no necessarily apprehensible phonic shape for individual elements of grammar.[19] It begins to

[18]   Only to begin with, admittedly. Structures may later be equated when they display no common phonic or morphic element. The IE absolute construction is an instance: this is itself a paradox, being the attempt of inflecting languages to insert into a sentence an element which shall be free from the relational mesh inescapably imposed by the inflexions. And it is differently re-integrated into the framework of categories in each language. A plausible account, which need not detain us now, can be given as to why one case was chosen here, another there; and a statistical criterion may have to be adopted — e.g. the Gk. genitive provided a larger number of acceptable structures for such integration than did the dative (the participle-phrase could be taken as 'time within which' or 'sphere of reference' or some even more specialized use, as in Homer, Θ 118). But it would be wrong to deny a common origin and a like *valor* to the observed phenomena of this type.

[19]   W. S. Allen, *TPhS* 1956, 144f. This does not create any special difficulties

look as if one of the handling-concepts of general linguistics — the morph or palpable morpheme — may end as a tool used exclusively by comparative philologists!

The external corroboration needed in this study will be the demonstration that the supposedly equivalent grammatical elements do in fact operate in several different structures in each of the compared languages, and that all those structures are respectively related to similar contextual situations in similar fashion as between the languages. This will be a kind of 'compared' or 'collective' syntax which will be an essential part of comparative syntax; but it will differ in several ways from the establishing of degrees of 'affinity' (i.e. of operational likeness) between languages by the comparison of systems.[20] For one thing, the items compared will remain individual items, merely *implying* the existence of systems, in individually appreciated structures. The presence of an item in a structure plus its presence in another and yet another will simply extend the comprehensiveness of the check that it is paralleled in function by an item in another language, where the same sort of structures will be looked for; oppositions as such will be largely irrelevant. The criticism which this idea arouses, to the effect that systems alone are really or profitably comparable, and that it is wrong to identify, for example, what is called 'nominative singular' in one language with what is called the same (or even what the analyst feels it not unreasonable to call the same) in another — all this has been answered[21] by showing that the historian's question

---

for historians, who are used to the state of affairs described in the last footnote, and who can in many cases appeal to earlier stages of sound-history.

[20] See Allen, *TPhS* 1953, 89 ff. Or one might compare functional needs. The Latin 'historic infinitive', which is characteristically common in description of collective or simultaneous action, or of syndromes of behaviour, and is normally extended over several successive verbs, has obvious affinities with the studied avoidance of temporally marked verb forms in extended passages in other languages. For Dickens' use of this evasion, which "gives the activity of the whole scene an oppressive simultaneity, a timeless continuum", see R. Quirk, *Charles Dickens and Appropriate Language*, Inaugural Lecture (Durham) 1959, 9. For the Latin infinitive usage, see M. Schuster, *Festschrift für Paul Kretschmer*, 224 ff.

[21] By J. Ellis, *Lingua* 1958, 169.

is merely whether one form rather than another corresponds to a form elsewhere. Now this is certainly true when the forms are part of the argument for phonological equations, and once even the slightest and most impressionistic likeness of morphemes has been assumed the phonic equations thence deduced can be checked in quite other contexts (e.g. the -*s*/-*ḥ* relation extracted from *equus*/*aśvaḥ* is checkable in *equis*/*aśvaiḥ*, the -*u*-/-*a*- relation is corroborated by *ferimus*/*bharāmaḥ* etc.). But a more absolute identification is desirable in purely grammatical comparison; and more crucial is the objection that "a nominative in a four case system would ... necessarily have a different 'meaning' from a nominative in a two case or in a fourteen case system".[22] An answer has been offered to this too.[23] It is suggested that such compared 'nominatives' in fact have in their own systems the same share of the total range of possible case-functions, despite the differing numbers of co-sharing terms. But again this answer is better in theory than in practice. Only the nominative (unless we count the vocative as a case) really makes a fair show of 'sharing the range' in the same way in two even cognate languages; and even this fails when broad categorization is left behind. The Lat. nominative does not 'mean', as does the Greek, that the subject of a reported verb is identical with the subject of the reporting verb, apart from structures of the *dicor*, *videor* type. The real counter-objection is to ask whether, as is involved in this attack, the criterion of contrastive substitution should be so elevated over that of distribution. A school of thought devoted to paradigmatic relations might believe that it should: but it would have none the less to admit that whereas phonemes, for instance, have a wide potential of commutation at least somewhere (in English *pin*, *bin*, *tin*, *din*, *kin* etc., despite the restriction in the context *s-V*; or in the full vowel range in stressed syllables as against the severe limitation in unstressed), morphemes on the other hand rarely commute plurally, commonly do so in binary fashion, but

---

[22]   J. R. Firth, *TPhS* 1951, 85 (= *Papers in Linguistics, 1934-1951*, 227). This is meant in the sense that 'meanings' are determined by the inter-relations of the terms in the grammatical systems set up for the language concerned.
[23]   By Ellis, *loc. cit.*, 168 fn. 128.

very often indeed do not oppose one another at all. This is too readily forgotten.[24] To speak of a range of opposed cases is to ignore the overwhelming restrictiveness of most structures: *mitto litteras Roma/am/ae* may be possible, although the last is unlikely; *proficiscor Roma/am* shows a reduction of the possibilities; in *puer amat puellam* all cases but one are precluded for the second noun — and this is, statistically, the normal type. *Facit/faciat* is a permissible opposition in a few clauses in classical Latin and even in these it is neutralized in favour of *faciat* by the presence of *ne:* elsewhere the syntagm determines the morpheme. Grammatical choice is commonly between a single possible and a multitude of impossible forms, a fact which reduces the importance of contrastive substitution considerably at this level of analysis. It is untrue to say that "syntax is concerned with free forms only".[25] Practically all terms stand, in most employments, in a one-term system; and a multiterm analysis really leaves an uneconomical number of phenomena to be handled by 'neutralizations' or 'contextual effects' or as 'instances of *parole*'.

If these answers are valid, comparison of syntax in the historian's sense is possible. It is also idiosyncratic, in that it deals with atomic elements (as presumable systemic terms), and not with systems *per se*; in that it is interested in degrees of identity only when seeking an initial basis for comparison, and not as part of its ultimate findings (which must be of the 'yes-or-no' type, with a large residue of 'don't know'); and in that it will tend to set up starred categories in a starred proto-language or in an unattested stage of a known language, a procedure without interest for the general linguist. What may interest, what may indeed alarm the general linguist, is the historian's readiness to establish as nonstarred actualities in an attested language categories or terms which do not seem economical or necessary to a purely descriptive uni-

---

[24]   But it has been clearly put in a recent paper by R. H. Robins (*Arch. Ling.* XI (1959), 91 ff., esp. 102, 109, 111).

[25]   S. Potter, *Modern Linguistics*, 104. (Concord should be taken into account here; the phenomena may be handled as single but discontinuous morphemes — so Z. S. Harris, *Methods in Structural Linguistics*, 165 f. — but the inherent 'tying' function should not be ignored).

lingual statement (even when this statement has been part of the historian's material in the first place), or which would never even occur to one making such a statement. On what evidential basis would a descriptive synchronic analyst of the classical Latin verb-system set up, as separate terms, the present-tense and past-tense *valores* of the perfect forms, when there is no formal distinction to be observed? Is such a separation any more defensible than the synchronic distinction of the instrumental from the ablative function within the formal bundle of the 'sextus casus' of the noun?[26] One may point to tense sequence (which is fairly stable, despite occurrences like *in antiquorum numerum reiciuntur, cum aliquid novi luxuria commenta est quo ipsa se obrueret* Seneca, *Ep. Mor.* 86, 8): but the alternation *oravi ut parcat/oravi ut parceret* may owe its difference of temporal reference, as of possibility of fulfilment, to the *parcat/parceret* commutation alone.[27] Thus it is to be admitted that all sociative/locative opposition may be carried by the pre-positions in the pair *cum nave/in nave* (where in the form of the

[26]   Quintilian first made the latter distinction (see Robins, *Ancient and Mediae-val Grammatical Theory in Europe*, 59). There is a whole group of functions answering to the single IE morpheme which is called 'sociative-instrumental', quite apart from those functions which, historically, we speak of as becoming syncretized in the Latin ablative. And this lack of internal case-unity in inflected languages is curiously partnered by a lack of clear difference *between* cases in many contexts, the more remarkable in view of the absence of free choice for the most part — so in Greek sometimes acc. = dat. = gen.: εὖ ἔχειν τὸ σῶμα καὶ τὴν ψυχήν Plato, *Gorg.* 464 a 8; οὕτως ἐχόντων τούτων τῆι φύσει Dem. *de Cor.* 315; ἀνδράσι μέλλουσιν εὖ σώματος ἕξειν Plato, *Rep.* 404 d 5. These considations make it difficult to establish separate terms in the category of case unless there is a clear-cut formal difference. Otherwise, even where there might be contrastive substitution, this is very hard to be sure of; does *tota erras via* (Ter. *Eun.* 245) mean "you err all along the line" (loc.), "... from the whole true course" (abl.), or "... by a whole street's length" (instr.)? Is there any point in trying to decide?

[27]   The point is that a co-present element, which (like *yesterday* or other 'lexi-grams') appears to determine an oppositional value of an element elsewhere in the grammatical structure, may be regarded as itself the true and only vehicle of the opposition, and then all that may be said of the other elements in the structure is that each is compatible with it. (This difficulty is much exploited by Gonda, *op. cit.*, 63, 89, 104). Of course, if there is formal difference, the privilege of co-occurrence with particular lexigrams is the grammatical mean-ing of the particular forms of the other elements.

noun, as in the case of the various perfect forms of the verb, syncretism has favoured what was the special form of one of the originally opposed terms); though this opposition is, after all, the entire function of the items *cum* and *in* — which is certainly not true of the items *parcat* (etc.) and *parceret* (etc.). The perfect might, therefore, be best analyzed as temporally neutral, except for its abiding implication of some past action. Yet the historian knows that the IE perfect (a present tense) and aorist (a past tense) have formally contributed to this category in Latin, and he finds a parallel functional distinction consistent and tractable.

Another, and possibly a novel, example. Historians would probably find it both convenient and logical to introduce into their statement of Latin, even in the classical period, the 'indefinite' or 'categorizing' subjunctive; not, that is, as a particular employment of the mood in certain subordinate clauses, but as a major term of analysis. A synchronic description might start with a single subjunctive *valor* — the mood of 'non-assertion', for instance.[28] But the co-occurrent *non/ne* alternation cannot, in main clauses, be applied as a separate and supervening opposition, because wishes (even vain ones for the past, which are tantamount to statements of past recommendation: cf. Gk. ὤφελον) colligate with *ne*, subjunctive statements (however non-assertive of fact) with *non*, while expressions of obligation vary between *ne* and *non* (according to whether the speaker's own will is expressed, for an action which may yet be carried out; both conditions must be fulfilled to ensure *ne*). A ternary opposition is suggested; and this is enforced by the tense distribution, which differs signally for the three *valores* just mentioned, as any text-book will show. Now historians, or analysts who permit themselves diachronic assistance, have curiously followed the same path, normally setting up will, wish and potentiality as the three *valores* and deducing, by very varied means, all complex structures from these.[29] Curiously, because there is an

[28]   This is the *valor* assigned by Waldo E. Sweet, *Latin, A Structural Approach*, 340.
[29]   See E. A. Hahn, *Subjunctive and Optative; their origin as Futures*, §190 ("the three standard categories for the Latin subjunctive"), and the review

obvious and troublesome skewness in that two of these functions, will and wish, are in the nature of pleas (or at least concern obligation), while potential expressions deal with, even if they do not 'assert', fact.

The copious speculation on the IE non-indicative, non-imperative forms has at least made it clear that the establishment of two formal moods in Vedic and early and classical Greek but only one in Latin, on the basis of roughly the same scatter of formal elements, must indicate that (a) an opposition exists which is applicable to, but dimensionally distinct from, all the meanings common to these non-indicative forms, but (b) this opposition is in practice not clear-cut enough to maintain itself over long (philological) time and ethnic differentiation.[30] This renders unacceptable any uneven ascription of *valores* to these moods at IE level, such as three to the optative and two to the subjunctive or vice versa,[31] and makes questionable any similar unevenness in the historical analysis of any known language, such as wish + potentiality (optative)/will (subjunctive) in Latin.

Just as, when 'non-assertion' is employed as vehicle of the speaker's desire or preference, the will/wish opposition is itself an example of the difference but closeness of subjunctive/optative function, so also, when 'non-assertion' appears simply as a vehicle of the speaker's opinion, the same duality may be expected to manifest itself consistently. If some future sense is noted in subjunctive structures, it argues for a remoter future sense in optative structures; likewise, a potential force in the optative ("one could or might find this happening") commends a nearer, merely non-particularizing, force in the subjunctive ("one finds this happening"). In this connexion the much-quoted verse δ 692 ἄλλον κ' ἐχθαίρηισι

---

of opinions in §§190-195 generally (and add E. C. Woodcock, *A New Latin Syntax*, §107, to the trinitarians).

[30] So two recent theorists, differing elsewhere, see just this kind of subjunctive/optative opposition, statable but subtle. Hahn, *op. cit.*, §§95ff. and §209, characterizes the distinction as vivid/remote; Gonda, *op. cit.*, 51, as of visualization/visualization + contingency.

[31] So, respectively, Delbrück, *Vergleichende Syntax*, ii 368f.; Brugmann-Thumb, *Griech. Gramm.*[4], 573ff.

βροτῶν, ἄλλον κε φιλοίη is especially revealing. It is not a plea
and it does not refer to the future: it is simply a non-particularizing
statement of what kings are known to do, with no assertion of
time or space relations. The double κε indicates that the regal
attitude is always a matter involving contingency; yet a subtle
difference is appreciable between subjunctive and optative, in that
one can be somewhat surer of a king's enmity than of his friend-
ship.[32] (In fact the whole passage contrasts the particularized
Odysseus with the non-particularized kings, in respect both of
their relative instability of behaviour and of their natural inclina-
tion to enmity). Probably all the attested uses of these moods can
be derived from the thoroughgoing application of some such
Grundbedeutung as 'non-assertion', provided one allows for their
operation as a closely-matched pair (and also for the interplay of
'subjunctivus pro optativo' and the reverse, noted above as a
natural enough phenomenon). There is no need to make their
future sense[33] an origin, as Miss Hahn does; it will be merely a

[32] Gonda's translation (72) is therefore too cumbersome and misses the
essential distinction, while Miss Hahn's comment (§113) "his hate is much
more certain than his love" goes to the other extreme. Monro (*Grammar of the
Homeric Dialect*[2], 253) has "a king will (is sure to) hate one, he may love another", which is better, as long as one remembers that the Eng. "is sure to"
is by no means matter-of-fact.
[33] For the problem of whether contiguity of a future indicative and a subjunctive (or an optative) proves or disproves identity of grammatical meaning,
see Gonda, *op. cit.*, 74 ff. (In disagreeing with Hahn and Walter over π 437, he
proposes to translate ... οὐδ' ἔσσεται οὐδὲ γένηται "... shall not live, nor can I
imagine the birth of such a man". But this leaves the opposition still largely
lexical, which is precisely Miss Hahn's point, §108.: it also puts what Gonda
calls the "emphatic" future (ἔσσεται) in a non-climactic position and gives
more force to the, as he supposes, weaker γένηται. In any event, "shall not
live" — if intended as an almost threatening future, like those quoted by
Gonda, 77 — is quite out of point here. And one may think of the clearly
menacing force of the *subjunctive* ἕλωμαι in A 137).
    Handford (§100) rightly sets up, as Kroll and Thomas before him, the future
valor of the Latin subjunctive. But his classical examples are unreliable;
most of them are consecutive clauses, while Virg. *Aen.*, I 283 ff. shows a stylistic
variation (in the clause *cum dominabitur* Jupiter states the factual future, and
implies his purpose therein: in *qui terminet* he states his purpose, and implies
that it will in the future be implemented — a typical syntactical hazard for the
analyst).

specialization of their 'non-particularizing', indefinite/potential, force (Gonda's 'visualization'), for this must have its realization — if it has any: similes have none, for example — in the future, in the sort of sense that parallel lines meet at infinity. As has been said, the application of these moods to desire rather than opinion (a slight enough shift: English 'is to' + infinitive covers both) produces the will/wish pair of functions. These three pairs of major functions will serve to explain the attested phenomena, as long as historical development is permitted within the analysis. The simple future sense does not last long in Sanskrit and Greek, and is rare even in the early Latin evidence (where a subjunctive/ optative difference of function is invisible in this *valor*). But this should not arm those who would deny Latin this modal duality altogether; will and wish are undeniably distinct in the language, a fact which supports our desire to see a functional distinction in the non-particularizing statements (which remain, unlike the future application, alongside the will/wish functions) — that is, indefinite statement (IE subjunctive)/potential statement (IE optative). The best number of basic uses of the subjunctive in Latin for a historical comparatist to set up may therefore well be five.

And so it is. It is really much more convenient, in a description based on historical considerations and concerned with probabilities of development, to admit this 'general-indefinite' subjunctive in Latin on a par with the potential. It is only a misleading preconception which forces renderings like "you never could (would) hear ..." (instead of "you never hear ...") etc. for *hoc numquam verbum ex uxore audias*.[34] Classical Greek restricts this *valor* to subordinate clauses; but for Latin one may say, with Gonda[35] "it may be important to recall that in Latin constructions of the type Plaut. *M.G.* 736 *qui deorum consilia culpet, stultus ... sit* the hypothetical tone is ... maintained through the whole sentence"; and *unum*

---

[34] Plaut. *Mil.* 689. But Hahn (fn. 21) gets it right, and Gonda (98) correctly translates "from A wife". This is the "ideal second person" construction (But Miss Hahn's derivation of it from a future function, §10, is not convincing).
[35] *Op. cit.*, 106 fn. 3.

quom noris omnis noris[36] clearly shows this subjunctive in both parts of the sentence. To 'fuse' this function of the non-indicative forms with its close but separate partner, the potential, in Latin as a whole is to store up for oneself the subsequent toil of disentangling the two, and of extracting an obviously non-potential sense from the potential. To make the potential answer, *inter alia*, the question "what sort of ...?" is specious enough in ambiguous structures like *is est qui amicos deserat* (which will probably yield the sense "a man who would desert" as reasonably as "a man who deserts", by any test); but it will not do for *absolvite eum qui fateatur*,[37] where the reference is certainly not to potentialities (the jurors are not told to acquit anyone who could or would or might confess or who "looks like a confessor" — that would fit neither the passage in question nor Roman legal practice in general — but only "a man who confesses", where the expression is indefinite but an actual person's confession precedes the acquittal). The subjunctive categorizes. In *quo redibo ore ad eam quam contempserim?* the girl is put into a category (jilted women) because the characteristics of that class of persons give point to the utterance.[38]

---

[36]   Ter. *Pho*. 265; cf. *Andr*. 10 (these are often mistaken for futures by editors). One must not confuse this use with that ideal second person which really *is* potential — i.e. the other category of the pair. For examples, see Handford, *op. cit.*, §120. The general-indefinite subjunctive mentioned above is practically identical with Gonda's IE subjunctive of 'ideal existence' or 'visualization'; but he extends its scope to complex syntax (104f.), in a way which seems perversely to fly in the face of the obvious, as does his refusal to set the 'will' sense apart (89, 91).

[37]   Cic. *Verr*. ii. 3, 221 (the whole passage is sarcastic). Treated as potential by Woodcock, *op. cit.* §155; but the subjunctive is only generic: it puts the defendant into that class of persons whose PAST actions, including above all the confession, make the blood boil at the very idea of acquittal. Woodcock has to say that the subjunctive in normal generic clauses has "lost its potential force": in fact it never had it.

[38]   Ter. *Pho*. 917 (and so often; cf., in the same play, 60, 537). That "the antecedent is definite and the verb refers to a fact" (Martin, *ad loc*.) is irrelevant; both the person and the fact are 'categorized'. In *quem ego viderim in vita optumum* (*Pho*. 367) the subjunctive conveys the category within which *optumum* applies; by a surprising but pardonable development the category is limited to one member at *Andr*. 973 (*solus est quem di diligant*). The causal, concessive and consecutive senses which supervene upon this basic structure

Several troublesome usages thus fall more easily into place.[39] And it would be immensely simpler to conclude that the subjunctive in clauses of indefinite frequency is only another direct application of this general *valor*. True, it might be so derived and yet be a Grecism.[40] but such a loan would have filled no gap, as a regular indefinite-frequentative employment of tenses of the indicative was available (cf. Woodcock, §§194(*b*) and 217(*c*)), and it is more economical to believe in a native application of an inherited general function.[41]

From this is follows that historical comparative syntax (of IE, for example) has to do with progress, first from broad starred types to small-scale and particular applications in the early evidence of known languages, and thence to broader types again within the later history of those same languages. (It is therefore wrong in principle to complain that syntacticians are "resorting overmuch to analogy" or that a certain category in a known language is "too

---

are well discussed by Woodcock, *op. cit.*, §§156f. That these senses *are* secondary, and that they are not clearly distinguished, is shown by Handford, *op. cit.*, §178 (but one is unconvinced by his suggested origin for them, §179).

[39] Non-particularization is essential after negative expressions generally, hence the type *nil reticebo quod sciam*, probably giving rise to the wider use of *quod sciam* = "as far as I know", as Gonda suggests, 98 fn. 1.

[40] In Greek the necessity of referring these clauses at least sometimes to the past induced a stereotyped subjunctive/optative temporal opposition. The optative probably entered here originally in a general-indefinite rôle ("pro subjunctivo") by the sort of interplay allowed above (see J. T. Allen, *TAPhA* 1902, 101 ff.). That the subjunctive here should have ἄν (usually) does not indicate that it is itself contingent or potential, for the corresponding optative does not have it; rather the non-indicative clause was at one stage especially felt to induce a contingent force into the main clause (cf. ἄν with a main indicative verb, when the sentence contains a frequentative optative clause; e.g. Thuc. VII 71, 3). On this matter, which involves a migration of ἄν from that part of the sentence where it should logically appear, see R. H. Howorth, *CQ* 1955, 84 ff.

[41] Either way, the absence of primary tenses of the subjunctive in temporal clauses of this kind needs explanation. Probably the usage in 'circumstantial' *cum*-clauses exercised a restrictive effect. What seems quite improbable is Handford's notion (§192) that only the Greek conditional-frequentative was borrowed. Woodcock, *op. cit.*, §196, derives the whole frequentative subjunctive range from "the descriptive or generic": provided one allows for the objections raised above to his treatment of generic clauses, this comes nearest to the mark.

restricted in its range of usage to make it likely that is should be the forerunner of any broad types".[42] Historical syntax well knows this sort of odd concertina-like effect. To give an example from a field where there has been a take-over rather than a development of function, the familiar syzygy of case-syncretism + emergence of prepositional direction involves not only the replacement of one type of structure by another and a shift from one kind of broad systemic function to another, but also an interim period, here of maximal complexity, in which the alternation possibilities of the terms of the one system are multiplied (theoretically, at any rate) by those of the terms of the other. Classical Greek is still largely in this condition: consider the three ranges of oppositions — of cases, of prepositions, and of both together — seen in:

(i) παρὰ τοῦ Κύρου / παρὰ τῶι Κύρωι / παρὰ τὸν Κῦρον

(ii) ἀπὸ Θράικης / ἐπὶ Θράικης

(iii) $\dfrac{\text{παρὰ τοῦ Κύρου}}{\text{ἐπὶ τοῦ Κύρου}} \left| \dfrac{\text{παρὰ τῶι Κύρωι}}{\text{ἐπὶ τῶι Κύρωι}} \right| \dfrac{\text{παρὰ τὸν Κῦρον}}{\text{ἐπὶ τὸν Κῦρον}}$[43]

The end-position is like the start; there are broad types (now prepositional and not casual) with manifold syntagmatical nuances.

It is the relation of the starred broad types to the small-scale applications which poses the acutest problems, problems of probability and even credibility. For instance, a preterital *valor* is a feature of three verbal forms (or groups of forms, allowing for the systemic differentiation of person and number) among those which any description would find it reasonable to list as tenses in known IE languages — imperfect, perfect and aorist. Now to account for the evidential phenomena within a comparative historical framework, the following *petite histoire*, or something very like it, is required:

---

[42] So Handford, *op. cit.*, §113. Yet he himself is more accurate in §21 ("the syntactical usages of language do not generally begin as broad types ... but as particular idioms, restricted at first to limited range").

[43] Respectively, 'from'/'with'/'to'; 'from'/'towards';

'from'	'with'	'to' .
'in time of	"in power of'	'against'

1. (a) The present denoted an action in course of occurring or a state of affairs in process of becoming.

(b) The perfect (set apart by stem metaphony and internal apophony and special endings) denoted simple state, but presupposed a completed process, as against the uncompleted process of the present.

(c) The aorist (set apart by stem apophony) denoted the momentary aspect of action as against the durational aspect of the present.

(All these, while usually called aspectual relations, are ultimately temporal distinctions.)

2. The perfect implied pastness without referring directly to it. The aorist not merely implied pastness but could not refer of itself to any time other than the past, except under special conditions of neutralization, because a non-past action cannot be known to be momentary (use of the aorist along with some other signal of, say, futurity is a different matter). These facts superimposed a simple time-relation (now — then) without removing the possibility of combining duration with pastness. Hence emerged the past present (imperfect), distinguished from the present only by the endings (ignoring, for the moment, the unstable and sporadic augment).

3. The following tense possibilities (with or without the retention of aspectual *valores*), relative to the speaker's time, then resulted:

(a) The perfect might stress the reference to the present (state) or to the past (action or process) — although, if the verb was lexically such as to have no 'aftermath', the past action could only be its beginning and the present state its continuing: hence the perfect would convey present action, inescapably, with such verbs.[44] If the reference was to the past, the perfect might become the normal narrative tense or it might not; if it did not, it might specialize in bringing the action close to the speaker's time or in leaving it remote, with equal reasonableness.[45]

---

[44] Called 'non-transformatives' by Ruipérez (*op. cit.*, 53). The Greek 'anomalous' perfects, with the sense of present action, are here in point ἀλάληµαι, δέδορκα, κέκραγα, etc.), as against the two different but normal types τέθνηκα/πέποµφα.

[45] The psychological reaction of speakers to states, actions or experiences

(b) The aorist might become the normal narrative tense or it might not; if it did not, it might specialize in denoting either the remote or the recent past.[46]

(c) The imperfect might become the normal narrative tense or it might not; if it did not, it might acquire a special rôle but was more likely to maintain itself by virtue of its aspectual usefulness (conation, intention, 'eyewitness' etc.).

(d) Any tense-form might be lost as long as one remained to carry the preterital *valor* (otherwise the language concerned ceases to be evidence).

(e) Any two tense-forms might lose their functional opposition but be retained as formally distinct conjugational variants (so the imperfect and perfect, in Hittite, are retained as, respectively, the preterite of the -*mi* conjugation and originally the preterite (subsequently, with the addition of the presentive marker -*i*, the present) of the -*hi* conjugation).[47] Conversely, any two tense-forms might be formally fused but still functionally differentiated (so the perfect and aorist in Latin). This latter event needs, for epigraphic languages, to be proved by conditioned variants in the syntagm and conditioning variants in the context (with all the difficulties noted above impairing the findings).

This is not, perhaps, an altogether incredible schema of development,[48] but it already shows an awkward amount of differentiation,

---

divides largely along ethnic or political frontiers. The divergent specializations mentioned above are characteristic of the Latin (and English) and the Sanskrit perfects respectively; that the Skt. perfect reports facts not witnessed by the speaker (so Macdonell, *Sanskrit Grammar*³, 206; Ellis, *Proc. VII Cong. Ling.*, I 125) is only a further specialization of its ⸱remote' use. For its shift from present to past reference, see T. Burrow, *The Sanskrit Language*, 297.

[46]   The use with reference to the recent past is seen not only in Skt. (Burrow, *op. cit.*, 295), but occasionally in Greek: cf. ἐξῆλθον (Eur. *Med.* 214), ἦλϑ'ἦλθε χελιδών ... (Rhodian Spring Song) or νῦν ἔγνων τὸν Ἔρωτα (Theoc. III 15).

[47]   See J. Kuryłowicz, *Proc. VIII Cong. Ling.*, 236ff.

[48]   The account of the IE tense and aspect development offered by Burrow (*op. cit.*, 296) prompts many objections. As to the evidence of Hittite, there is no reason to regard this as reflecting the IE position most accurately: in phonology Greek preserves the vowel reflexes better, and in morphology the fact that it is the past forms of the *hi*-conjugation (presumed on the evidence of the Anatolian languages) which correspond to the IE perfect forms argues a

and even of diametrically opposed applications. But nothing less will account comprehensively for the preterital systems of Hittite, Sanskrit, Greek and Latin — that is, for a small part of the verbal functioning of a mere handful of languages in one cognate group. Yet a failure to attempt to account for all such complexes, with whatever degree of complication, nullifies all the apparent progress made even in studies of historical phonology; in any case, such a failure disprizes Sir William Jones's famous remark which sparked off our IE historical research, and which spoke in particular, it must be remembered, of "the roots of verbs and the forms of grammar".

These considerations, positive and negative, have seemed worth putting forward as empiric findings. Other observations are more safely couched in the form of questions. If these questions are rightly posed, the greater is the hope getting helpful answers. Here the following problems obtrude themselves:

1. To what degree may an *Ursyntax* diverge in details of 'taxonomic hierarchy'[49] from the structures of the evidential languages? Some fixed points of such a hierarchic arrangement (e.g. 'sentence' and 'word') must be common to, and alike in, all the compared idioms and the starred reconstructions.[50] At other points differences

---

developed state for Hittite. The aorist may therefore have been lost there. There are those who think this about the feminine gender, and that is clearly a comparatively late IE formation. The ablaut arrangements of the aorist show it to be early, and probably more or less contemporaneous in origin with the perfect. As to the evidence of Greek, a thoroughgoing 'extension' of the pres./aor. distinction INTO the moods and infinitive (which is Burrow's suggestion) involves an apparent shift from a temporal to an aspectual opposition; but the reverse shift is, as suggested above, more feasible and indeed logically necessitated. As to the Indian evidence, why should a similar formal 'extension' be visible in the Vedic moods (where also the distinction is to be seen) if, as Burrow's notion entails, Sanskrit more or less preserves the IE (purely temporal) *valores*? Aspect can hardly be assigned to the earlier form of the language on this view; yet without it there is no motive for the 'extension'.

[49] For this term, see M. A. K. Halliday, *Studies in Linguistic Analysis*, 58f. (the important element being the 'unit'). The same notion is conveyed by Haas's term 'functional relations' (*TPhS* 1954, 56f.).

[50] Hence one must disagree with Ellis (*Lingua* 1958, 169) who, like Allen, rejects the possibility of starred sentences. The implausibility of any individual attempt to construct one is another matter.

may manifest themselves between languages and between historical stages (e.g. 'phrase' may be a dispensable unit). 'Clause' is probably unnecessary for IE (the balance of opinion being now strongly against a conjunctional force in items like *$i̯o$-), and sentential parataxes in proto-Greek, proto-Latin etc. will suffice. If a 'number-of-units' variation is admitted between IE and its 'dialects', would a 'kind-of-units' variation be permissible in any similarly studied group?

2. What variation of morphological typology[51] is permissible without vitiating the historical comparability of languages? It is often taken for granted that inflexion is the type-character of IE. But English is now largely isolating (cf. phrasal verbs), Sanskrit partly polysynthetic (one thinks of forms like *dhūsarakambalakr̥ta-tanutrāṇena*), and IE itself has sometimes been credited with vestiges of agglutination (if, say, the 'ego' element in all verb-forms is to be referred to a common element *-Hm-). Is any classification admissible at any stage, provided it does not preclude at an early stage a purely inflectional type (with its typical 'solidarity', as of number and case in Latin — 'portmanteau morphs' is Hockett's term — and wide allomorphism)?

3. Using a language means making a succession of choices. The different stages of grammatical choice will be mentioned shortly; for the moment it may be noticed that, where the choice involves significant opposition of equally admissible forms, this opposition may be of these kinds:

(a) If simple, binary (e.g. masculine/feminine) or plural (e.g. masculine/feminine/neuter).

(b) If complex, alternative (i.e. fully exclusive: thus the Greek

---

[51] See C. E. Bazell, *Linguistic Typology* (Inaugural Lecture, 1958), 10, for the analytical significance (in the matter of relating segments to classes) of the traditional types. This problem does not arise in pure phonology — cf. Bazell's remark (5) that "phonology ... would seem a most unfavourable domain" (i.e. for typological study). In this field, all that have so far been offered under the heading of typology are observations on the co-existence or apparent non-co-existence of particular bundles of phonematic features; indeed, this has been done, but even more sporadically, with grammatical elements (see R. Jakobson, *Proc. VIII Cong. Ling.*, 17 ff.; V. V. Ivanov, *Voprosy Jazykoznanija* 1958, 34 ff.).

infinitive may show either present/past time reference or durative/ punctual aspect, but not both); or co-existent (i.e. non-exclusive: thus a Latin singular or a plural verbal function must combine with a first or a second or a third person agent-function, and inextricably fuses the formal expression of the terms of the two systems); or successive (i.e. partly exclusive: thus after the choice has been made between the Sanskrit indicative opposition present/past, choice of the latter opens the further possibility of choosing between imperfect/aorist/perfect).[52] (In this case the imperfect will, if chosen, stand in opposition to the aorist and perfect in one respect, to the present in another; so this oppositional type may equally well be called 'multidimensional'). Practically any combination of these modes is possible within a successive complex.[53] What rules are therefore formulable by which to exclude impossible relationships (of history) between complexes? Are any relationships impossible?

4. Even when we are satisfied with the comparability (in terms both of *mutata* and of *mutatio*) of certain oppositions in different languages, or at least of individual oppositional terms, which is all that matters for historians, and of the nature of the choice which they impose, it remains necessary to relate this comparability to a more general view of grammatical procedure. Thus:

(i) the speaker decides between what is grammatically acceptable at all and what is not. *Balbus canem mordent* or *Balbo canis mordet* is rejected: *Balbus canem mordet* or *Balbum canis mordet* is accepted.

(ii) of the accepted possibilities, the speaker rejects those which entirely fail to convey the information he wishes to impart. *Balbus canem mordet* is excluded if only *Balbum canis mordet* is 'true'.

(iii) the speaker prefers those structures which cater for the

---

[52] Ruipérez (*op. cit.*, 23f.) is however unfortunate in thinking that this type of successive opposition is parallel to the phonological relation $n:d/t$, for these phonemes, in use, are equipollent.

[53] Thus, in the Greek verb,

infinitive > fut./pres./past   *or*   durative/punctual

finite   >   indicative   > pres. (> state/process)/past (> durative/punctual)

non-indicative > {subj./opt./impv.
{*and* durative/punctual

context, linguistic or situational (as far as they are separable).
If the hearers know the dog's propensity for biting but not its latest
victim, the probable preferred form will be *Balbum canis mordet*:
if they are aware of Balbus' proximity to the dog but not of the
result, the utterance will become *mordet Balbum canis* or *mordet
canis Balbum*.[54]

(iv) then there is room for further refinement, according to the
stylistic rating of individual structures. Of the two final possibilities
in (iii) either may be the final choice, but as artistic considerations
(e.g. of sound patterns) decide.[55]

No particular type of mechanism need be tied, even in one language, to a particular stage of choice. Morphemic oppositions
enter into (i), (ii) and (iii) in Latin and Greek,[56] intonation-pattern-
ing into (ii) (e.g. questions *versus* statements) as well as (iii) in
many languages. Word-order operates in Latin at (iii) and (iv),[57]

---

[54] Of this 'context-realization', in terms of 'given' and 'new' information,
I owe my understanding to M. A. K. Halliday (see, for example, *Studies in
Linguistic Analysis*, 61). In spoken utterances the relationships can be conveyed
by contrastive intonations, with further subtleties if the 'given' is accepted
but the 'new' questioned, etc. Otherwise grammatical features of word-order
or even morphemic opposition come into play. For the arrangement in Latin
cum-clauses, see Woodcock, *op. cit.*, §235 note ii: in these, the past subjunctive
conveys the 'given', if this falls within the subordinate clause, and the past
indicative is used if this clause handles the 'new'. Failure to appreciate this,
a by-product of the subjunctive's power to non-particularize, leads Handford
into a series of misunderstandings (*op. cit.*, §183).

[55] Rather than suggest a time-sequence of 'stages' or positive 'rejection'
by the speaker, it may be safer to say that stage (i) involves syntagmatic restrictions of form, stage (ii) those reflexes of situational relations which have
paradigmatic exponence, stage (iii) those reflexes of the situation (e.g. relative
prominence) which have only *ad hoc*, heterogeneous exponence, and stage (iv)
a (presumably supervening) restructuring.

[56] The *cum*-clause distinction (see earlier footnote) is largely matched in
Greek by the distribution of the conjunctions ἐπεί (directing a clause containing
the 'given') and ὅτε (directing one which conveys the 'new').

[57] Hence A. A. Hill, *Introduction to Linguistic Structures*, App. B., 476, is
hardly correct in saying that "order of sentence elements is linguistically without
significance in Latin, but is a feature controlled by the stylistic situation,
and so meaningful on the stylistic level". This confuses stages (iii) and (iv),
and creates an unwanted schism between stylistics and linguistics. Hill is
right to reject the rigid idea of a 'normal' word-order in Latin, but this should
not be pressed so far as to deny quantitative proof of favourable arrangements

in English at (i), (ii) and (iv) regularly, at (iii) somewhat less readily.

Clearly, the operational position (in terms of these stages of choice) of mechanisms will not only diverge as between languages, but in a cognate group will diverge to a degree proportionate to the spatial and temporal separation of these languages. How much freedom can be allowed within such a group in this matter? At how many of these stages must fruitful comparability be established for any comparability to be universally recognized at all? Where, in other words, is the threshold of grammatical identity for a historian's purposes in a cognate language group?

These and similar queries may seem a trifle naive; but, in the absence of an answer or at least some reassuring words on such points, historical comparative syntacticians must be forgiven for showing a touch of diffidence.

---

of order (e.g. participle at end of phrase, $A^1A^2VN^1N^2$ in the poetic 'golden verse', etc.) which are widespread enough to be the basis of variations. Robins also perhaps goes too far in claiming that "immediate constituent structure and postional order of units ... bear scant correspondence in Latin" (*TPhS* 1959, 139). In any case, word-order in Latin as an exponent of (iii) is admitted by C. F. Hockett, *A Course in Modern Linguistics*, 250; he calls this 'deep', as opposed to 'surface', grammar.

7. LINGUISTIC MODELS: A HISTORIAN'S USE – (I)

Grammatical analysis has always relied on a base theory representing space relations, logical order relations and controlled choice.
The theory has not everywhere been obtruded or even formulated.
It so happens that the current fashion is for explicitness in that
direction as in others; and also current is a return to traditionalism
in two respects, the gathering together, under the banner of grammar, of levels of language for many years studied in fairly strict
separation, and an analogical appeal to the theoretical frameworks
of other disciplines. As the genetic hypothesis in linguistics has
long been tacitly underpinned by the biological model or by the
palaeographers' 'stemmatics' model of manuscript relations (and
as phonology has been seen as homologous to natural genetics,
cf. Jakobson, 1962, xxviii and Sebeok, *Lg.* 39, 1963, 466), so now
a mathematical or a geological or a chemical model guides the
newer theories of grammar (see Strang, 1965). Sapir's dictum that
all grammars leak has caused historians to suspect that evolution
is incompatible with total and adequate explicitness as to what
comprises a given language at a given time (unless evolution is
staccato succession, which returns us to Zeno's paradox of the
arrow's flight), or that general linguists can prompt diachronic
study only by virtue of their own inadequacies. And it is a fact that
scarcely any linguistic theory of the kinds we may call 'structural'
and 'quantified' (as taking account, respectively, of paradigm/
syntagm dimensions and of the type/token aspect), during the first
half of this century, deliberately offered any help to historians.
If historians have tried to glimpse their explanations by the light
of general theories, such as phoneme theory, that is another
matter; and yet another thing, to be considered in the next chapter,

is the eagerness of recent formal theorists of the MIT persuasion to handle diachronic problems. What follows here is a subjective review of the sporadic assistance history may derive from non-projective and non-generative concepts of grammar.[1] Yet even the fitfulness of the light of descriptive theory can itself lead to the discovery of important shifts and emergences.

1. *Immediate constituent analysis*

In order to set out genetic divergence in terms of specific shifts of sound and form, we seek comparable 'bits' as between our data languages. The comparability of these bits is guaranteed by their location in morphs of like function (but not necessarily identical function or frequency) in their respective language systems.[2] It might be thought that a type of operational analysis of which the end-product is an inventory of the morphemes of a language would be a boon to a historical enquiry. But IC analysis is not helpful in that particular way. Its preoccupation is less with ultimate constituents than with the cuts, and the hierarchy of those cuts, to be made successively in the text of an utterance. Moreover, it can assert nothing as to the historical comparability of the ultimate (or penultimate) entities of two or more languages, whereas it is

---

[1]   A starting-point may be Hockett's famous contrast (1954) of the two models of grammatical description, item-and-process and item-and-arrangement. IP employs 'derivation' from presupposed categories and items — explicit projection and generation are types of the derivation process — and is characterized as inevitably historical in bent (although this is denied by Robins, 1959, 136, for both IP and word-and-paradigm grammar, a model he sees, unlike Hockett, as reasonably close to IP; cf. 119): hence chapter 8, below. (WP is ignored here; it is an inflexional speciality and yet its discounting of the morpheme level obscures inflexional history). To IA belong space-conscious, manipulatory models, like immediate constituent analysis, dependency grammar, and glosscmatics (even if Holt equates 'compound' with 'derivative', 1959, 52; 1961, 71). One might suppose 'realization' grammars to be as much part of IP as 'mutation' types, their process being implementation by rules which change shapes; yet Lamb, 1964, 111 and 116 fn. 9; 1966; 36, sets his face against process as properly only diachronic. Harris' model is poised between IP and IA, declaring itself a middle ground between IC analysis (cf. Wells, 1947, *et al.*) and transformational grammar (1962, 18 ff.).

[2]   For the reason why not, see Hoenigswald, *IJAL* 28, 1962, 211.

just this comparability (in relation to morphs and word-forms, as the expressions of those entities) which the historian is at pains, and often at a loss, to justify. IC analysis does not repair the damage done by the absence, when one language is set beside another, of like formal environments of items above the word (an absence which occurs even in bilingual texts, where inter-translation merely ensures the more or less equal overall response-to-context of two partial implementations of different grammars). As to the mere extrication of morphemes in the languages separately, these readily parade before the eye or ear of anybody of even moderate linguistic sensibility, because of the recurrent patterns of grammar. If the intuitively recognised smallest segment is larger than a morpheme — as with 'word' languages — it, too, is inescapably marked by graphic or accentual devices.

But IC analysis does provoke some new lines of thought about evolution. Those items which, standing within constituents, signal information about constituents are sometimes divided into two types. There are (a) those which mark sub-constituent relationships (predicative verbs, prepositions, conjunctions), and those (b) which indicate the kind of constituent within which they are enclosed (the *and, or* connectives, for instance).[3] Type (a) is credited with constituent membership, and thus differs from (b) in status as well as function — and so also, possibly, in origin. One may argue, *prima facie*, that type (a) markers are more likely to have evolved from semantically 'full' but essentially sub-constituent items (often adverbal or adnominal) set apart by a comparatively late cut. The earlier role of type (b) items is, however, more reasonably extra-constituent (interjection) or self-constituent (single word operating as a sentence); in Latin, the former origin is typified by *et* ('then again', cf. Greek ἔτι), the latter by *uel* (# 'choose' #). As for type (a), *mane dum scribit* (Plautus, *Bacch*. 737) is the hackneyed example of a conjunctional marker derived from a full adverb, as if from *mane; dum scribit* or *mane dum; scribit* (*dum* = 'the while'). The expected transitional hesitation is visible in Catullus' double

---

[3]   See Hockett, 1958, 153f., 191f., 197. Type (a) is entitled 'impure markers' as 'pure markers' cannot be members of constituents.

entry *sic uirgo, dum* ('as long as') *intacta manet, dum* ('so long') *cara suis est* (62, 45) on this, see E. A. Hahn, *Hommages à Max Niedermann*, Brussels 1956, 154 ff. (Within this type, shifts move towards exocentricity of the affected subconstituents, as with evolved prepositional phrases. There may be delay: so ⟨Verb-Adverb-(verb-linked case-marked)Noun⟩ can pass either to ⟨Verb— preposition+(case-restricted)Noun⟩ or to ⟨preverb+Verb — (case-marked)Noun⟩.[4] But in the latter event, where the prefixed verb is still endocentric, the move to exocentricity follows: the meaning of the compound verb ceases to be a loose conjoining of the meaning of its parts (cf. *understand*, ἐφίεcθαι, etc.), and the simple and compound forms become syntactically divergent (cf. *uidere* and *inuidere*)). It seems that the evolution of conjunctions from interrogative or demonstrative elements is as justified as it is traditional. But there are type (*b*) markers already at very early stages, at least of Indo-European history, which by their non-prominence and minimal substance offer the historian who is prompted by IC analysis no more than a suspicion of their former role. One thinks of the enclitic *$*-k^we$*, for which the incidence of Mycenaean -*qe* suggests a possibly larger original function than merely that of a connective.

Endocentric structures (positively defined, so that the exocentric type represents 'the rest' and can here be ignored) assign syntactical equivalence to their totality and one or more of their constituents. Hence the constituents which are not signal elements must bear complexities of internal and external relationship. Internally, the specific problem is that the 'head' or 'nucleus' or 'nuclear model' may be linked either identically or differentially with the 'attributes' or 'partners'. Further, the manner of linking is theoretically variable through time. So it has been argued that, in the still much debated history of the Latin gerund and gerundive, sequences like

(*equum ← comparandi*) *copia* and *equi comparandi copia* and/or

---

[4] E.g. ἀμφὶ ... | χαῖται | ὤμοιc | ἀίccονται (*Il*. 6, 509 f.) and περὶ ... | ζώνην | βάλετ' | ἰξυῖ (*Od*. 5, 231) pass to ἀμφ'ὤμοιcιν ἐδύcετο τεύχεα (*Il*. 3, 328) and περιβαλλομένουc ... τεύχεα (*Od*. 22, 148).

(*equi → comparandi*) *copia* simply reflect shifts, whose direction is beyond proof by this means, between hierarchic and simultaneous head-to-attribute relations.[5] However, genetic connexion does not by any means preclude divergent status, from language to language and period to period, of classes of even congeneric items within endocentric structures. English adjectives usually act as subordinate attributes (so Robins, 1964, 236, cites (*clever*) *boys* — things like *slow and easy goes far in a day* are limited to paroemiac expressions). But Latin adjectives are commonly co-ordinate alternative heads: so *saeui* (scil. *principes*) *proximis* (scil. *hominibus*) *ingruunt* (Tacitus, *Hist*. 4, 74). The Latin elasticity is possible because of its tight noun-adjective concord, with a high proportion of actual rhymes; yet, aside from the hint it possibly gives as to early adjective-genitive equivalence (see chapter 8, pp. 183f.), *aerarium hostium* (+ noun gen.), when set against *aerarium hostile* (+ adj.), shows the misleading limitations of concord-expression in this regard.

IC analysis involuntarily fixes boundaries between functional elements. The order in which it makes its cuts reflects a scale of prominence of these boundaries (and their markers), from one extreme, long silence, to the other, minimal separation feature. The relevance of this to the phonetic environments which condition sound shifts is obvious. At the lower end of the scale a crucial sequence may be unimpaired; as we return upwards the prominence of boundaries increases, sequences cease to be such and relevant environments (other than pause) tend to vanish. Pedersen and others considered morpheme boundaries as an interference factor in sound history, but a guiding principle is lacking. The interference is sometimes held to inhibit shifts altogether, sometimes to slow down their progress; in the latter event, it is not always clear if the result is one of articulation (the shift moving part of the way in the mouth, so to speak) or one of time (with the possibility that the arrested feature be held suspended in a form susceptible to a

[5] Cf. R. G. G. Coleman, *Journal of Roman Studies* 55, 1965, 259; L. R. Palmer, *The Latin language*, 1954, 321f.

competing shift).[6] Quite another matter is the revising of the place
of the boundary on the scale of prominence. If only there were
regular exponence of the scalar differences, one might link this
revising to historical reassignment of syntactical rank to units;
the movement parataxis → hypotaxis → syntaxis ($\langle \# S_a \# S_{b1} \# \rangle >$
$\langle \# S_a \,(\text{conj.} + S_{b2}) \# \rangle$) could be charted through all stages.[7] But
it can be argued (and demonstrated from the incidence of pauses
in the speech of television commentators) that the more marked
separations occur often at what are, in terms of IC cuts, the lowest
and latest boundaries. That is, the places in the utterance where
there is maximum syntactical — but not logical — predictability of
the ensuing item (as after *the*) are exploited by speakers in full
flow for thinking (about choice of words and emphasis and so
forth), with a reduced danger of losing the grammatical thread of
the discourse. Nevertheless, an averaged large-sample acoustic
differentiation applied by *Verschiebeprobe* (see Glinz, 1961) to
hypotactically and non-hypotactically ordered pairs (especially
within congruences such as *he went to town and saw a show* against
he saw a show and went to town) might well give descriptive shape
to what is at the moment a historian's hopeful name (hypotaxis)
for a presumed interim condition. Finally, the crossing of boundaries (or partial control of one constituent by another in the syntagm) can be handled with some profit under the heading of

---

[6]   As if SOME shift were due. For simple inhibition, it is easy to point to the
pattern-linking made possible by a morpheme-boundary: *duco*: *deduco*:: *signo*:
designo (-*VsV*- retained); or Myc. *-$k(h)w$- > -$k^w k^w$- but -$k(h)|w$-, as in *iqo* but
tetukowoa (cf. *araruwoa*), which shows that later τετευχώς etc. are not the
result of simple early loss of *w*. But *pos-se* or -*is-se* infinitives do not hold
*uel-se (> *uelle*), nor *dis-cedo* hold pre-boundary *s* in *dirimo* (< **dis-emo*).
Ἐρέττω (with **ty* > *tt*, not *s*) links up with ἐρέτ-ης, ἐρετ-μόν, but is unaffected
by εἰρεσ-ία (a deviation akin to those which preoccupy Chomsky, like *pirate-
piracy*). Allen, 1958, 116, 119, speaks not of time-delay in the shift-process but
rather of a rallentando in the movement of articulatory position, and of a
'more' (vs. less) 'advanced development' of the change of organic production
of the sound. This whole notion, of Pedersen and others, needs a more careful
exploration.
[7]   Although 'particles', as connectors within units above the sentence, seem to
perpetuate the intermediate stage, as an alternative organization of discourse.

'cohesion'. But this concept responds better to the devices of 'scale and category' grammar.

2. *String analysis*

Harris's peculiar side-swiping sort of analysis (1962) has as its ultimate relict a single, complete, minimal sentence. The basic form of that sentence, $SV(O)$, deflects the criticism which has been levelled at ordinary IC procedures,[8] namely that the prime cut is made between main subject and verbal predicate, the most closely knit group in lax concord languages and that which has, arguably, the deepest linkage everywhere. In theory, one should be able first to establish the relicts of favourite-form sentences in what are presumed to be genetically close languages, and then by comparative reconstruction to arrive at the basic *Ursatz* formula. A further calculus of the order and placing of adjuncts, in spatial relation to the centre string, should improve the formula into a credible pattern for adequate communication in the proto-language. But in fact there are so many incomparables and imbalances of testimony and evolutionary permutations that little can emerge; perhaps only negative indications, such as the unlikelihood of the order *VOS* in PIE.

Yet this approach can make very clear some subtleties of syntactical difference between *états*, and registers, of a language; and it can therefore open our eyes to possible, and even plot the course of actual, lines of diachronic movement. The embedding of part(s) of the centre string within one or more of its own adjuncts is the direct converse of the normal process envisaged by Harris; it may, however, be a diagnostic deviant feature of poetry. In Latin prose an adjunct is embedded at one place only in the basic sentence, and suffers interruption only to accommodate other adjunct elements subordinate to itself; the centre string resumes after the adjunct's completion, as does the prior adjunct after completion of the subordinate. In poetry, however, partial embedding of the centre string, or of prior adjuncts, is admitted, in such entwinings

[8]   See M. Grady, *Glossa* 1, 1967, 68-74; cf. Longacre, 1965, 73 fn. 16.

as *2uerso 1dominus 2pede 1pressit 1harenam* or *2quae 1tamen 2odit 1habet* or, as an extreme, *1quantum terrae potuit ... parari /2hoc 3quem 3ciuiles 3hauserunt 2sanguine 3dextrae.*[9] Such hyperbaton is rejected in prose; and string analysis thus makes clear (to fix on one example) why unified forms evolve as conjunctions, like *antequam, priusquam, postquam.* The shift from *fuimus ante* (advb.) *Rudini* by way of *ante rorat* (+ *quam pluit*) to *non defatigabor antequam ... percepero*[10] occasions an infringement of the prose rule once the comparative clause has become an inescapable expansion of the adverb; quasi *2ante 1rorat 2quam 2pluit.* The item *ante* etc. is shifted to conform, in this case allowing the unamended version to co-exist as an occasional marker of the precious style.

3. *Dependency grammar*

This model shares with IC analysis a concentration on "tactic relations among elementary units". Its own special contribution is to combine, in presentation, the cuts which the analyst makes in the utterance with the procedural sequence — and hence hierarchic status — of the cuts. The end-product is a series of spatial diagrams, sometimes called configurations of '*nœuds*', sometimes 'D-trees'.[11] For convenience (that of historians, at least), and without much falsification, one may thus far conflate the work of Tesnière and Hays. There seems, frankly, little of direct help to diachrony in Hays' particular formalizations and evaluating procedures. One may perhaps salvage such a general aphorism as that co-occurring items like Noun and Adjective have a mutual interrelation of occurrence (of actual exponents), to be called

---

[9]   Ovid, *Metam.* 8, 869; *Amores* 3, 11B, 20; Lucan 1, 13f.
[10]   Ennius, *Ann.* 377; Varro, *de ling. Lat.* 7, 58; Cicero, *de orat.* 3, 145.
[11]   Cf. Tesnière, 1959; Hays, 1964. The trees are commonly equated with 'P-markers', but the latter are context-free hierarchic dispositions of elements of which trees are just one type of display (see W. S-Y. Wang, *Lg.* 41, 1965, 457 fn. 3, and his reference to the Ohio discussion). 'Government' and 'dependence' are not entirely foreign to IC grammar (*pace* Hays, 1964, 520), which distinguishes 'head' elements from others, and are commonplace for IE scholars.

mutual 'valences'. It would be possible to build on this base a graduated table of syntagmatic environments, from a high to a low degree of probability; this might be a useful corrective to the flightier essays on supposed conditioning environments in historical change.[12]

The model might be expected to offer a positive lead on the question of ultimate priority of Noun or Verb, with prime dependency answering to chronological sequence. In fact, and no doubt salutarily, it underlines the idiosyncrasy of languages in this respect. Tesnière regularly speaks as if dependency is ultimately on the Verb, but allows that a Noun-central statement fits most non-European idioms better (61). Hays does not categorically delimit the root-element at the top of his (inverted) trees; in the actual English examples which he employs the Verb is placed there.[13] An interdisciplinary bridge might be built with one foot resting on Tesnière's division of 'empty' words into 'junctives' and 'translatives' (respectively, connectors like *and* and those of the prepositional kind, for instance). The theory sees a preposition as converting a noun into an adverb. It follows that a 'concrete case' morpheme — on these cases and the others see chapter 8, fn. 34 — must be equally accounted a translative (*Romā = ab urbe*). Now the 'concrete cases' are distinct both from the 'grammatical cases' (like the nominative) and from such systemic markers of situational facts as number and sex-based gender; also, the other cited 'translations' (denominative verbs; adverb becoming unmarked adjectives,

---

[12] The concept of 'assignment function' (cited by Hays, 1964, 512, from Bar-Hillel), the distribution of forms to functions and vice versa, could lead to handy empirical theorems if worked out over successive *états* of one language. It could be that morphological ambiguity arising from shift or attrition or analogy cannot pass beyond a calculable saturation point; in a given sector, further loading may occasion either a predictable phonological revision of morphs (as in Latin the imperfect *-ā-* is supplemented and largely replaced by *-bā-*) or a formal collapse in the particular system (as with English noun-cases).

[13] Bar-Hillel's algebraic metaphor of syntax (1953), wherein a sentence (s) is formed by the arithmetical product of noun (n) and verb ($\frac{s}{n}$) and so forth, appears to be equally arbitrary in its choice of fundamental category (n). Its formulations of word-classes and syntagms could be simply re-written on the basis of $\frac{s}{v}$ (noun) $\times$ v (verb), etc.

as *un vin extra, iste post phaselus*; relative clause operating as adjective, etc.) are clearly latecomers. One of two things must be true. Either the 'concrete cases', despite their close tie with the context of the situation, are comparatively recent phenomena and are not to be set on an earlier evolutionary plane than the peripheral parts of speech. Or else they result from early 'translations', but the crucial role of the 'grammatical cases' and the power of the basic dependency *nœuds* have reduced them to items wholly contioned by rules of syntax (as with items controlled by 'dative verbs', or the shrinking of optative and subjunctive to clause-subordination signals, in the classical languages). Then 'retranslating' will be necessary. One can predict, or 'retrodict', the replacement of 'concrete case' values by prepositional phrases, and the shift of 'full' verbs to modal status, and like rearrangements in other sectors. The basic dependencies of a given grammar will presumably permit fewer and briefer disruptions. But history knows reorganisations of a pretty fundamental kind; and dependency theory has no power to predict those of extra-grammatical causation. Where Greek transforms an indirect object into the subject of a passive verb no morphological novelties are involved; the influence is almost certainly pattern-analogy between the trees of semantically similar sentences. The evolution of English *he is given a book* is quite otherwise, probably by way of reinterpretation of the element before the verb (*hym was brought a sop in win*) when an originally dative noun occurred in that basically pronominal position. The general loss of noun case markers and the consequent promotion of word order as a feature of syntactical exponence have, in this particular type of sentence, occasioned gross shifts of tactic relations (overriding pronoun case marking) as compared with the Greek example (which has nothing so fundamental as a change of nominative subject to object-included-in-passive).[14] There is no single diachronic path swept by this theory from tree to tree.

[14]   For Greek, see E. Schwyzer and A. Debrunner, *Griech. Gramm.* II (Munich 1950), 240f.; and *Word* 19, 1963, 236ff. For English, see W. van der Gaaf, *English Studies* 11, 1929, 1-11, 58-67. The Greek process fits better into the mechanics of 'gradience grammar'; see below.

4. *Glossematics*

The Saussurian dichotomies had perhaps their greatest exploita-
tion in the Danish model of 'immanent structure'. The depressing
judgement that glossematics simply excludes history (Chikobava,
1959, 161 f.) may be somewhat discounted. This model elevates in
importance the written form of language (cf. Spang-Hanssen, 1961,
147 ff. and, for genetic relevance, Hjelmslev, 1954, 171 f.), to the
satisfaction of epigraphic diachronists. Again, its recognition of
'substitution' as well as 'commutation' — that is, that two terms
may differ only in one or other of the two planes of language,
content plane and expression plane — permits a readier understanding of the processes and transitional awkwardness of, for
example, case-syncretism (where an interim stage may reflect only
loss of differential marking OR only loss of significant difference of
meaning in given syntagms). It also gives a basis for understanding
why syncretism and morphological suspension fail to preclude each
other: each is a form of substitution which can reach the limits of
the tolerable, but the mechanisms for salvaging content-difference
are in the former case syntagmatic and in the latter case paradigmatic.[15]

Otherwise, however, the historian will sift profitlessly the rather
dusty archives of this theory. The esoteric terminology (cf. Haas,
1956, 105 ff.) reveals, or obscures, nothing new for his purposes,
and no detective insights come from the generalized application of
glossematic method. But it is to be noted that when this model is
credited with applicability to historical studies, the assertion is made
in respect of the formal, abstract, dimension. Diachrony is, indeed,
seen as a constant series of laws of restructuring, applied to the
formal, non-substantial, entities of language, and based on an
adequate typology of those entities.[16] Now the mechanics, although
not the reconstructions, of phonological history demand substance;

---

[15]   Respectively, by the insertion of prepositions or the choice of conjunctions,
and by the coexistence in other paradigms of the relevant expression-difference.
Spang-Hanssen, 1961, 160, sees glossematics as neutral in the antithesis of
synchrony and diachrony; cf. below and fn. 16.
[16]   So Hjelmslev, 1966 (esp. 128, 171 f.).

besides, when it is a matter of historical causation, one can handle the glossematic dimension of form rather more easily in connexion with the plane of content. Therefore one seeks to apply the theory to diachronic problems where organised semantic categories figure, namely within the field of grammar, strictly defined (at least to the exclusion of phonology). One may then pause over Holt's (1961) calculus of the "order of content entities" in grammatical complexes; if the presence of one category logically depends on the presence of another, some sort of chronology of evolution might answer to this. It need not; and Holt is careful to reject the connecting of his 'order' with time and space. But empirical discovery of such a connexion anywhere would be there a powerful historical asset. And there are some prima facie grounds for think-ing the search worth making. In Greek λείπονται < *$leik^w$-o-nt-o-i the extremes of closeness to, and remoteness from, the lexical element are represented by the aspect marker (root ablaut) and the present time marker (-i); among the semantic categories which the total form signals these are respectively, in evolution, not im-probably the earliest and quite certainly the latest. We need a field in which there is no doubt as to (*a*) the presence and the posi-tioning of elements of expression, preferably in a single spatial direction relative to the lexical segment of a word, and (*b*) the fragmentation of meaning and the mapping of the fragments on to morphs. Then it would help to have a guide to the relative time of emergence of (some) markers. Agglutination is the obvious field; and Holt cites Turkish, asserting that there number logically precedes case, apparently on the grounds that it spatially precedes it (cf. *ev-ler-in* = lexical item + plural + genitive). Now if case is 'late' in Turkish, coming after even personal possessive (cf. *ev-ler-i-(n)de*), one might just speculate on the possible connexion with the developmental fact that case is a curiously 'superlinguistic' category, easily related neither to experiential phenomena — as are number and gender — nor to a counterpart in other disciplines. Yet the chronological implications are obscure. So with number: this may be the earliest variation feature in the utterance, in view of its possible 'priority' in the noun. But nothing prevents its historically late emergence, if, once noted, it seemed so crucial as to deserve special re-ordering of existing markers.[17] These animadversions are not gratuitous attacks on a position which has never been intended to be held. The slightest sign of regularity in the relationship of logical and chronological precedences would be of immense value to historians; to know for sure that such a glimpse must always be an ignis fatuus would save time and heartache.

5. Scale-and-category grammar (or slot-plus-filler categorization)[18]

(a) 'neoFirthian' grammar. The first articulation (Halliday, 1961), though it prompted no answers to particular historical problems, did suggest some novel questions (which have been ventilated in chapter 6, pp. 124 ff.). Nobody has yet proved that what seems, in terms of descriptive theory, to be gross operational difference between two états de langue must be regarded as a doubtful piece

---

[17] Turkish evleri answers without phonic or graphic distinction to the meanings 'his/her houses', 'their house', 'their houses'. As nothing elsewhere support the view that 'plural' is here a morphological prosody of varying domain, there may be historical truth in the pedagogical device of forming the expression of 'their houses' by applying haplology to *evler + leri (cf. the process 'dovetailing', chapter 2, pp. 38). Holt's Latin examples (67 f.) unhappily do not work, quite apart from the inextricability of the morphemes in (as he quotes) hortī etc. The presence versus absence of inflexional distinctions (e.g. in nom. and acc. pl. patrēs versus nom. sing. pater, acc. sing. patrem) is spoken of as though identical with that of the content entities themselves, which confuses the two 'planes'. The judgement, from the example above, that in Latin "distinction of case depends on number" is offset by e.g. nom. sing. and pl. nūbēs versus abl. sing. nūbe, abl. pl. nūbibus, which seems to show distinction of number depending on case; again, masc. sing. seruō, fem. sing. seruā versus masc. and fem. pl. seruīs in the ablative shows gender depending on number, against Holt's idea that "the whole syntagm is first inflected for gender". Gender is a late affair in IE.

[18] It is not a coincidence that these two fall together. For Halliday, scalar operations fit interdefined categories into a coherent scheme, but then structure needs a pinpointing of its 'elements', 'at' which the systems of classes of units occur. Tagmemics conversely starts with an entity which is at once slot and filler ('function-set'), but then requires a ranking scale to handle structures of structures (inclusive and included constituents) — or even two such scales: one for functions (tagmeme, syntagmeme) and one for structures (from morpheme to discourse).

of history. Thus this model does not offer, any more than taxonomic models in general, any control on historical speculation. Neither 'delicacy' (increasing detail in the statement of the structures of units) nor 'exponence' (the realizing of elements of structures, as (systems of) classes of lower units) is demonstrably more susceptible to, or more preclusive of, any one kind of redesigning as opposed to another. A language may, in evolving, lose from among the secondary elements of a structure some exponent which has so far operated in a two-term system (such might be a fairly typical gender loss). This would much alter the statements of exponence and delicacy at that unit-rank; but it is scarcely feasible to predict or explain such a reduction within a theory which sees 'the grammarian's dream' as maximum permissible delicacy and as much movement down the exponence scale as possible. A scale of 'depth' has been introduced (Huddleston, 1965, 585) to measure the complexity of sentences; but it offers no theorems to a diachronist, whose reconstruction of proto-sentences must be extremely crude, if performed at all.

Still, some help, at least in handling phenomena, does come from both the older (1961, 1963) and the newer (1966a) version of the theory. Halliday has always leaned heavily on the concept of (downward) rank-shift, to cope with recursive structures. A clause may operate as a group (phrase) or as a word, a group as a word, even a sentence as a word (*my come-what-may philosophy*), which is not to say that a clause IS a group etc. One aspect of evolution may be dimly reflected here. PIE can be reconstructed without the rank of clause, a unit derivable from post-PIE sentence-parataxis. Moreover, only the attributive adjective used as 'modifier' enforces the unit-status of the group, as otherwise nominal and verbal groups arise from the later application of apposition and periphrasis to original noun and verb univerbals. But where PIE has only just four sub-paragraph ranks, the increase to five is virtually complete before the comparative evidence (on the basis of which we accept or reject ranks as apparent proto-ranks) presents itself. The redesigning is a regularization of a kind of rank-shift whereby sentence operates in sentence-structure, or at least makes respectable the flaunting of rank-hierarchy. (If to interpret the shift parataxis $>$ hypotaxis in this way seems, as combinations of 'like' units do to Huddleston, 1965, 579, to trivialize rank-shift, one may follow him in regarding all such couplings as 'complexes'. Then the changing of coupled sentences to interrelated clauses, or the creation of multiverbal verbs, means that the complex is recognised as a new, in each case higher, rank. At the rank of sentence, the new unit takes the old name). In any case there is re-ranking to avoid a sort of mezzanine,[19] and rank-shift otherwise loses its evolutionary power, a fact which may reward exploration by theorists of history.

Upward rank-shift is not officially recognised.[20] Critics have not proved that anything more is needed than the regular ability, within the rules of the model, of any single unit to form the whole structure of a unit of the next rank above (the structure of which has n elements, where $n \geqslant 1$) and so from bottom to top. However viewed, the process may answer to the useful but intractable notion of 'ellipse', safer in diachronic than in synchronic studies. The model's means of accounting, with maximal grammatical statement, for things like the sentence *Yes* (cf. Halliday, 1961, 253 fn.31) may be used to point up just what has happened in (to take a

[19]   Of course, a bound word is practically equivalent to a morpheme (*very* in *very happy* $=$ -*est* in *happiest*), and a bound clause traditionally substitutes for a noun (group) or an adjective or adverb (word). A bound unit, therefore, is virtually always in rank-shift. But the bound unit, or at least the bound-free distinction, justifies the rank (because a free unit is co-terminous with a simple unit of the rank above and need not be set apart, and a compound upper unit implies a lower unit that can be bound). Therefore all ranking rests ultimately on rank-shift.

[20]   By Halliday, 1961, 251, 1963, and 1966b. Matthews' objections (1966, 104 ff.) over the place of function of English *of* and -'s do not enforce it. Nothing prevents permitted downward shift from coping with e.g. *your beautiful young sister's*, as a word, like *John's*, in which *your beautiful young sister* is (a rank-shifted group operating as) a morpheme, like *John*. To handle thus the celebrated problem of *the king of England's hat* points up both the solution and the counter-intuitive awkwardness which makes it such a problem. Matthews' stronger case (106 ff.), against elliptical *and*, as in *I should have stayed sober and kept to the path* — where, even if itself assigned rank-free status, it tiresomely joins non-units — is somewhat answered by Huddleston's idea of unit-complexes. But Longacre (1965, 74, 76) recognizes upward rank-shift ('level-skipping') as well as downward ('backlooping').

deliberately transparent example) the Sanskrit 'periphrastic' future. 'I shall give' > 'I am a (potential) giver' = *dātāsmi* (*dātā* + *asmi*); but in the first person plural less than the full complement of morphemes — and so systems — forms a word or, historically, there is ellipse of a number marker: *dātā* + *smaḥ*, and not **dātāraḥ* + *smaḥ*. Again, third plural *dātāraḥ* (not **dātāraḥ* + *santi*) shows ellipse of the finite item or, in Hallidayan terms, here a single word forms a verbal group.

There may be a historical value in the notion that like systems operate at different ranks (on rank-free items see fn. 20), and that the higher the rank at which a system can be located the better. A shift and its path may be made clearer if a calculus of functional place and importance can be applied.[21] We lack examples, however. Those IE languages which reflect both categories, seem to have their mood-system statable at the rank of sentence and their case-system at the rank of clause. But this distinction is immaterial to evolution; English has only vestiges of each system, Italian has kept the subjunctive mood and lost the noun cases, Modern Greek still has much of the case-system but the mood has gone. It is possible that 'structural cohesion', defined by Halliday, 1964, 304, as concerning "the relations between clauses in sentence structure" or "presupposition at the rank of the sentence", can be invoked to explain how some demonstratives become specialized as reflexives, or why verbal mood becomes statable at so high a rank. Latin has a well-known contrast in subordinate clauses between plain and 'virtual oratio obliqua' structures (*Paetus omnes libros quos frater* suus reliquisset *mihi donauit* Cicero, *ad Att.* 2, 1 versus *Gaius iratus fuit Herennio Macro quod* illum *Gaium* salutauerat (not **... se ... salutauisset*) Seneca, *Dial.* 2, 18). This is clearly a contrast of cohesive clauses within a sentence and non-cohesive clauses. The concept permits the theoretical subsuming and historical uniting of events usually set apart: subordinated mood, mood or tense 'sequence', modal 'attraction', indirect reflexion, protasis-apodosis relation, choice of conjunction. The limit is

---

[21]   But for a discounting of the historical role of functional load, see Robert D. King, *Lg.* 43, 1967, 831 ff.

set by the empirical difficulty of finding 'proto-cohesions', especially with fewer ranks in the proto-language; and only a very small degree of isomorphism in this respect is to be found even between, say, Greek, Latin and Sanskrit.

The newer form of the model (1966a) offers *inter alia* (such as the splitting of feature-environment from feature-realization) the concept of a system-network. This is displayed as a flow-chart of the properties of given units, the exponential path through the chart making it clear whether the applicable systems occur together, preclude one another, or are hierarchically ordered. The whole thing makes explicit the notional 'scale of delicacy', and the germ of it had occurred in the adumbration of such interrelations in what appears now as chapter 6 above (pp. 124f.). The networks are not affected by historical change in items of spoken or written expression or their formal organisation (Catford's 'medium-form'). But any redistribution of items of medium-form to ultimate exponence of systemic terms, or any rearrangement of the properties themselves, will show up in startling clarity in the flow-charts, if these are continued through to final exponence and compared at different états. Perhaps the clarity, and the degree of complication shown, will be excessive. For instance, it is diachronically a very slight and trite matter indeed when Sanskrit extends the co-occurrence of its *mā* negative from 'injunctive' forms to prohibitive uses of the imperative. Yet in a combined display of system-network and morph-occurrence there appears to be a minor revolution:

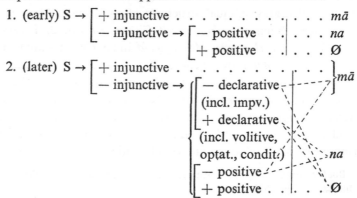

— and even this is worsened by the occasional semantic equivalence of optative $+ na$ to prohibition.

If, however, two systems appear to be interpreclusive at one point in a network but alternative at another, and the ultimate exponents are in either case identical, we have with fair certainty the reflex of a transitional stage in diachronic supercession of one system by another. The Greek verbal systems of aspect and tense are alternative after the earlier choice of non-finite (infinitive); once co-occurrent elements are logged (and the theory is not clear on how this is done) they become interpreclusive, in that a prolative infinitive cannot have tense and an oratio obliqua infinitive does not have aspect, and so on. Choice of finite non-indicative rules out tense, again; but it is the combined alternating/preclusive role of terms whose expression is indistinguishable which suggests that one set of oppositions is becoming the other. Only the direction of shift remains uncertain. Finally, it may be that extended search would uncover a relation between isomorphism of categories and properties and genetic connexion; 'translation at rank' (cf. Ellis, 1966, 42 ff., 127 ff.) may help to bring out *parenté*, but may also be hard pressed to set it apart from areal *affinité*.

(b) *Tagmemics.* Under this heading one may include the theories of interlocking modes and variant perspective (leading to statements of constituent-relations, matrix presentations and particle-wave-field dynamics) to be found in the writings of Pike, Longacre, Pickett and others of this persuasion (cf. Pike's checklist in *Current Trends in Linguistics* III). Some of what is relevant to diachrony is discussed elsewhere,[22] and the general similarity of this model to Halliday's is scarcely to be missed (much of what has been said above could be repeated with mechanical transposition of terminology). Tagmemicists seem to ignore history as determinedly as do

---

[22] On matrices, see chapter 2, pp. 26 ff. On unit boundaries, see above, pp. 132 ff. Tagmemics is verb-centred (Longacre, 1965, 65 f.) but abhors trees (*ibid.* 72 and fn. 15). Syntagmemes above the sentence (cf. Pickett, 1960, and Waterhouse, 1963) do not matter to historians, who (if they get as far as reconstructing sentences with connectives) need merely to presume just one such unit; paragraph reconstruction is a myth.

all taxonomists; indeed, sometimes their tenets actually discourage historians. For example, Kuryłowicz (1964, esp. 22f.) has proposed a simple arithmetical test to determine the direction of an apparent shift of the systemic (contextual) values of the terms of a paradigm: if an opposition is expounded by a single difference of expression it is older than a formally cognate opposition which, in debased or inflated fashion, is expounded by more than a single difference. Let us return to the Greek shift between aspect and tense, mentioned above with its direction left undecided. Where Greek tense is not relevant to the opposition, as with imperfect indicative versus aorist indicative, the aspect difference is first marked by the vocalic ablaut-grade in the root syllable alone; the Sanskrit basic distinction, of present versus aorist tense (in Kuryłowicz's view), is marked by BOTH root ablaut AND primary versus secondary desinences: ἔλειπον:ἔλιπον but *sárpati: ásṛpat*. Hence the Greek state of affairs is the earlier and, in view of the formal comparability, one may lay down that in IE tense derives from aspect. But this victory is denied us if we accept Longacre's ruling (1964, 18; but a long-standing tenet in him) that one syntagmeme does not affectively contrast with another at all unless the observer can point to a dual structural difference. The best that can be salvaged from such insistence on two or more markings is some assistance in the nagging problem of contrasts like *hodie regit*/*cras reget*. Here some would deny that the terms of the Latin tense-system can be elucidated with the semantic help of the time-reference in the opposed adverbs; these latter alone, it is argued, carry the opposition of meaning for which they are used, the verbal morphemes being in that respect empty co-occurrents.[23] The tagmemic point (perhaps aided by lexical dualities of difference-marking, and the feature of redundancy — *gravely ill* but *grievously wounded*) seems to be that the opposition resides in both items in the syntagm, and the verbal

---

[23] For instance, Gonda (1956, 104) denies that 'volition' is a semantic clue in the history of the IE subordinated subjunctive, specifically in Latin 'indirect commands', on the grounds that this sense is carried lexically by the main verb in the stock citations.

morphemes are not to be denied full semantic status just where we have a clue as to what the semantic opposition is.

6. *Stratificational grammar*

This model alone actually recoils, with apparent horror, from involvement with language history (cf. Lamb, 1964, 111 and 116 fn. 9); it seems unfair to underline its general inapplicability to a task it tries hard not to begin to do. Still, even for descriptive purposes it is difficult to locate in its stratal systems some of the phenomena which a student of Indo-European, or of any time-expired inflecting morphosyntax, handles as commonplaces. There is the element — or, if you prefer, the abstraction — 'stem', as *puella-* or *mone-*; it may be misty but it is crucial for the reconstruction, across paradigms, of the real syntactical variables. *Puellās*, *puellīs* etc. are clearly, in Lamb's terms, lexemes in the lexemic knot pattern, passing to lexemic signs in the lexemic sign pattern. *Puell-* and *-ās, -īs* are morphemes passing to morphemic signs, with similar pattern placing, in the next stratum down. How are stems to be handled? (A question which matters here, as it does not in models which do not offer realizations, or which terminate at the morpheme.) Scarcely as lexons, combining in the lexemic sign pattern; combination of nonsignificant parts of entities (not so divided above or immediately below) is not allowed for in the model. Nor within the morphemic alternation pattern, for the model offers no 'ordered downward AND' in that pattern; and in the morphemic tactic pattern only if the 'stem vowel' had separate theoretical existence in the sign pattern. Again, where does one locate semantic elements like 'contingency', the *Gestalt* achieved by the syntactical combination of different clause-types becoming the conditional sentence? The 'hypersememes' are not adequately exemplified to suggest that they are sufficiently abstract or generalized (as opposed to complex) in meaning for this purpose (31 f.).

But historians should not dismiss the theory entirely. The subtle feature termed 'anataxis' (difference in the ordering of units as between levels, not necessarily as between strata) may prove to be useful as a general formalization of several methods and devices used by historians. When anataxis occurs between strata, "the lower tactic pattern always takes precedence over what is specified from above" (Lamb, 1966, 22), a rule exemplified by the way Zoque phonotactics, by precluding consonant sequences of palatal semivowel + stop, enforces a re-ordering of the morphons after the morphemic stratum has produced a provisional arrangement of them: $\{y + ken + hay + pa\} \rightarrow$ /kyenhapya/. Such metatheses are common in description and in history, without always being shared by both disciplines. The whole procedure known as 'internal reconstruction', at least in the formulation of Hoenigswald where it is really internal and non-comparative, is aimed at removing precisely those obstructive anomalies of paradigm-data which arise where phonotactics has amended morphological realization. The rule fails, as does the procedure, with loan-forms and similar mavericks; hence it diagnoses and extracts them. We have noted the common belief that morphological boundaries control phonic movement (p. 77, and fn. 6 above), which might seem to be a counter-case. But the boundary marker, the physical factor, is a degree of juncture, and unplaced in the theory. It is at highest a morphon, and thus is not significantly other than a unit at the upward limit of the phonemic alternation pattern; it does not place the origin of the interference with sound shaping in the higher stratum, certainly not in the higher tactic pattern. As for the assimilating pressures, normally of morphological origin, which diachronists call collectively 'analogy', these fall equally within the anataxis rule. They operate purely in the morphemic stratum even though their ultimate effect is upon sound realizations; they simply restrict the variety of morphons to be called up into the morphemic sign pattern, and the complexity of the nodes of the sign pattern itself. But the anataxis rule and the facts of evolution can be in danger of conflicting. Let us suppose that, at a comparatively late *état de langue*, the lexotactics includes a downward node of a degree of generality unknown in earlier *états*, and that one or more morphemic units now become needed for the first time. The morphological patterns are revised under pressure from a higher stratum, and unless the tactics are amended the rule is contravened. A Greek internal development allows a verb in 'oratio obliqua' or 'interrogatio obliqua', when directed by a main verbal item in a past tense, to have either the mood of the 'original' ('oratio recta') or the optative; yet its tense form must be that of the 'original' utterance. The consequence is that a brand-new lexeme has to be made available at a previously unknown tense-mood intersection: hence the 'future optative', operating in this function only. Then the 'downward ANDs' of the morphotactics must arrange themselves otherwise.[24] The reason is that without fresh patterning there the anataxis rule, when the model is applied synchronically, will be falsified, all the more because in this case no actual new morphemic sign is created. It follows that (a) if two stratificational grammars of two temporally close états of the same language show linked novelties in two contiguous strata, a single (if complex) evolutionary fact is discovered, and (b) if the novelties in the higher stratum — and these alone — are realized by units of the lower stratum in a novel taxis, then the downward direction of the causation of the diachronic movement is discovered.

7. Gradience grammar

The notion has long been current that language relationship subsists between systems rather than items, and is of the nature of 'more-or-less' rather than of 'yes-or-no'. Allen (1953), imposing even an arithmetical calculus of system-comparison, used the revelation as a means of attacking traditional genetic history (esp. 91f.). But Bolinger (1961) deserves the credit for establishing the principle of graduated likeness in linguistic analysis, and his term 'gradience' may serve to entitle this approach. More recently, Quirk (1965), adding to this concept that of 'delicacy' (a term taken

[24] In order to allow a node at which the existing morphemes e.g. λυ-, -c-, and -οι may now join, in that order. No rearrangement is needed to accommodate an absent 'future subjunctive' (a fact which, in Latin, Gleason, 1964, 81, handles under semotactics only). Whether the formal identity between the putative realization of that lexeme and the existing aorist subjunctive (e.g. λύcηι etc.) is cause or effect of the absence, I cannot say.

over from McIntosh and Halliday), has cogently demonstrated not only the greater descriptive adequacy but also the explanatory power (in that it explains structural creation) of what he calls 'serial relationship'. The presentation is too partial and informal to be called a model, but it corrects other models and must interest historians.

In effect, matrices are constructed to plot sequences (of varying size, most often clauses or sentences). The horizontal dimension represents items of presumed similar function or lexical interplay (one might list *want(s)*, *intend(s)*, *seem(s)*, *require(s)*). The vertical columns represent the structures into which at least some of the items enter, and are differentiated by the presence or absence of potential features (like the possibility of inserting specific adverbs) or transformational features (like the change from active to passive) — so *he X to come, he would X to come, he X that we come, he is Xed to come* etc. The columns operate as syntagmatic parameters, and their judicious ordering shows, as well as can be done in the absence of polydimensional displays, a gradience in each matrix of infinitely delicate degrees of congrammaticality, to borrow Hiż's term.[25] It is interesting that, say, similar English verbs such as *like, persuade, help, tempt, oblige, say, feel, know, think, make, elect, declare, regard* are subcategorized in terms of infinite variability in many dimensions. It is more compelling that "vertical agreement in the matrix is actually generative" (Quirk, 1965, 211). Items which, by sharing incidence in structures, have cellular agreement in one or more columns may extend that congruence to further columns; and this may happen without involving a recognized transformational linkage between the newly affected column (that is, the structure-type which it represents) and some non-affected column (representing what would seem an apparent source-structure). Thus *they know/say that he is* Adj and *it is known/said that he is* Adj sponsor a spread from *he is known to be* Adj to *he is said to be* Adj; the absence of spread from *they know him to be* Adj to **they say him to be* Adj is immaterial. This is seen to accommodate

[25]   But see chapter 2, fn. 10; and note that gaps in a pattern do not destroy that pattern or necessarily cause instability.

diachronic statement (Quirk, 1965, 214); and the complex syn-chronic interaction of patterns is likened by Winter (1965, 487) to simple facts long noticed by historians, above all to diachronic 'analogy'. The diagram of the paradigmatic creation of structures (Quirk, fig. 8) shows pattern-descent in diverging lines and the more normally conceived — but in fact often absent — functional projection in the horizontal dimension. If this figure were re-orientated by a 90 degree twist, it would be an intriguing analogue of the configuration used in palaeographical stemmatics. There the normal process of text-transfer from exemplars is shown verti-cally, and is synonymous with the genealogy of the manuscripts themselves. But the possibility is not excluded that co-existing manu-scripts may cross-affect one another, and show readings neither unique nor prompted by what is in each case the undeniable parent codex. Turyn (1952, 15) has called this phenomenon 'horizontal influence'.

This explanation has its difficulties. It does not matter as much as one might think that Chomsky has since abandoned the notion that structures, at least sentences, derive from other (kernel) surface structures by rules located in the transformational part of the gram-mar. By including all the potentially needed items (like Passive, Interrogative) in the base component,[26] and activating them by phrase structure rules, he has done more than make the active → passive relation irrelevant; he has uncharacteristically opposed traditional attitudes, not to mention native intuition, in respect of this relation and others. But even if surface-to-surface T-deriva-tion is out and the enemy has to be given fresh faces, Quirk's pat-tern-spread disposes of much of what commonly passes for evolu-tionary logic, particularly the idea that the existence of a structure of one given set inevitably implies the (prior) existence of a struc-ture of a second given set, or (if you like) that only categories breed. On the other hand, to identify pattern-spread is not enough.

[26] Chomsky, 1965, 103 ff. This does not, however, make irrelevant Quirk's argument for the posteriority of *John is easy to please* to *John is eager to please*; transformational grammar, assuming coexistence, has never explained WHY this 'deep' difference is not retained as the grammar moves to the surface.

Historical statement must cover the reasons or conditions (of environment and period) which govern the incidence of spread. Why is spread sporadic? Why is influence unidirectional (despite the Quirkian dislike of this term, one notes that *know* affects *say* but not the reverse: *I am saying that he is* Adj but **I am knowing that* etc.)? Hockett's and Bolinger's 'blending' (*Lg.* 37, 1961, 52 and ibid. 366 ff.) and its diachronic partner, classical 'contamination', need the careful weighing of all the factors present in individual syntagms; mere context-free mixing is less convincing, as a diagnosis of what happens in each speech occurrence, than the relating of each individual syntagm to the general dynamics of thought.[27] And nice as it is to see that old diachronic warhorse, analogy, given a fresh grooming, it needs here in syntax the guiding principles which Kuryłowicz and Mańczak have tried to supply for it in morphology.

Yet this approach is conscious of history. It is not so much generative, in the technical sense, as creative (which is why it is admitted here, despite the remarks in this chapter's opening paragraph). It allows no non-terminal forms of frankly unhistorical status; it needs no deep relations; its adducing of item-linked sequences entails the prior existence and use of some particular sequences to others, with no doubt about this meaning priority in time. Hence the exposition has an air of puzzlement over the closeness of its own hypothesis to language development, and over the obviously evolutive role of its derived forms; appeal is constantly made to Jakobson's (1961, 248) plea for 'dynamic synchrony'. What is being recognised, almost inadvertently, is that history is a crucial component of linguistic operation and should therefore figure undisguisedly in description and formal theory. This is so, not because of the constant factor of evolution which makes all grammars leaky; nor because history needs description (and its

---

[27] General 'contamination' is no trouble: cf. the interesting and credible development of syntactical identity by the originally very different Latin verbs *interest* and *refert*. But for the ad hoc nature of most such classical phenomena, and the different types of semantic re-interpretation of utterances, see *Greece and Rome* 22, 1953, 130f. (And as to one of Quirk's examples, 215, see the same fascicule of *Language*, 291).

underlying theory) to enable it to see the true face of its own data; nor because of sporadic parallelisms in diachronic and synchronic rules — though all these facts are true, and the next chapter will explore them further in a particular vein. It is because synchronic properties of grammar are simultaneously creative properties; and grammatical relations, once we leave the universalities which people the extreme depths, are by necessity evolutive and operate in communication on that understanding. Diachrony and diatopy are parts of synchrony.[28]

REFERENCES

This list is not intended as an exhaustive inventory of the writings on each of the theories treated in the chapter, any more than the discussion above is intended to evaluate the models. Only those papers which are cited or useful for the present arbitrary and eclectic purpose are included; for what is omitted, often fundamental to particular models, the reader is referred to the standard bibliographies (including Bursill-Hall, 1962).

Allen, W. S. 1953, "Relationship in comparative linguistics, *TPhS* 1953, 52-108.
—— 1958, "Some problems of palatalization in Greek", *Lingua* 7, 113-133.
Bar-Hillel, Y. 1953, "A quasi-arithmetical notation for syntactic description", *Lg.* 29, 47-58 (= *Language and information*, 1964, Jerusalem *et al.*, 61-74).
Bazell, C.E. 1949, "On some asymmetries of the linguistic system", *Act. Ling.*, 5, 139-145.

[28] Some linguists, notably J. P. Thorne and P. A. M. Seuren, have recently proposed a sort of 'implicational' grammar, to cover e.g. the skewed relation of *he can go* and *he can't go* to *he must go* and *he mustn't go* (or, if you like, the semantic distinction of the 'must' negations *he mustn't go* and *he needn't go*). The solutions involve the separating out of 'places' of structure (quasi 1) *it is essential* | 2) *he ... go* — or even 1) *I make the proposition* | 2) *it is essential* | 3) *he ... go*, in order to pierce the opaqueness of surface identity by differential placing of the negation; so *I don't say he should go* = negation at place 1), *I don't think he need go* = negation at place 2), *I don't think he should go* = negation at place 3)). Seuren sets up 'nuclei' and 'operators', as in his forthcoming book *Operators and Nucleus*, Cambridge. Thorne's ideas are to appear in *Journal of Linguistics*.

The pedagogic usefulness is obvious; it is brought out how French structure commonly reflects these separate 'places' *(il se peut que ...)* which English obscures, and the deep conditioning of the Latin choice between e.g. *quisquam* and *quiuis* now leaps to the eye. More complex place-and-sememe permutation is needed to cope with e.g. *nobody here knows two languages* versus *two languages are known by nobody here*. Until these notions are crystallized into a coherent theory, we may simply note them in passing.

Bolinger, D.L. 1961, *Generality, gradience, and the all-or-none* (The Hague).

Bursill-Hall, G.L. 1962, "Theories of syntactic analysis", *Stud. Ling.* 16, 100-112.

Chikobava, A.S. 1959, *Problema jazyka kak predmeta jazykoznania* (Moscow).

Chomsky, N. 1965, *Aspects of the theory of syntax* (Cambridge, Mass).

Ellis, J.O. 1966, *Towards a general comparative linguistics* (The Hague).

Gleason, H.A. Jr. 1964, "The organization of language: a stratificational view". In Stuart, 1964, 75-95.

Glinz, H. 1961, *Die innere Form des Deutschen* (2nd. edn.) (Bern, Munich).

Gonda, J. 1956, *The character of the Indo-European moods* (Wiesbaden).

Haas, W. 1956, "Concerning glossematics", *Arch. Ling.* 8, 93-110.

Halliday, M.A.K. 1961, "Categories of the theory of grammar", *Word* 17, 241-292.

—— 1963, "Class in relation to the axes of chain and choice in language", *Linguistics* 2, 5-15.

—— 1964, "The linguistic study of literary texts", *Proceedings of the ninth International Congress of Linguists* (The Hague), 302-307.

—— 1966a, "Some notes on 'deep' grammar", *JL* 2, 57-67.

—— 1966b, "The concept of rank: a reply", *JL* 2, 110-118.

Harris, Z.S. 1962, *String analysis of sentence structure* (The Hague).

Hays, D.G. 1964, "Dependency theory: a formalism and some observations", *Lg.* 40, 511-525.

Hjelmslev, L. 1953, *Prolegomena to a theory of language* (transl. F. J. Whitfield), Baltimore (=1943, *Omkring sprogteoriens grundlæggelse*, Copenhagen).

—— 1954, "La stratification du langage", *Word* 10, 163-188 (reprinted in 1959, *Essais linguistiques*, Copenhagen).

—— 1966, *Le langage* (transl. M. Olsen), Paris (=1963, *Sproget*, Copenhagen).

Hockett, C.F. 1954, "Two models of grammatical description", *Word* 10, 210-234 (=1966, *Readings in linguistics* I[4], ed. Joos, 386-399).

—— 1958, *A course in modern linguistics* (New York).

Holt, J. 1959, "Pleremics", *Proc. Univ. Durham Philos. Socy.* I (Ser. B.) 6, 49-53.

—— 1961, "Order of content entities", *Language and society* (Copenhagen), 65-72.

Huddleston, R.D. 1965, "Rank and depth", *Lg.* 41, 574-586.

Jakobson, R. 1961, "Linguistics and communication theory", *Proceedings of symposia in applied mathematics* (Providence), 12.

—— 1962, "Concluding remarks" in *Proceedings of the fourth International Congress of Phonetic Sciences* (The Hague), xxv-xxix.

Kuryłowicz, J. 1964, "On the methods of internal reconstruction", *Proceedings of the ninth International Congress of Linguists* (The Hague), 9-29.

Lamb, S.M. 1964, "On alternation, transformation, realization, and stratification", In Stuart, 1964, 105-122.

—— 1966, *Outline of stratificational grammar* (Washington, D.C.).

Longacre, R.E. 1964, *Grammar discovery procedures* (The Hague).

—— 1965, "Some fundamental insights of tagmemics", *Lg.* 41, 65-76.

Matthews, P.H. 1966, "The concept of rank in neo-Firthian grammar", *JL* 2, 101-109.

Pickett, V.B. 1960, *The grammatical hierarchy of Isthmus Zapotec*. *Lg.* diss. 56, suppl. to *Lg.* 36.

Pike, K.L. 1958, "On tagmemes, née gramemes", *IJAL* 24, 273-278.

Quirk, R. 1965, "Descriptive statement and serial relationship", *Lg.* 41, 205-217.

Robins, R.H. 1959, "In defence of WP", *TPhS* 1959, 116-144.

—— 1964, *General linguistics: an introductory survey* (London).

Spang-Hanssen, H. 1961, "Glossematics", *Trends in European and American linguistics 1930-1960* I (Utrecht, Antwerp), 128-164.

Strang, B.M.H. 1965, *Metaphors and models* (Newcastle upon Tyne).

Stuart, C.I.J.M. 1964, ed. *Report of the fifteenth annual (first international) Round Table meeting on linguistics and language studies (= Monograph series on languages and linguistics*, Georgetown Univ., 17) (Washington, D.C.).

Tesnière, L. 1959, *Élements de syntaxe structurale* (Paris).

Turyn,A. 1952, *Studies in the manuscript tradition of the tragedies of Sophocles* (Urbana, Ill.).

Waterhouse, V. 1963, "Independent and dependent sentences", *IJAL* 29, 45-53.

Wells, R.S. 1947, "Immediate constituents", *Lg.* 23, 81-117 (=1966, *Readings in linguistics* I⁴, ed. Joos, 186-207.

8. LINGUISTIC MODELS: A HISTORIAN'S USE – (II)

In the last chapter several types of 'realization grammars' were lumped together without, one hopes, being confused. 'Mutation grammars' deserve separate consideration as a historian's tool-set, and this for two reasons. First, proponents of mutation grammars reveal an implicit kinship with historians; secondly, they frequently make explicit claims of historical relevance for their methods and their findings. In the evaluation which follows, diachrony in general will be represented by genetic history, and mutation grammars by the generative variety commonly called 'transformational';[1] the convenience is obvious, and some judgements of relevance may be made.

---

[1] The various kinds of diachronic study are set out, somewhat esoterically, in Ellis, 1966. Generative grammar has until recently been rather a descriptive device of traditional linguistics, sporadically applied. Among contemporary 'formal' grammar with a base in modern logic, the particular theory of mental rules controlling a repertory of universal elements, familiar since 1957 in the writings of Chomsky, which explains intuitive skill and is loosely called 'transformational' grammar, is the strongest and most coherent doctrine; no rival within the type has as yet passed beyond adumbration. (Bibliographies of the theory so far are to be found in e.g. Chomsky, 1965, 237-245, which is very incomplete, and Dingwall, 1965; a new phase of the theory may be said to have begun around 1965. Ruwet, 1967, is a convenient handbook). Beyond the general characteristics of a mutation grammar, namely generation by projection and explicitness — hence the name 'generative' — the transformational model has a further essential feature: a rules component comprising multiple rewritings, switchings, deletions and manipulation of variables, and including enforced ordering of at least some of the rules. A generative grammar need not be transformational, but the converse is not true in anybody's practice. Further, generative grammar separates language 'levels' not by arbitrary subject-difference, but according to the stage or nature of the process involved (e.g. interpretive as opposed to generative); therefore phonology is included and bulks large in the discussion in this chapter. The 'applicational generative model'

As to kinship — or, at least, rapport — between T-grammar and diachrony, it cannot have escaped the dullest notice that the new generative enthusiasts set up two targets of especial detestation, not to say mockery: these are sterile taxonomy applied to what is superficially observable, and antimentalism (with poor Bloomfield often figuring as Empusa in both demonologies).[2] Now the attitudes of the descriptivists of the thirties, forties and early fifties towards historical study, and particularly towards 'comparative philology', ranged from the distant to the contemptuous.[3] What, then, more natural than kind words and understanding nods from transformationalists to those unloved by the previous occupiers of the linguistic limelight? Inadequacy in formal theory may well go along with shortage of human sympathy.

Nevertheless, transformationalists and historians have serious lines of linkage:[4] (1) Both employ the concept of 'generation', but the historians have been more timid and more spasmodic in its use (the 'subjective' and 'objective' genitives of the classical languages are among their rare explanatory successes). (2) Both lay bare previously obscured formal and semantic relationships, these centring on grammatical entities defined in the old, wide, sense of grammar (including phonology). (3) Both make use of signs which

---

of Šaumjan (see his writings from 1963, listed below), for all its interest, does not yet take the primitive concept 'transformational series' beyond the major parts of speech (stem-classes and generated word-classes) — beyond, in fact, what Šaumjan calls the genotype level (his use of 'genotype' and 'phenotype' is quasi-biological and quite other than Osgood's employment of them in respects of language universals). Hence it is useful for historians only in two places (*a*) at the level of sentence structure, where their work in protophenomena is at its weakest, and the 'atomistic' method of historical linguistics (cf. Ellis, 1966, 21 and 26) is thus precluded; and (*b*) in the 'noun first or verb first' controversy, and this Šaumjan does not enter. It has not seemed worth while exploring this model further as yet.

[2] See especially Chomsky, 1964 and Katz, 1964.

[3] But certainly not valueless in a provocative way: cf. the salutary countercritique of Allen's (and others') searching objections by Ellis, 1966, App. B.

[4] The differences are obvious: e.g. the arrows cannot cross boundaries between languages, where '>' can; '*' in history does not indicate unacceptability in grammar but merely that the item is not attested. But dummy markers, and items zeroed and switched, are paralleled in history easily enough (cf. *H*, *ṇ*, *Hu̯/u̯H* and so forth in IE).

import (*a*) evolution (→, ⇒, >), (*b*) citation-worthy non-existence
(*). (4) Both limit their development rules by (*a*) environmental
restrictions (curiously called 'context-sensitivity' by the transformationalists), and (*b*) order of application. (In case it is surprising to some to hear this latter limitation cited as a crucial feature of
diachrony, here is a simple, clearly differentiating example. In
the history of PIE > Greek, feature-shifting in phonologically
related PIE obstruents must precede dissimilatory loss of aspiration where a form inherits closely consecutive aspirates, whereas
the reverse order must operate within PIE > 'Pelasgian'; otherwise
we fail to arrive, respectively, at e.g. πυϑόμενος and πυργός as
end forms[5] — see Georgiev, 1958, 407-410; Brandenstein, 1954,
23). (5) The most luminous examples offered by Hoenigswald of
the 'principal step' in comparative reconstruction (that is, the major
reduction formula for protophonemes, precluding the unreality
of having a separate proto-form for every different reflex-equation)
involve not merely segmental analysis applied to phonemic ortho-
graphies but also the recognition of archiphonemes. These, by
splitting the reflex-range in one language, set up superficially
misleading, and merely apparent, equation-differences (cf. the
Sanskrit suspension of the $/d^h/$-$/d/$ opposition in *dehí-* etc., which
produces the irrelevance of d/d alongside dh/d, for the pairing
Sanskrit/German). Taxonomists have never cared for the archi-
phoneme, and some scorn the 'segment'; but transformationalists
(nothwithstanding their rejection of the full implications of
phoneme theory) accept segments. What is more, they are prepared to represent them where possible by a specification of "less
than their normal complement of features", an effective rehabilita-
tion of the archiphonemic principle, so useful to historians (compare the implications of Hoenigswald, 1950 with Halle, 1962,
61 fn. 4; likewise in 1964b). And to these five points of likeness one

---

[5]   Merlingen, in *Lingua* 18, 1967, 163, sees a form *pət, 'feed', underlying
φάτνη/πάϑνη, 'manger'. Apart from etymological difficulties in tying this in
with *pāsco* etc., the aspirate dissimilation would have to occur *after* the *Lautverschiebung*. One must clearly make up one's mind just what one wants to
treat as firm and what as fluid in this not-altogether-believed-in language.

may perhaps add the general similarity of behaviour (as noticed by Hockett, 1965, 186 ff.) between the new generativists and the neo-grammarians — the 'Young Turk' syndrome. Not that historians, I think, have failed to notice transformationalists' chivalrous interest in them: it is, however, akin to receiving a hearty handshake in a public place from a beaming stranger wearing a faintly familiar tie.

At the most simplicistic, it is obvious that any one type of evolutionary statement can employ the conventions of another: any historical shift may be cited in the form of a rewrite rule.[6] Two points then arise. First, by the law of averages alone (given that the data of historical and descriptive linguistics are common, at least in part), the two disciplines must sometimes arrive at identical formulations. Morphographemic rules for, and notation of the history of, Greek 'contract verb' forms will show congruence; each will rewrite τιμάομεν as τιμῶμεν, δηλόηις as δηλοῖς, and so forth; and probably each will agree, in this sector of the inflectional component of a language which favours a word-and-paradigm statement, in the particular choice of lexical base-forms and morphemic items. This congruence may lead to valuable generaliz-ations: if vowel contractions are handled in terms of respecifica-tions of distinctive features, one can in fact say for ancient Greek dialects such things as "when within a word two successive vocalic segments are replaced by a single segment, it is always diagnostic of East Greek (from West Greek) that segmentally successive specification-unlikenesses of the feature 'grave' (and/or 'flat') are replaced by a single '+ grave' (and/or '+ flat')".

Feature specification also enables diachronists to see more clearly certain environmental phonetic processes, and so to elabor-ate their own universals of co-occurrence and determination under-lying these processes. Historians have treated the phonetic aspects

[6] A recent example is K. Kohler's handling of Middle Scots phonetics at *TPhS* 1967, 32 ff.; cf. D. T. Langendoen, *Lg.* 42, 1966, 8 f.; Kiparsky, 1966-1967, 1967 (and references there), and above, chapter 2, p. 34. See also part III of Chomsky and Halle's forthcoming *The Sound Pattern of English*. Cf. the remark of Watkins, in Birnbaum and Puhvel 1966. 31: 'to use the generative model, which may profitably be applied to dialectal problems, we may ask, How early is the rule?' See also Thomas, 1967.

of their reconstructions either too timidly (partly because of a natural reluctance to fall into circularity of argument, partly from a less understandable disinclination to operate inside the trade with 'workshop forms' so to speak — see *Arch. Ling.* 8, 1956, 119f.), or else too boldly, as if typology did not impose some constraint at least. Too rare are such welcome guidelines as those of Allen (1958). Let us consider his universal ruling (107) that, in the sequence *VnC*, most commonly the nasality prevents friction in the following consonant; or, if friction is established, the nasality passes (with 'compensatory lengthening') to the preceding vowel, and may be lost altogether. As a T-formulation this latter process may be presented as a chronologically related (cf. Klima, 1964) pair of optional rules (wholly determined features having been catered for elsewhere in the grammar):

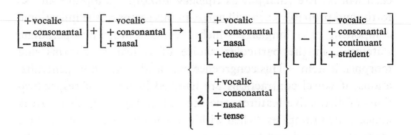

Of course, the facts are still a historical discovery. But a large number of such shifts may hide, as many now known long did hide, their relevant likenesses beneath a mass of unanalyzed complexes of features and a multiplicity of co-occurrences. Were each evolutionary statement featurized as above, and fed into a computer with the most elementary pattern-retrieval programme, the environmental conditionings of prevention or inducing of shift (switch, loss or addition) would tabulate themselves suggestively before many a microsecond had passed.

How we employ distinctive features is a wide-open matter of personal knack and enterprise. Hockett, for instance, lays out a kind of high tension field, with particle trajectory and nuclear fission within it (1965, 201ff.). For him, allophones in sequence are connected by 'most probable paths' of phonic transition, the points on which paths are 'local maxima' whose components are the distinctive features — though not according to the Chomsky-Halle quantization. Different paths traversing an allophone split it; and subsequently the ramifications of restructuring make a return to the original impossible (the principle of irreversibility, which "alone ... renders the comparative method of linguistics possible", 203).

Nonetheless, there are two (if not more) serious limitations on the applicability of T-grammar procedures to historical study. Of these, the first may be named the 'sbis' problem, after a recent essay (Foley, 1965) on morbid transformations — which is what (one supposes) one will have to call generative processes in a dead language. This author makes no pretensions to actual existence for his interim forms,[7] that these derivational steps have themselves 'appeared phonetically', as he oddly phrases it. But historical and comparative relevance IS claimed; and for example, Lachmann's law (more correctly, the law of Lachmann and Maniet) is used as a high-level morphographemic rule (59 fn. 1). The interim forms include, as 2 sing. fut. ind. of *esse*, *sbis* (64) — clearly, by the rules structure, not a terminal form and so not cited as *sbis or *esbis* — and the rules include '2: $\#C + C \to \#eC + C$' and '4:$s + b \to s$' (along with a thoroughly historical rhotacizing rule) — whence finally, *eris*. It does not matter that idiosyncratic processes of prothesis and epenthesis ($s + m \to s + um$ etc.) are introduced; they simply replace, and are no worse than, widespread skewing and waywardness in the traditional historical morphology. What matters is (a) the creation of morphological generalia for a language in which they clearly do not exist (thus -*bi*- cited as THE future tense marker, much less safe than so handling -*bā*- as the imperfect formant), and (b) the suspension of sound shifts (e.g. in this case the well established shift $s +$ voiced consonant $>$

---

[7]   I prefer this term to the usual 'non-terminal'. Where internal reconstruction is applied to the morphophonemic sector of a language, starred forms will emerge (for use in comparative reconstruction) which display a proportionately greater congruence with generated interim forms.

(:+) voiced consonant) which ARE general for the data. 'Sbis'
therefore represents to a historian not even a potential form (which
is convenient to use but difficult to realise) but a mythological
chimera. It may also stray beyond such limits of plausibility as
are imposed by generativists, tacitly, on their own citations.

The second limitation is this: strict ordering of rules, applied
to historical statement, may impose an unwarranted and unwanted
causality. In citing that part of Grimm's law (alone) which
concerns the PIE apical obstruents, one need not assign pre-
Germanic time precedence between $/t/ > /\theta/$ and $/d/ > /t/$. T-
grammar, however, with the rewriting ordered as 1. $/d/ \rightarrow /t/$,
2. $/t/ \rightarrow /\theta/$, will generate ungrammaticalities like $*\theta a\acute{\imath}hun$ (for,
despite the protestations of Chomsky, 1966b, 1 ff., T-theory has
many affinities with digital machine-computation, not the least
being the necessity to keep out of an address-location any item
which one does not want to be affected by a subsequent operation
directed at that address). Therefore the converse order is enforced
and, if used historically, must import the equivalent chronology.
Where the historian, even if committed to systemic causation,
need not decide whether he is dealing with gap-filling (after $/t/$
becomes empty) or shouldering-out (after $/t/$ becomes overloaded),
T-mechanics urge not only a prima facie case for teleology itself
but also that gap-filling is the correct answer to an enforced
question.[8]

Not that we are without a body of orthodox, and comparatively
subtle, doctrine governing this area of possible collaboration. It
can be called the Halle-Closs programme (Halle, 1961, 89 ff.;
1962, 64 ff.; 1964b, 344 ff.; Closs, 1965. 402 ff.).[9] Halle has seen

---

[8] An example of phonological gap-filling for its own sake will be found at
Fudge, 1967, 10. Shouldering-out is a possible process in generative terms if,
and only if, we can accept Halle's notion that the grammar at a deep level can
retain pre-merger forms not used on the surface (see the discussion below).
Even then we would have to decide (a) whether the base component of a T-
grammar needs ordering of rules at all, and (b) if deep rule change reflects
historical change at all.
[9] This programme seeks to locate historical events within the generative
processes. The converse — to assign to items or rules of generative grammar
a birth-date of *floruit*-date in time — has not been seriously attempted (outside

two points of disciplinary intersection (at least in the phonological component), which may be examined in order:

(1) 'SIMPLICITY'. Transformational simplicity in the phonological component is definable as the most economical citation of the distinctive features necessary to the morphophonemic exponence of the sentences of the given language, this citation deriving from a calculation of the entries both in the lexicon and in the phonological component itself. Halle opines in general, that "considerations of simplicity ... usually play an important role in reconstruction" (1962, 67), especially in determining the necessary chronological priority of one sound shift to another. He declares, in particular, that Grimm's law must by this criterion precede Verner's, whereas within Grimm's law itself the shifts $/b^h/ > /\beta/$, $/d^h/ > /\eth/$, $/g^h/ > /\gamma/$ are chronologically unplaceable, in the absence both of documentary proof and of considerations of simplicity of generative statement.

General objections occur to the mind at once. Not that historians often reject the simple (although indeed they do: a recent essay throws out the neat pre-Latin form *breuimā, with which we were all so happy as the precursor of brūma, in favour of '*$mr^e/_o$ xuisemā') — for diachronic simplicity and T-simplicity are very different animals.[10] One may point out that relative chronology, where it is

---

student essays). Yet it would be most useful to have a rationale of 'T-history', based on succession-patterns, causality theorems, calculus of factors conditioning survival, and so forth. The theoretical relation of 'innovations' and 'mutations' (as defined by Closs; see here p. 166) to deep and surface structures, and to changes within the lexicon, is discussed in the final part of (Mrs.) Closs (Traugott)'s forthcoming study *Deep and surface structure in Alfredian prose* (see also the reference in fn. 13).

[10] As is clear from Saporta's interesting view (1965, 223) of hypercorrection as being equivalent, transformationally, to a pair of 'mirror-image' rules. The simplest process which generates hypercorrect forms from standard forms is admitted to need only one rule of the proposed pair; so that the historically crucial intervening stage ('familiar') is actually obscured by T-simplicity. (To argue that the hypercorrect *état* may count as containing both the hypercorrect and the familiar alternants of the forms is to be sophistic over definitions.) Clearly, adequacy in T-grammar and adequacy in history can be as oil and vinegar. In dialectal study likewise Thomas (1967, 195f,) rejects Halle's

essential to the correct formulation of shift laws, is already known or can be inferred by common sense (from the particular way in which a formulation which ignores it fails to account for the data).[11] Indeed it is always true for historical linguists that their difficulty in plotting a development rises in proportion to the comparative insignificance of that development. Much more important is the way in which Halle, in relating reconstruction to obtrusive transformational features, virtually restricts accepted shifts to the role of single, additional rules inserted at points of break in an existing (adult's) grammar.[12] Now 'existing grammar' is no sound basis

---

simplicity criterion on the grounds that genetic sequence and generative paths are, in his experience, only sporadic in their coincidence, and the choice of the simplest generative path in any sector is often in fact counter-historical. He also rejects the presentation of the total grammar of a group of dialects in the guise of the extended grammar of one dialect of the group, because experience regularly reveals non-identity of the total grammar with that of any single dialect, unless it is slanted — a consideration relevant when temptation is felt to identify → with >.

[11]   It has also been overplayed: Ščur, 1967, 123 f., claims to deduce the chronological order of development of certain formal categories of the verb in one Germanic language from the known order of like events in another (Afrikaans ~ Icelandic). But congruence in time-order is not an inescapable feature of like or identical historical processes, even in closely cognate languages. E.g., in Greek the shift 'vocalis ante vocalem corripitur' precedes, and comes to an end before, the shift /ei/ > /ẹ:/ (cf. nouns in -είᾱ, λεῖoc etc.), whereas in Latin it is after the frontal monophthongization that the still operative process of vowel shortening shapes forms like (*sei-u̯e > *sei̯u̯'- >) *sei̯u̯ > sẹ̄u̯ > sĕu̯ (still disyllabic, as till late in neuter) > seu (monosyll.). This is the relevance of relative chronology: precisely such anisomorphisms are used to defeat speculations on sub-proto languages (such as 'Italo-Celtic'; see Watkins in Birnbaum and Puhvel, 1966, 33).

[12]   Halle's contention is partly corroborated by Sigurd, 1966, who offers the set of ordered morphophonemic rules for the masculine a-stems in Old Swedish as an instance of the reflexion of historical shifts in time-order. Of the block of fourteen basic rules, numbers 8-14 are relevant (46). The corroboration is only partial, because Sigurd's rules are presented as still the best generative statement for this paradigm; this means that later speakers of Old Swedish (not a matter of one generation) found the additive and cumulative nature of the innovations identical with the optimal restructuring demanded of them by the Halle-Closs theory — which would be unusual, at the very least. Also, rule 12 (a hiatus rule) relates to the history of Old Swedish proper, while rule 13 (an assimilation rule) is appropriate to runic Swedish, which is earlier; and of rule 11 (a devoicing rule) only part is a reflex of diachrony. But Sigurd well appreciates the close relation of T-grammar to internal reconstruction (36).

for calculations of simplicity and/or obtrusiveness when it is 'that postulated for the proto-language', precisely because that postulation itself rests on no separate foundation. The very construction of the proto-grammar is conditioned all along by our success or otherwise in reconciling with it the grammars of the evidential languages. Its simplicity is manipulable (even at the level of data), and is itself a controller of data-relevance. It also seems true that, even when we are not dealing with a proto-grammar, an artificial homogeneity, imposed on the bulk of a grammar through several historical stages, seems to be the sole convenient base for comparing, in a quasi-historical fashion, successive organizations of rules in one sector (say, the pronominal systems of the given language — so Klima, 1964, 2).

'Simplicity', however, is in this context an ambivalent term. Halle sees the primary mechanism of phonological change as the addition of rules, with special preference for the addition of single rules at the ends of different subdivisions of the grammar.[13] He further holds that this additive element in the grammar of adults is replaced by a fundamental restructuring of the whole relevant sector in the grammar which underlies the competence and performance of their children (provided that the children's learning of the language is at least not completed before the historical shift occurs). The new generation is exactly that, in both senses. The child's typical construction of the simplest grammar capable of generating all and only the grammatical utterances of the language produces discontinuity — but not mutual unintelligibility — between historical periods.[14] On these concepts Closs erects the following 'five proposals':

---

[13]   Subtraction of rules is likely to leave interim forms in an intractable condition for ensuing rewritings, and to impose further revision on a whole sector of the grammar. But some (e.g. Voyles, see fn. 18) discount the role of 'natural breaks'; and, for diachronic change as including subtraction or simplification, see Mrs. Closs Traugott's forthcoming 'Toward a grammar of syntactic change'.
[14]   Closs (402) sees the constraint of intelligibility as limiting the discontinuity between generations. Halle (e.g. 1962, 66) sees it as restricting the placing and complexity of the amending rules. It is not certain that these amount to the same thing.

(1) that the adult's addition of a single rule is the effective process of language change: this process is to be called 'innovation'.

(2) that innovations occur at natural points of break in the grammar.

(3) that the imitative child constructs the simplest grammar which will produce the same utterances as the adult's innovated grammar.[15]

(4) that the child's construction may involve comparatively radical restructuring: this relationship is to be called 'mutation'.

(5) that mutations are rare.

If the order of the rules as dictated by synchronic considerations is to "mirror properly the relative chronology of the rules" themselves, this guide is available only when no more simplicity is to be achieved by any further means than the initial addition of a rule at a grammar-break, and when the addition does not affect the overall simplicity of the grammar (as Halle sees). Mutations, which need leave no single trace of the shifts which precipitate them, are not directly visible to a historian's atomistic spectacles;[16] as Closs

---

[15]   The transformationalist view of children's competence needs a fuller statement than has so far been given. Those divergences from accepted usage which allow us to say that children are not speaking the language as normally defined may perhaps be dismissed — so as not to spoil the picture of the children working like beavers at their generation's grammar-construction — by being assigned to performance rather than competence. But what is the relation of their faulty performance yet adequate competence, on the one hand, to their (when adult) adequate performance but no-longer-constructive and degenerated competence, on the other? When is maturity? Or the various maturities? Their new grammar is relevant, after all, as such only when it is complete. Must all those of a generation be optimal constructors? And have identical starting grammar? Historical survival depends on the answers.

[16]   See Ellis, 1966, 26. But in 'subgrouping', within a quasi-genealogical presentation — which remains the basic metaphor for historians — 'atomism' gives way. Innovations are then relevant if, and only if, they are (a) shared by given languages, (b) exclusive of others, (c) preferably morphological, especially in a non-lexical sense, and (d) 'structurally' disruptive. Otherwise they reduce to mere coincidences, like Grassmann's Law in Greek and in Indo-Aryan. Best of all is such a series of characteristics where (e) what is shared is a minority failure to innovate (this not only produces a node on the historical tree, but places it chronologically). Still, it is hard to see how T-grammar can help (pace Hoenigswald, in Birnbaum and Puhvel, 1966, 12 fn. 30) in respect of (d),

says (402), synchronic grammars reflect innovations and not mutations. Therefore historians must restrict their concern to adults'
additive reconfigurations, forbear to compare fundamentally
different grammars, and ignore most tinkerings with otherwise
single grammars. This said, these proposals have nevertheless an
interesting converse, even when only considerably different surface-
structures are our data. If any two chronologically separate stages
of one language, of known sequence, are compared in respect of a
given sector of their optimal grammars (G1, G2): and if the generative powers of G2 can be grafted on to G1 by simple additive
adjustments to G1; then the additions must reflect — and if they
are maximally simple, i.e. single, rules, will actually express —
precise historical shifts.[17]

---

which results in substantial restructurings of whole sectors and hinders even
identification, or (e), which does not show up in T-terms at all.

[17] Closs (403 fn. 6) has a sane note on the application of generative grammar
to the limited corpus of a dead language: she argues that scholars gain a
secondary 'native intuition' after years of association with the data, and that
the corpus-grammar should when necessary be based on unobserved data.
If a corpus is a closed set of accepted sentences and if T-generation produces an
open-ended set of acceptable sentences (on a scale of acceptancy; see Chomsky,
1965, 148ff.; Bazell, 1962, 140; Quirk and Svartvik, 1966, is also relevant),
then a real T-grammar is only possible on a pseudo-corpus. But treating the
remains of a dead language as a really open-ended pseudo-corpus is no more
and no less awkward than treating its graphic data as phonetically known, a
thing we regularly do. Otherwise we increase the complexity of the description
intolerably (see Lyons, 1963, 19).

   More crucial is the nuisance that only when the corpus is treated as closed
for purposes of appeal has the linguist a control comparable to the appeal
to native intuition (i.e. susceptible to multipersonal check). For instance, it is
untrue that, if S_1 and S_2 have the same syntactic structure and S_1 is grammatical,
then S_2 is grammatical: syntactically *John admires sincerity* and *sincerity
frightens John* do not sponsor *sincerity admires John* and *John frightens
sincerity*, even though 'dominating constituents' elsewhere in the sentence
permit such things as *one cannot frighten sincerity* — cf. Chomsky, 1965, 157;
and ibid. 141: "the grammar does not, of itself, provide any sensible procedure
... for producing a given sentence" (Bazell, 1962, 140f., calls such an S_2 'parasi-
tic'.) Hence I do not see how to defend, in T-terms for surface structure at
least, Closs's reference to characterising 'the sentences of the corpus, and so
the infinite set of unobserved sentences which pattern with them'. In theory,
the T-grammarian cannot dispense with ultimate appeal to native reaction for
EVERY generated sentence; and if the set of a language's acceptable sentences

At once, a question of evolutionary importance suggests itself. How can we, and do we want to, rule out the possibility that additive reconfiguration is regularly the reaction of the change-acceptors to an already fundamental restructuring on the part of the change-initiator (and that it is this reaction which submits to the control of mutual intelligibility, whereby mutual unintelligibility leads to rejection of the potential shift)? On this view, the initiator (of what starts as a mere ungrammatical deviation) is potentially a prophet of the optimal structuring of rules of the next generation, his grammar being already, possibly, radically mutated from that of his contemporaries. The need for maintained intelligibility, satisfied by certain limitations on number, complexity and placing of added rules, will prevent some deviants (indeed all but those 'most likely to survive' — Halle, 1962, 66) from becoming anything more; that is, the role of adult grammar is to inhibit a *panta rhei* situation. But deviants which impose little or no strain on the intelligibility checks will be admitted as innovations. This answers to the dynamic-versus-static tension so obvious, and so precarious, in language; it also answers to the principle of 'économie', in that if shift-initiation (as well as adults' acceptance of shifts) were itself purely additive, it would only be by accident that language avoided evolving into the more and more cumbrous. Further, after a child's optimal grammar (G2) has hidden all direct reflexion of a shift in G1, the child on attaining adulthood is not inhibited from accepting as further shifts (now handled additively in G2 under the conditions of acceptance) forms which infringe or repeat the original shift-rule in G1. (It is in these terms that we may handle what are normally called 'secondary' phenomena, after the identical primaries have been lost.)

To return to Halle on particular chronologies; the "all but uni-

---

(let alone mere candidates for acceptance) is infinite, he has a time problem on his hands, at the very least. (In passing, another general point. It is also untrue that, if S_2 is an expanded form of S_1, and S_2 is grammatical, then S_1 is grammatical. Chomsky, 1965, 21f., supports a third meaning for *I had a book stolen* by the expansion *I almost had a book stolen, but they caught me leaving the library with it.* By my intuition, in any context at all, for this meaning some expansion of this S_1 is indispensable).

versal agreement" that Grimm's law (at least partly) precedes Verner's law is for historians almost certainly based on the greater item-economy of traditional diachronic statements which is achieved if that time-order is adopted. As anybody can work out for himself, if Verner's law is put first the inventory of pre-Germanic stops and non-strident continuants differs in post-Verner and post-Grimm counting (e.g., to cite one series, $/b^h/$, $/b/$, $/\beta/$, $/f/ > /\beta/$, $/p/$, $/f/$), whereas to put Grimm first is to level both counts at $/\beta/$, $/p/$, $/f/$ etc. But Halle is right to corroborate this by appealing to the greater generalizing power of a Grimm → Verner succession, whereby both the shifts $/f, 0, \chi/ > /\beta, ð, \gamma/$ and $/s/ > /z/$ come under one context-sensitive rule applying to all continuants in non-post-tonic position (Halle, 1964b, §IX, puts this point most clearly). Not only must this general rule come after the generation of (non PIE) $/f, \theta, \chi/$, and therefore Verner's law must post-date at least part of Grimm's; but it is also impossible to construct even on the basis of simultaneity of these laws a block of rules as compact as the form needed for the Grimm → Verner hypothesis.[18] But none of this should blind us to the fact that we already know the answer; Halle cites cases where neither T-grammar nor traditional history has solved the problem, but no case where T-grammar has and diachronists have not. Here, then, is an offer: let us plot certain well-known, but chronologically uncertain, Greek vowel shifts in transformational-Jakobsonian terms and see what conclusions follow.

[18]   Were it not for the sibilant shift, one could posit simultaneity of the 'laws'; e.g., the rules 1. $/'p/ > /'f/$, 2. $/b^h/ > /p/$, 3. $/p/ > /\beta/$, 4. $/b/ > /p/$ would cover both, and the non-historical status of rule 2 (alone) would be of interest. But the shift $/s/ > /z/$, as (inter alia) it does not apply to $/'s/$, inevitably adds to the inventory of rules, and economy, as compared with the usual and the Hallean citations, is lost.

Voyles (1967, 642 ff.) establishes the following sequence of rules: 1. $/p/ \rightarrow /p^h/$; 2a. $/p^h/ \rightarrow /f/$, $/b^h/ \rightarrow /ƀ/$; 2b. non post-accentual $/f/ \rightarrow /ƀ/$; 3. $/ƀ/ \rightarrow /b/$ before $/n/$; 4. voiced $C_1n \rightarrow C_1C_1$; 5. $/b/ \rightarrow /p/$. This is not compact, although each single rule uses the fewest possible features; the application of the principle of simplicity needs some guidelines. Verner's Law (= rule 2b) is set early within Grimm's Law in this 'chronology'; its application to sibilants is ignored. It is interesting that Voyles discards the notion of 'natural breaks' in the grammar; his new rules apply as blocks to 'lexical entries' (637).

First, one needs to tabulate the feature-specifications, based on widely accepted phonetic diagnosis, of the ancient Greek vowels:

	[u	ǫ	ɔ	a	ε	ẹ	i	y]
flat	+	+	+	−	−	−	−	+
compact	−	−	+	+	+	−	−	−
diffuse	+	−	−	−	−	−	+	+
grave	+	+	+	−	−	−	−	−
acute	−	−	−	−	+	+	+	−

(Undifferentiated features, + voice, + continuant, are ignored. So also + tense, which is irrelevant to the qualitative shifts — unless perhaps that of [ǫ] > [u] — and is at first a mere delaying factor and more recently an automatic concomitant of stress.)[19]

Does this display offer greater clarity or dynamic causality for developments in the vowel system? The overall redundancies are clear: e.g. ⟨+ diffuse ⊃ − compact⟩ and ⟨+ compact ⊃ − diffuse⟩. If it is supposed, as is most likely (see chapter 1), that Attic-Ionic shifts [u] > [y] (that is, reduces its differentiation from [i] yet retains the effect of (lip-)rounding), one can measure the 'systematic size' of this change as against that of, say, [ǫ] > [u] (again see chapter 1, for the possible linkage of these rearrangements). Theorems of causality may then be possible, as between different matrices; but a more sophisticated rationale will have to

[19] For e.g. Attic, the citing of a separate 'matrix' for ⟨−tense⟩ must involve non-specification for [ε] and [ɔ], at least until αι > ε (a monophthongization shift which is irrelevant to the present consideration of pure vowel shifts and which heralds the period when 'vowel length' is a stress-feature). For dialects with no evidence of the 'spurious diphthongs', [ε] and [ɔ] will be absent in the ⟨-tense⟩ citation, and [e] and [o] in the ⟨+ tense⟩ citation. But if Allen (1959, 244f.) is correct, Attic has both a relatively close and a relatively open long vowel of 'e' and 'o' type, and a single mid short vowel of each type; this complicates the matrix, by necessitating ⟨+compact and − diffuse⟩, ⟨−compact and − diffuse⟩, and ⟨−compact and +diffuse⟩. But the theorems of redundancy mentioned above are, as it happens, in no way affected. (Note that Greek α, probably representing a plumb central articulation, is deliberately *exempli causa* specified as ⟨−grave, −acute⟩; it conditions labiovelar reflexes unlike acute vowels, but choice of preceding kappa (not koppa) unlike grave vowels.)

be evolved than hitherto, if we are to be convinced that matrix A will or will not induce matrix B, and so forth. The effects of the separate stages cited (1. [u], [i]; 2. [y], [i]; 3. [u], [y], [i]). in terms of redundancy rules, are:

at all stages α i⟨+ diffuse ⊃ − compact⟩, ii ⟨+ compact ⊃ − diffuse⟩

β ⟨+ grave ⊃ + flat⟩

at stage 1   γ ⟨flat ≡ grave⟩

at stage 2   γ ⟨flat ≡ grave⟩ is replaced by δ ⟨− flat ⊃ − grave⟩ (see fn. 19 as to Gk. α)

ε there are added i ⟨+ diffuse ⊃ − grave⟩, ii ⟨+ grave ⊃ − diffuse⟩

at stage 3   α β δ remain; ε is excised.

Stage 3 can be calculated, according to different criteria, either as more or as less simple than stage 2, and so forth: is ⟨flat ≡ grave⟩ more or less economic in a mentalistic context than '⊃ type' redundancies? When rules of this degree of generality are involved, simplicity is of no easy calculation. It can at least be argued that one is unlikely to find (as here one does not) a shift merely contraverting the specific rearrangement, and that only, imposed by an immediately prior shift. Simultaneous counter-balancing is possible; later, unlinked, revision is quite to be expected; but is anything else?

If this notion of comparatively deep redistribution of redundancy is applied in the case of the crossing shifts ϙ > ϙ and ϙ > ϙ a deduction as to relative chronology may be made. The former shift (of ε) itself is first evidenced by the confusion of ε and αι in papyri from the early second century B.C., the latter (of η) by the spelling εὐϲεβήαϲ in the same period; but convergence of some kind is already shown by the form Δεμήτριοϲ from 260 B.C. Now these shifts need not cross each other in the symmetrical way denoted by Sturtevant's crossed arrows (1940, 39 fig. 4). However, it will be seen that the shift ϙ > ϙ, importing the amendment [− compact] → [+ compact] in the sixth column of the feature alphabet table, makes no change in the more general implicational rules; whereas the shift $e > e$, importing [+ compact] → [− compact] in the fifth column, now makes it true that X ⟨+ compact ⊃ − acute⟩, and Y ⟨+ acute ⊃ − compact⟩. (The subsequent shift, $> i$, makes no further fundamental difference). Moreover, after the operation of BOTH shifts, amendments X and Y are cancelled. The argument from simplicity must therefore be that simultaneity of these historical processes — notwithstanding the admittedly largely fortuitous documentation — is most likely, because this avoids supposition of not one but two directly opposed successive reorganizations of general feature implications, and the basic phonological geometry, so to speak, is untouched. (Completion of the shift $e > e$ before the start of the other change is ruled out by the documentary evidence, and one cannot suppose a substantial, causality-removing, time-gap.) Which in turn suggests that, while Sturtevant's documentary evidence is inadequate as a basis for a chronology here, his diagram is correct after all; and the crossing-point (which reflects maximum uncertainty in the [compact] feature specification in both phonemes, and is bound to precede the spelling hesitations caused by the completion of the crossing) may be as early as the fourth century B.C., if any weight can be attached to Aristotle's derivation of ἠθική from ἔθος (*Eth. Nic.* 1103a 17). And, for T-based history, the interesting thing is that in this instance simultaneity is argued, whereas in the case of the Germanic consonant shifts it was shown to be less likely. This new tool has at least a desirable flexibility.

Still, this virtue must not be overprized. Simultaneity, for example, may be suggested where it is known to be impossible, For example, there is no doubt of the correctness both of the occurrence and of the nomenclature of *die erste* and *die zweite Lautverschiebung*. But an additively amended PIE grammar can take us straight to NHG, for PIE non-word-initial apical consonants, (−grave, −diffuse, −flat) /d/, /t/ and /dʰ/, may be transformed into NHG /s/ (*ss*), /d/ and /t/ (ignoring, for convenience, the well-known inhibiting effects of certain clusters) by an added, ordered, three-rule block of hypothetical 'T-history'; (PIE → NHG express):

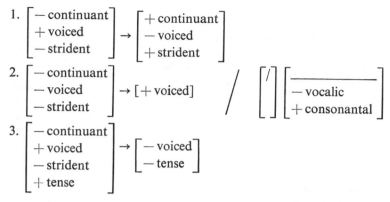

Yet no insertion, for none is needed, corresponds to the actual circular evolution $*/t/ > /\theta/ > /\delta/ > /t/$ in non-post-tonic position, so that even additive simplicity effectively disguises (or by contrastive omission, actually denies) known *états de langue*. The existence of the successive stages for which a T-rationale is evolved must be itself pre-established by either documentary evidence or traditional comparative methods.

(2) 'DORMANCY'. Halle's second point of T-grammar relevance to historical study (1962, §§11, 12; 1964, §§XI, XII) may be described as catering for feature-complexes which are functionally dormant but descriptively surviving. It is supposed that the T-dictionary, in assigning phonemic shape to its entries, may retain complexes of features which are no longer phonetically actualized (a high level rule will subsequently exponentially merge these with the complexes which have historically swallowed them). No historian will cavil at the example given by Halle from Russian dialects, where by maintaining a conditioning feature-difference between certain accented vowels, despite its exponential loss, the analyst can neatly state the distribution of non-diffuse vowels (following a sharp consonant) in the preceding syllable. This is to say no more than that internal reconstruction demerges phonemes, and reconstructs lost phonemes in at least rough phonetic shape: the distribution of Sanskrit /c/, relatively to /k/, is more understandable if the cases of following /a/ are supposed to hide a merger of mid front with

mid back and central vowels; or (to quote, like Halle, a sound divergence within one short paradigm) Vedic 1.s. pf. *cakắra* and 3.s. pf. *cakā́ra* pose no problem, as to the distribution of odd variants of the 'strong' form of the lexical root syllable, if some lost item (invented ad hoc, but defended and defined thereafter by comparative evidence) is held to inhibit Brugmann's law, by which *-orV-* > *-ārV-*, in the 1.s. pf. form (*$k^u ek^u orAe$*, against 3.s. *$k^u ek^u ore$*). Historians are, in effect, thus avoiding 'non-recoverable deletions' of once visible explicanda in their process of working back to proto-grammar; this is akin to the idea behind the newer T-technique of using base-component 'dummies' (see Chomsky, 1965, 144ff., 1966b, 39). But this recitation of the trite is followed, in Halle's essays, by speculation on the incredible: namely that coalesced items may re-emerge in precise correspondence to their pristine identities; and in particular that a late shift may affect only those (morphemically distributed) tokens of a feature-complex which represented that complex before a given earlier shift. Now secondary shifts carry along all real tokens of the relevant feature-complexes (not approximations, for example for rhyming purposes), if the shifts really are secondary, as defined. The common-Greek > Attic shift of *$\bar{a}$* > *ę̄* has sometimes been formulated — to cope with the systematic exceptions where *i*, *e* or *r* precedes — as a rule for all environments, to which a secondary, reversing, shift of *ię̄* > *iā* etc. is appended. The obvious drawback (whether the result of the first shift is [ɛ:] or [æ:]) is that the secondary shift must rest on natives' ability to pick out, from the total set of *ię̄* sequences in the language at the relevant time, those and only those which reflect an original *iā* etc. (so separating ἰήσομαι from ἵημι, and so forth). In this relatively tractable case extrication is arguable: the overloaded Greek mid-front long vowel sector did not at once resolve itself to a single systemic exponent, and the maintained non-identity of the reflexes of original /a:/ and original /e:/ is betrayed by different spellings (⊟, E) at least in some Ionic islands (even as late as the fifth century in Ceos). But the principle is tendentious, and Halle's extension of it will shortly be considered further. Even if — unlikely as it is, in view of speakers' common inability even to identify phonic variants without the help of functional frontiers (as Fry's perception and recognition experiments have shown) — even if adults, with amended grammars, can maintain the necessary rules to store these dormant distinctions, it is not explained how the children, in constructing their own optimal grammar (on which the only control is its own adequacy to generate with maximal simplicity the grammatical sentences of the language they hear), can conceivably be induced to build into their lexicon this otiose information. Only if all languages were, operationally, internally panisomorphic and non-heteroclitic (and speakers needed strict pattern), and if the best method of imposing pattern-generality on a given sector were always to appeal to history, would this proposal seem other than a sort of blind-eye history, matching in generativists their occasional 'tin-ear practical phonetics' (Hockett, 1965, 202 fn. 39). The diachronic principle, empirically arrived at, of irreversibility is too precious to be jettisoned (cf. Hoenigswald in Birnbaum and Puhvel, 1966, 7).

Closs's special contribution (1965) to this interesting programme is to validate three of the proposals in the syntactical sector also. Her step by step commentary on the evolution of the verbal auxiliary in English leads her to reject only (2) the confining of innovations to natural breaks in the grammar (cf. Voyles, 1967), and (5) the rarity of mutations. These later generalizations are assigned to the area of phonological change alone. This is theoretically sound; the battle against the presumption of a thorough parallelism between phonology and grammar (even, in T-terms, between phonology and syntax) has long since been won.[20] Also, the judgement that greater frequency of deep and extensive restructuring is the ultimate expression of syntactical change follows naturally from the empirical fact that rebuilding in that sector is comparatively rarely a simple reshuffling of bricks. The trouble here lies in the role assigned to 'point of break' in the grammar; it arises from the shiftiness of that concept (cf. footnote 18), and because such breaks are individually as much subject to dispute and re-location

[20] A particularly trenchant proclamation of this victory is made by Bazell, *Journal of Linguistics* 1, 1965, 95.

as are most frontiers. For the syntactical component Closs's watersheds are (414):

phrase structure//lexicon//transformational subcomponent

with a further break between the whole syntactical component and the morphophonemic component. But, as well as further refinements peculiar to particular sub-models (see Closs, 414 fn.23), other revelations of the quasi-spatial relationships of the parts of T-grammar are not lacking. In Chomsky's recent formulation (1965, 16f., 135f., 141) the lexicon's immediate frontier divides it from the categorial subcomponent, and these together form the base component which marches with the transformational sub-component (and 'phrase structure', in so far as it exists at all, resides in the rules and markers of the whole base).[21] Besides, the semantic component on the one side, and the phonological component on the other, "are purely interpretive" (141), with no generative power. This suggests that there is little in common between the frontiers which separate them from the syntactic component and the divisions within the syntactic component itself, whereas there would seem to be a likeness linking the break between syntax and phonology as a whole with the break between what are traditionally called morphophonemics and phonotactics (cf. Matthews, 1967, 145). In fact, there seems little point in historians fussing themselves over this aspect of the matter until transformational theory sorts itself out.

Let us concentrate on the base and the transformational part of the syntactic component, and the frontiers of each. Here an attempt has been made to diagnose the evolutionary differentials within the morphosyntax of comparable sentences in an inflected (WP-favouring) language — namely the problem of noun-case syncretism in Latin. To take one sub-sector, the classical *casus sextus* responds to generative statement in a manner suggestive for history.[22]

---

[21]   This is all visually presented by P. H. Matthews, *Journal of Linguistics* 3, 1967, 144, plus an 'improved' version of his own (145) with the frontiers altered yet again.

[22]   The exemplification here given rests in part on a 1962 graduate paper by one of my Pennsylvania students, Mrs. Carlota S. Smith. The presentation has

The relevant data may be expressed as extant sentences (some in non-expanded form, the difference between cited and contextual form being immaterial) with, where appropriate, apparent prior kernel sentences on the left,[23] as follows:

been changed, both in the Latin data and the T-formulation, and the findings are somewhat other than hers. But my thanks are due to her for an interesting insight into Latin case-evolution. On the associative-instrumental, one notes its ready extrication from the rest of the 'casus sextus' by Quintilian, 1, 4, 26.
[23]   The current view of kernel sentences, since the critiques of Schachter and Heidolph, is that they have intuitive but not generative significance (cf. Chomsky, 1965, 18). Nevertheless, they are useful here; the differentiae are more readily appreciated than via P-markers and T-markers of the neo-Chomskian kind. However, a presentation of e.g. derivations 2 and 3(a2) based on Chomsky, 1965, 129 ff. (diverging only in the omission of the step 'Predicate-Phrase', which allows for the separate representation of 'Aux' from VP, incorrect for these Latin verbs), would be:

2.

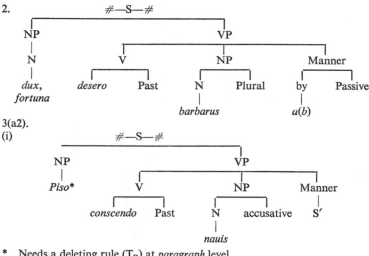

3(a2).
(i)

* Needs a deleting rule (T_D) at *paragraph* level.

(ii)

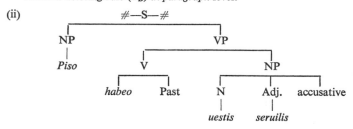

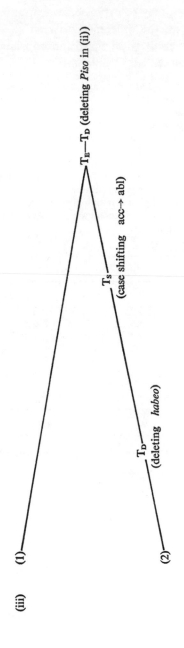

1. (a) Albae constiterunt, in urbe opportuna. Cic. *Phil.* 4, 2, 6.

1. (b) num montes moliri sede sua paramus? Livy 9, 3, 3.

1. (c) se in castra equo contulit. Caes. *B.C.* 3, 94.

2.   (dux et fortuna eos deserunt) → ab duce et a fortuna deser-
    ebantur. *Caes.* B.C. 5, 34.

3. (a1) (*i* celeriter currunt ⎱ → incredibili celeritate ad flumen decu-
      ii incredibile est) ⎰ currerunt. Caes. *B.G.* 2, 19.

3. (a2) (*i* nauem conscendit   ⎱ → ueste seruili nauem conscen-
      ii uestem scruilem habet) ⎰ dit. Cic. *Pis.* 38, 92.

3. (b) (*i* militiam subterfugit ⎱ → (insimulant eum tragoediae)
     ii simulat insaniam) ⎰ simulatione insaniae[24] militiam
     subterfugere uoluisse. Cic. *Off.*
     3, 26, 97.

3. (c) (*i* Cethegus conticescit
     ii (aliquis) litteras   → Cethegus recitatis litteris repente
     conticuit. Cic. *Cat.* 3, 5, 10.
     rccitat)

Examples 1a-c are the products neither of generalized Phrase-
markers (involving recursive replacements, by #S#, of S′
within #S# (Chomsky, 1965, 134)), nor of the rewriting of dummy symbols in a Phrase-marker (ibid., 132). Examples 2 does
involve the latter (in the revised treatment of the feature Passive,
which was earlier regarded, for our purposes more conveniently,
as a paraphrastic optional transformation). Examples 3a-c derive
from the filling out of recursive S′, followed by the switchings and
zeroings necessary to produce the surface structure. It springs to
the eye that the regroupings within the case-form scatter which
historians have made for an earlier stage, partly on semantic and
partly on syntactic grounds, are at least to some extent reflected,
and refined, by the transformational picture. There are three
distinct behaviour patterns. The locative is restricted to sentences
with transformational history of type 1, the separative enters also

---

[24] Possibly via *simulatio* + genitive + *est* (cf. Cicero, *Acad*, 2, 46, 140);
hence *celeritatem habent* in the 'history' of 3(a1)? Then 3(a1) comprises the
model origins for all $\widehat{N \langle N + Adj \rangle}$abl or V *cum* + Nabl uses; 1(b) ultimately
generates comparatives, and so forth.

into type 2, the associative-instrumental engages in types 1 and 3.[25] Furthermore the type 1 function of the latter answers to (rather, receives interpretation as) an instrumental 'sememe' alone (cf. fn. 25), for the semantic fusing of associative and instrumental (which has proved historically irreducible) appears only in the complex type 3. Thus we establish a prime facie likelihood (i.e. on syntactical, as well as on impressionistic-semantic grounds) for (a) the fact that there IS case fusion here, though not necessarily in Latin, or pre-Latin, as opposed to PIE; and (b) the comparative lateness of the syncretism of the instrumental (and hence the associative-instrumental) into the traditional 'ablative' case.

Several recent essayists have taken notice, directly or indirectly, of the generative-genetic connexion.[26] Their suggestions are not without interest or methodological importance. Nevertheless, to keep the really fundamental in view, it may be helpful to conclude with some comments on the attempts which are currently being made by formal theorists to elicit the structural-conceptual basis of language evolution. Interesting above all is the problem of universal primes and their relative priority, as reflected in the 'noun first or verb first?' debate.[27]

---

[25] It is arguable that, because associative and instrumental are never mentally distinct for IE speakers during the period of the formation of the respective exponents of the list of cases, *equo* in 1(c) and *ueste* in 3(a2) should not be separated. That I do separate them is not because their syntax is somewhat different in classical Latin (the associative *N*abl usually — but, *pace* the average grammar, not always — has an accompanying *Adj* or *cum*). It is because the same kernel sentences which were used to produce 3(a2) will still produce a semantically identical sentence by a different T-process of embedding (e.g.→ *cum nauem conscenderet uestem seruilem habebat*), whereas a similar handling of sentence 1(c) would not be successful in that way, but needs lexically different kernels (e.g. *equo utitur*).

[26] Most are noticed in this chapter. Cf. also Harris, 1965, 396f.; O'Neil, 1963; Thomas 1967; Kiparsky, 1967; Stockwell's paper on "Realism in historical English phonology" at the Linguistic Society of America meeting, Dec. 1964.

[27] Universals as such are not among the agenda of this chapter. For their relevance to history, see the essays of Hoenigswald and Cowgill in Greenberg, 1963, and Kiparsky in E. Bach and R. Harms, *Universals in Linguistic Theory* (forthcoming). On genuine universals in grammatical theory, see Matthews, 1966, 157f.

Chomsky's decision (1965, 115f.) to prefer "selecting Verbs in terms of Nouns ... rather than conversely", and to make Nouns 'selectionally dominant' in directing his selectional rules — even if these are 'rather marginal', ibid. 153 — has led to the question (by P. H. Matthews, *JL*. 3, 1967, 131) whether such a priority reflects any linguistic intuition of value. Notionalism, of course, finds nouns easier to classify than verbs; but, rather than reject as facile (for that reason) a notional, noun-first, hierarchization of grammar, we see that it is possible and attractive (primarily, but not solely, to transformationalists) to accept notionalism and its evolutionary implications. This is what Lyons (1966) has recently done. His major contentions (that is, most relevant to a historian's purpose) are (a) that Noun is a primary category (substantive universal) of grammar, like Predicator and Sentence; and (b) that the distinction between Verb and Adjective is a fine (and not, as between languages, a constant) supervening variation within the Predicator (Jespersen's 'secondaries'). The first point is, of course, in no way new: the earliest Indian grammarians fought on this battlefield, and Gārgya may be held to represent the nominalists against the verbalist Śākaṭāyana; nor does Pāṇini, for all his verb-root approach, impose pseudo-derivations on what may be called prime Nouns.[28] But the distinction between deep structure, which when adequately stated may be found to be universal, and surface structure, which is ultimately specific to the given language — together with the locating of the Verb-Noun relation (and hence the focal nature of the Verb) in surface structure — opens the way to a resolution of what may turn out to be a pseudo-problem anyway. These considerations link up with the preoccupations of the mediaeval schoolmen. Do they lead to improved history? If the elements of ultimate deep structure are universally identical, historical research lies in the comparison of the details of the movement from deep to surface structure, as between non-kindred and kindred languages, or within each group or between periods of one language. A quantitative statement of divergence may be made possible (as in lexicostatistics, hopefully). But in fact Indo-

[28] Despite the references at Lyons, 1966, 231.

European evolution seems only partly to help, and be helped by, the nominalist and notionalist approach.

First, the IE cases have a syntactical characteristic of revolving around the verb, as the focal point of their interdetermination; and their exponential forms, despite the inflexional difficulty of mapping segments of meaning on to segments of form, reveal some system of likeness and unlikeness. Yet the genitive responds best to a basically nominal relationship in syntax: and formally, for example, its plural, alone of all the PIE plural forms, has no marker s; indeed, such marking as at all differentiates its singular form from that of the nominative is demonstrably adjectival in character. Not surprisingly, it has been thought that the earliest PIE syntax is adnominal. This may result in the genitive's either being earlier than the verb or marking a parallel alternative syntactic evolution from the preverbal era. The basic sentence form could then be $\widehat{N_1 N_2}$, sememes of 'object' and 'action' being indifferently handled by N; and N_1 being assigned existential priority but N_2 logical priority (since the latter is defined in terms of the former, not unlike *gas man, holiday hotel*[29] etc.) — thus e.g. $\widehat{\text{PATR- EQV-}}$, $\widehat{\text{PATR- AM-}}$ etc. It is presumably, in this view, the subsequent separation of action from mere existence, and its special marking, which sires the duality wherein the new structure $(\widehat{NV})$ PAT(E)R AM(AT) stands alongside $\widehat{N_1 N_2}$ PATR(IS) AM(OR) or $(\widehat{Adj_1 N_2})$ PATR(IUS) AM(OR). (PATRIS AMOR is a sentence no less and no more than PATER is; intra-Latin enquiry perhaps takes us back before the PATER AMAT syntagm is readmitted and yet after the PATRIS AMOR syntagm is discarded as a full sentence type [see footnote 35]; but this is a historical accident.) Here the semantic

---

[29]   An influence in English is the s-less feminine genitive, as in *Lady Day* etc. It is, of course, no part of Lyons's theory (cf. 1966, 1967) that THIS is the universal basic sentence form, rather than $S \rightarrow \widehat{N\ Pred}$ and $Pred \rightarrow V$ or Adj or N (with *Pred* primarily locative). But while the distinguishing of 'action' from 'state' verbs is crucial, as the general and evolutionary equation of the latter with adjectives is defensible, formal cognateness of verb and adjective morphs is simply lacking at the PIE stage.

equality represents deep structure precisely as in Stockwell's equation of *John's arrival* with *John arrived* (*Language* 40, 1964, 483—despite the likely T-derived interrelationship of these surface locutions). Or one may note the common equation, even in surface structure, of 'possessor' (of noun) and 'subject' (of verb); cf. Allen, 1964, 338 ff. This makes sense, functionally and formally.[30] But there is no room, until a later stage — by which time even relicts like *patrius amor* structure with a centring verb (cf. Virgil, *Aen.* 1, 643 f.) — for the $\widehat{N_1 Adj_2}$ colligations which Lyons's essay would demand as early co-variants of a ⟨noun + predicator⟩ base (e.g. *pater* (*est*) *amans*): so that Ἡρακλῆς βίαιος post-dates Ἡρακληείη βίη or ἳς Ἡρακλῆος. What is more, the much used points of resemblance between Caucasian and Indo-European languages have occasioned theories of an ergative structure in PIE (cf. Vaillant, 1936, and, for a general report, Martinet 1962, 149-154). It may be that accusative-marked transitivity and ergative-marked agent-subject distinction are identical in deep structure (as suggested by Lyons, 1966, 228 fn. 7). But if so, they will represent late and surface clarifications, in form, of a possible syntactic confusion between nouns which have become linked in one syntagm by

[30] The evidence is as follows:

(1) on the form of the PIE genit. pl. see V. V. Ivanov, *Proc. 8th Int. Cong. Ling.* (1958), 250; on the formal congruence of genit. pl. and adj. at the earliest stage see A. Martinet, *Économie des changements phonétiques* (1955, Bern), 220, fn. 23.

(2) on the relation of PIE genit. sing. to nom. sing. note: (*i*) Myc. often ignores the formal difference (cf. E. Vilborg, *A tentative grammar of Mycenaean Greek* (1960, Göteborg), 57). Hitt. has gen. and nom. forms in -*aš*. (*ii*) The nom./gen. alternation -s/-$^e/_o s$ ties in with the adj. function of the thematic vowel (cf. esp. the ordinals). See L. L. Hammerich, *Proc. 7th. Int. Cong. Ling.* (1956), I. 175. (*iii*) the $^e/_o$-stem genit. sing. marker -io, differencing the originally identical nom. and gen. (cf. H. Pedersen, *Études lithuaniennes, KDVS/M* 19, 3, 23), is indifferently genitival or adjectival (esp. with ref. to place of origin or material characteristics); the distinction is largely terminological. (Cf. J. M. Aitchison, *Glotta* 42, 1964, 132-138, on the semantic history which finally produces a 'father's name' out of an originally objective adjective τελαμώνιος, 'possessed of a baldric'. So Wackernagel (Genetiv und Adjektiv, *Mél. Saussure*, 123 ff.) is right to see the 'adj' doing the possessive job before the 'gen'., though his functional and formal categories are injected from a later stage in time. (Sommerfelt's extension of this, *Diachronic and synchronic aspects of language*,

embedding transformations. One may then speculate on this evolution for PIE:

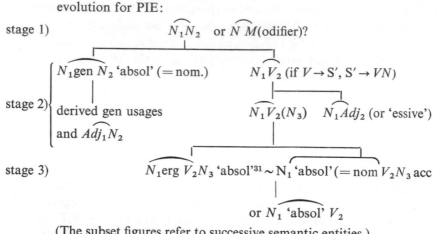

stage 1) $\widehat{N_1 N_2}$ or $\widehat{N\ M}$(odifier)?

stage 2)

$\widehat{N_1 \text{gen}\ N_2}$ 'absol' ($=$ nom.) $N_1 V_2$ (if $V \to S'$, $S' \to VN$)

derived gen usages $\widehat{N_1 V_2}(N_3)$ $\widehat{N_1 Adj_2}$ (or 'essive')

and $\widehat{Adj_1 N_2}$

stage 3) $\widehat{N_1 \text{erg}\ V_2 N_3}$ 'absol'[31] $\sim N_1$ 'absol' ($=$ nom $V_2 N_3$ acc

or $\widehat{N_1}$ 'absol' V_2

(The subset figures refer to successive semantic entities.)

1962, The Hague, 237ff., leads to his deriving the possessive from the partitive, within the gen. itself, which is unnecessary). Sommer's (1914, 443; cf. *Kritische Erklärungen*, 121) connecting of *$k^u os$-$\dot{i}o$-, with infection from cons. stem gen. -os, with Latin declined *quoiius*, then uniform *cuius* (Cic., Virg. archaic *cuium*). has been attacked for no good reason; cf. the meaning 'whose?' for the Greek ποῖος at e.g. Eurip. *Bacch.* 1273.

(3) Hitt. seems to show a (formally prompted) repetition of the PIE line of evolution within its own paradigms: *ku-ru-ra-aš an-tu-uh-ša-aš* leads to *ku-ru-ra-an an-tu-uh-ša-an* (N_1gen + N_2nom > Adj_1 'nom' ($\to$ acc) + N_2nom ($\to$ acc); as if Greek παιδὸς λόγος $\to$ *παιδὸν λόγον).

Watkins (1966, 38 and fn. 17, 1967 passim) sees the genitive as a very *late* emergent in IE. His reasons are its syntactic anomalousness (which Benveniste, 1962, 17f., declares to be reducible to the subjective-objective type, itself secondary in both function and derivation to the nominative-accusative opposition), the variety of $^e/_o$-stem gen. sing. forms (actually outweighed by the substantial uniformity shown in the other stems), and the Hittite facts combined with the absence of gen. forms in Luwian (in favour of 'relationals' in -*ašša/i*-). These last points rather fit the thesis outlined above: that 'Adj' form and syntax, 'gen' form and syntax, and 'qualificative' marking and use of N_1 in general are all alternant exponences of one deep relationship. Cf. for Greek the 'objective' *Adj* in κράτος ἐμόν 'power over me', (Eurip. *Bacch.* 1038); and for Latin Diver's remark (1964, 192) linking 'most uses of the genitive' with 'that chapter of the grammar that is concerned with the Adjective'. But as long as some clear difference is here accepted in the history of the PIE cases, T-grammar or its notionalist extensions reflect evolution.

[31] Note that in Kabardian the ergative is used for both the subject of a 'transi-

PIE shows both results of the bifurcation which produces stage 2 ($= N_1 P \rightarrow N_1 N_2$ ($\rightarrow Adj_1 N_2$) or $N_1 Adj_2$ or $N_1 V_2 \pm V \rightarrow S'$) and stage 3. Hence the coexistence of various structures in the known languages, where selection is governed by context, poetic effects, and so forth, as well as by historical accidents of prominence or favour.

In Latin one may thereafter offer (in the most tentative exemplificatory way, and allowing increasing semantic fullness to copula *esse*) the following parallelism and interaction, in part or whole:

A	and/or	B
N_1erg V N_2absol		N_1absol ($=$ nom) V N_2 acc
1. Romae (loc.) est domus		1. Roma continet domum
2. a. consuli est domus		2. a. consul possidet domum
b. consuli uenit pecunia		b. consul tradit pecuniam
3. hosti parcit dux		*3.

The structure $N_1 \overgroup{Adj_2}$ then permits:

4. consuli est domus magna	4. consul aedificat domum magnam
5. consuli est domus aedificata	5. consul habet domum aedificatam

— and, as the existence of B. 2.b. sponsors *anseres seruant urbem*, hence:

*6. a. anscribus (dat.) est urbs seruata	6. anseres habent urbem seruatam

By now have come in the 'concrete' elements, which may comprise the original general valor of dative and locative (this the prime case, Lyons, 1967, would claim) and clearly do so for 'ablative' (separa-

---

tive' verb and for the possessor (cf. Allen, 1964, 340, and his similar reference to Lakk). The parallel Latin sentences cited presume, boldly, an 'ergative' source for locative and dative, as well as showing the Caucasian type of semantic confluence; thus they may point up a shared innovation which could justify an 'overgrouping' of PIE and proto-Caucasian (cf. fn. 33). (In passing, one may say that the supposition that the ergative could actually sire the genitive leads to great difficulties (cf. Hammerich, *Proc. 7th Int. Cong. Ling.* II 534), and in this sketch the genitive remains a separate, stage 2, manifestation).

tive and instrumental);[32] then instrumental adjunct and agency marking ensue:

6. b. anseribus (abl.) est urbs
       seruata
7. a consule est urbs seruata   7. ($\equiv$ B. 5)

Interplay between the lines of descent then helps to produce the passive (see below); and B. 2. b. is recognized as the semantic partner to A. 7 and to

8. a consule $\begin{cases} \text{seruatur urbs} \\ \text{traditur pecunia etc.} \end{cases}$

while the confluence of *hosti parcitur* and *duci parcitur* (see A. 3) is disambiguated from **duci hosti parcitur*[33] to:

9. a duce hosti parcitur

For the sentences in the left-hand column a development is arguable from a basically ergative construction, although the Latin reflexes have been so processed and filtered as to be mere hints. In South Caucasian, dative and ergative stand side by side after a split which may be conditioned, as it is clearly maintained, by verbal tense-distinction (aorist *versus* perfect). Still, these left-hand cases (dative-locative-associative-instrumental) — because they are attached to situational features and are rationalised and subdivided into possession, location, affectedness and concomitance — are distinct from the purely formal-syntactical cases of the right-hand

---

[32]   The contextualization of these left-hand column cases does not readily extend to the separative, which must arise as a natural situational counterpart to the allative sense of dative or locative: *Roma scripsit Balbus* (Cic.) cannot be trifled with. Therefore Vaillant was incorrect in using a nom-abl. identity to support the 'PIE ergative'. These cases are only formally alike in PIE where the abl. is identical with the genitive; in the plural, and in the singular of the thematic stems, its own differential form is far from the nom.

[33]   This sentence is functionally replaced by the one below it for reasons parallel to those governing the dissimilation of (semantic) subject dative and (indirect) object dative in Georgian (cf. the use of the subject and object postposition in Harauti), except that in Georgian (and Harauti) it is the object marker which is changed (cf. Allen, 1964, 342f.). The relevant shared (IE ~ Cauc.) innovation here is the crisis, of course, not the solution.

column. This distinction answers pretty well to Kuryłowicz's dividing of the IE cases into the 'concrete' (locative, ablative, instrumental) and the 'grammatical' (nominative, accusative, genitive).[34]

After stage 2, the relation of deep to surface structure has altered so much that, within the surface representation, the Verb has become the epicentre of the focus of deep relations, as it were, and hence the focal element in IE sentences.[35] In the constructions on the right-hand side above, the $+/s/$ nominative marking of animates (if we ignore supervening formal loss, as in *consul*) preserves one deep characteristic: the dominance of animates in the role of 'initiator'.[36] It may be that it is the absence of this mark-

[34] 1949, 131ff. and fn. 19; cf. 1964, 179ff. The types of case go hand in hand with, respectively, marginality and centrality to the Verb, in the syntax and semantics of the état when the Verb is focal (see Regamey, *Proceedings of the 7th International Congress of Linguists* I 129ff., for a general *V*-central system possibly underlying Tibetan, Caucasian, Amerindian, Malay, Javanese and Eskimo syntax). The dative is first left in limbo by Kuryłowicz and then assigned to the 'concrete' group. (Cf. Woodcock, 1959, 1, for the maintenance of this sort of distinction within one case, the accusative, even at a late stage). Parallel derivation of 'existential' and possessive from locative is argued by Lyons, 1967.

[35] Latin, like the other IE languages, is too far developed, even in its earliest analyzable form, for us to see back beyond the prime syntactical structures (*a*) $\widehat{N_1 Adj_2}$ or $\widehat{N_1 N_2}$ (both nom) — which feeds from our stage 2 into our left hand column above — and (*b*) V — a post-stage 3 development. Cunningham (1965) sets up just these, glossing the first (sometimes called 'equational': see Julia A. Sableski, *Language* 41, 1965, 439 and fn. 2) by *Poeni foedifragi*; *crudelis Hannibal* etc., and the second by *statur* or *placet* or *ueni uidi uici*. From these forms — themselves, I would argue, a secondary basis — he derives the rest (e.g. the common $\widehat{NV}$ is for him an expansion of (*b*) by assimilation to (*a*); 27ff.) Possibly he would accept Kuryłowicz's (1964, 20) further conflation: *Ciceronem designauerunt* + *Cicero consul* → *Ciceronem consulem designauerunt*. But this is all very modern in IE terms; relevant here is the choice between taking $S \to V$ as a stage in Latin evolution (one of the earliest accessible by internal reconstruction) or as a side variant within our parallel columns of post-PIE processes. Diver (1964) reduces the Latin sentences to varied manifestations of a 'system of agency'; items which are not agentive or patientive are 'residual', especially the free-standing verb (*itur*, *pluit*, etc.). But nothing evolutive is implied, even as to the '3 sing. mediopassive' in *-r*.

[36] See Halliday, 1967, 42. Assigning this agentive function to $+/s/$ is preferable to seeing it as, in origin, a left-hand side ergative marker, as do many, from C. C. Uhlenbeck (*IF* 12, 1901, 170f.) onwards.

ing in the left-hand column which permits the fusion of 'initiator' with 'action' in the Verb, and leads to the 'middle' voice. So e.g. *pek^weto-i/r means 'cooking is being (got) done' ('involving' N). If the middle voice spreads to the right column and/or the nom. and acc. cases to the left (displacing erg. and nom.), we have the colligations *narah pacate, uir cingitur ferrum*; also, the simultaneous 'indirect object' semantic status of what is formally 'subject' is then denotable by the choice of the 'middle' form. Later 'initiator' and 'goal' are fused in N_1nom — partly by the return of the animate Noun to semantic epicentre, partly by the semantic necessities of certain lexical items. Then, the reflexive middle occurs (λούομαι 'I wash myself'); and if 'initiating' fades, the passive meaning — 'am washed' — and, later, special tense forms emerge,[37] 'agency' being a non-essential addition. Again, non-initiating inanimates, because they need no surface differentiation in the structures of either column to mark 'initiator' status, will offer a single absolutive-nominative-accusative form (the 'concrete' cases, once they respond to situational features, will then readily extend their scope to inanimates). The inanimate nominative may actually derive from a re-assessment of e.g. (a) *ciuibus* (erg > dat/abl.) *aedificatur templum* (absol) as a passive sentence (Ndat/abl + V + Nnom). There may be a subsidiary factor in the loosening of the inanimate-neuter gender link: that is, *a ciuibus aedificatur aedes*, with a quasi-animate marked nominative now in *aedes*, allows unmarked *templum* to possess that case.

This sort of semi-logical, semi-mechanistic essay is wildly speculative. If T-grammar had its own histories and evolutionary patterns worked out, it could replace speculation by probabilities. But we must be grateful that it at least indicates where historical strata are to be found. Formal theory seems likely to restore to historical linguistics (subject, like all historical disciplines, to the

---

[37]   E.g. the impossibility of killing inanimates leads to the interpretation of N_1nom + 'kill' med, where N_1 is animate and no other animate Noun is present, as involving N_1's being killed. Hence the passive. This lexical type does indeed tend to exclude middle or deponent forms in IE, in favour of a simple active-passive opposition.

law of diminishing returns) some of its lost dynamic and digging power. And diachrony may conversely be able to offer the generativist a separate but analogous model — that of a "universal grammar of language change", which will be in effect an empirical typology of the relationships through time of all the possible different subsets of linguistic universals.[38]

REFERENCES

Allen, W.S. 1958, "Some problems in the phonetic development of the *IE* voiced aspirates in Latin", *Arch Ling* 10, 100-116.
—— 1959, "Some remarks on the structure of the Greek vowel systems", *Word* 15, 240-251.
—— 1964, "Transitivity and possession", *Lg.* 40, 337-343.
Bazell, C.E. 1962, "Meaning and the morpheme", *Word* 18, 132-142.
Benveniste, E. 1962, "Pour l'analyse des fonctions casuelles: le génitif latin", *Lingua* 11, 10-18.
Birnbaum, H. and Puhvel, J. (ed.) 1966, *Ancient Indo-European Dialects* (Berkeley and Los Angeles).
Brandenstein, W. 1964, *Griechische Sprachwissenschaft* I (Berlin).
Chomsky, N. 1964, *Current issues in linguistic theory* (The Hague).
—— 1965, *Aspects of the theory of syntax* (Cambridge, Mass.).
—— 1966, "Topics in the theory of generative grammar", *Current trends in linguistics* 3, ed. Sebeok (The Hague, 1966), 1-60.
Chomsky, N. and Halle, M. 1965, "Some controversial questions in phonological theory", *JL* 1, 97-138.
Closs, Elizabeth 1965, "Diachronic syntax and generative grammar", *Lg.* 41, 402-415. (See also fn. 8, 13).
Cunningham, M.P. 1965, "A theory of the Latin sentence", *Classical Philology* 60, 24-28.
Dingwall, W.O. 1965, *Transformational generative grammar: a bibliography* (Washington).
Diver, W. 1964, "The system of agency of the Latin noun", *Word* 20, 178-196.
Ellis, J.O. 1966, *Towards a general comparative linguistics* (The Hague).
Foley, James 1965, "Prothesis in the Latin verb", *Lg.* 41, 59-64.
Fudge, E.C. 1967, "The nature of phonological primes", *JL* 3, 1-36.
Georgiev, V. 1958, "Das Pelasgische — eine neuentdeckte indoeuropäische Sprache", *Proceedings of the 8th International Congress of Linguists* (Oslo), 406-413.

---

[38] Helpful discussion of points raised in this chapter has come from Elizabeth Closs Traugott, John Lyons and Frederick Bowers. They are not to be blamed for its idiosyncrasies. No account is taken, be it noted, of any shifts in the underlying formal theory later than 1967, nor of the decided sentiments (in favour of viewing historical change ONLY via 'transformationalism') promised in Postal's *Aspects of phonological theory*.

Greenberg, J.H. (ed.) 1963, *Universals of language* (Cambridge, Mass.).
Halle, M. 1961, "On the role of simplicity in linguistic descriptions, Structure of language and its mathematical aspects", *Proceedings of symposia in applied mathematics*, 12 (Providence, R.I.), 89-94.
—— 1962, "Phonology in generative grammar", *Word* 18, 54-72. (See also 1964b).
—— 1964a, "On the bases of phonology", *The structure of language: readings in the philosophy of language* (ed. J. A. Fodor and J. J. Katz), 324-333.
—— 1964b, "Phonology in generative grammar", In Fodor and Katz, 334-352.
Halliday, M.A.K. 1967, "Notes on transitivity and theme in English", *JL* 3, 37-81.
Harris, Z.S. 1965, "Transformational theory", *Lg.* 41, 363-401.
Hockett, C.F. 1965, "Sound change", *Lg.* 41, 185-204.
Hoenigswald, H.M. 1950, "The principal step in comparative grammar", *Lg.* 26, 357-364. (= *Readings in Linguistics* I⁴ ed. Joos, 1966, 298-302).
Katz, J.J. 1964, "Mentalism in linguistics", *Lg.* 40, 124-137.
Kiparsky, P. 1966-67, "A phonological rule of Greek", *Glotta* 44, 109-134.
—— 1967, "Sonorant clusters in Greek", *Lg.* 43, 619-635.
Klima, E.S. 1964, "Relatedness between grammatical systems", *Lg.* 40, 1-20.
Kuryłowicz, J. 1949, *Esquisses linguistiques* (Wrocław-Krakow).
—— 1964, *The inflectional categories of Indo-European* (Heidelberg).
Lyons, J. 1963, *Structural semantics* (Oxford).
—— 1966, "Towards a 'notional' theory of the 'parts' of speech", *JL* 2, 209-236.
—— 1967, "A note on possessive, existential and locative sentences", *Foundations of Language* 3, 390-396.
Martinet, A. 1962, *A functional view of language* (London).
Matthews, P.H. 1966, "Latin" (In fascicule devoted to parts of speech), *Lingua* 17, 153-181.
O'Neil, W.A. 1963, "The dialects of modern Faroese: a preliminary report", *Orbis* 12, 393-397.
Quirk, R. and Svartvik, J. 1966, *Investigating linguistic acceptability* (The Hague).
Ruwet, N. 1967, *Introduction à la grammaire générative* (Paris).
Saporta, S. 1965, "Ordered rules, dialect differences, and historical processes", *Lg.* 41, 218-224.
Šaumjan, S.K. 1963a, "Poroždajuščaja lingvističeskaja model'na baze principa dvuxstupenčatosti", *Voprosy jazykoznanija*, 2.
—— 1963b, (with P. A. Soboleva) "Applikativnaja poroždajuščaja model'i isčislenie transformacij v russkom jazyke", *Izdatel'stvo Akademii Nauk SSSR*.
—— 1964, *Transformacionnij metod v strukturnoj lingvistike* (Moscow).
—— 1965, "Outline of the applicational generative model for the description of language", *Foundations of Language* 1, 189-222.
—— 1966, *Strukturnaja lingvistika* (Moscow).
Ščur, G.S. 1967, "On the connection between the Germanic finite and non-finite verbal forms", *TPhS* 1967, 77-124.
Sigurd, B. 1966, "Generative grammar and historical linguistics", *Acta linguistica Hafniensia* 10, 35-48.

Sommer, F. 1914, *Historische Laut- und Formenlehre der lateinischen Sprache* (2nd. edn.) (Heidelberg).

Sturtevant, E. H. 1940, *The pronunciation of Greek and Latin* (2nd edn.) (Philadelphia).

Thomas, A.R. 1967, "Generative phonology in dialectology", *TPhS* 1967, 179-203.

Vaillant, A. 1936, "L'ergatif indo-européen", *BSL* 37, 93-108.

Voyles, J.B. 1967, "Simplicity, ordered rules and the First Sound Shift", *Lg.* 43, 636-660.

Wackernagel, J. 1953, "Genetiv und Adjektiv", *Kleine Schriften*, 1346-1373 (= *Mél. Saussure*, 1908, 125-152).

Watkins, C. 1966, "Italo-Celtic revisited", in Birnbaum and Puhvel, 1966, 29-50.

—— 1967, "On the genitive", *To honor Roman Jakobson on the occasion of his seventieth birthday* (The Hague).

Winter, W. 1965, "Transforms without kernels?" *Lg.* 41, 484-489.

Woodcock, E.C. 1959, *A new Latin syntax* (London).

9. COMPUTATION AND LATIN CONSONANTS

I

The rules for Latin quantitative prosody are well-known, as are the variations in usage between pre-classical, classical and post-classical poets. Yet problems remain. One of the knottiest is the curious double-headed poser set by words beginning with *s*- plus another consonant (hereafter denoted by *sC*-, where *C* comprises *c* or *q*, *p*, *t*, or rarely *m*: another consonant in third place, *scr*- etc., does not affect the matter). The problem's two heads are these: first, most poets seem to be uncertain whether a short vowel, preceding such an initial string, forms the nucleus of a light or of a heavy syllable;[1] and secondly, all poets appear to be under some odd compulsion to avoid these initial strings altogether.

To begin with, the question may be expressed in a comparative metrical fashion. The syllable whose nucleus is a vowel, short or

---

[1] Vowels are short or long, open or close; syllables are light or heavy, unchecked or checked. Only an unchecked syllable with a short vowel nucleus can be light (i.e. "a light syllable is one which ends in a short vowel" — W. S. Allen, *Vox Latina* [London, 1965], 91). Vowels affect syllables, but the converse does not hold: for a 'vowel long by position' in the traditional phrase, one must speak of a 'syllable heavy by structure'; and, *Iambenkürzung* apart, all syllabic weight is so determined. See W. D. Whitney, *A Sanskrit Grammar* (Leipzig, 1924⁵), §79; W. S. Allen, *Phonetics in Ancient India* (London, 1953), 185, for this Indian terminology; and, for the relevance to Latin, Allen, *Vox Latina*, 89-94. For a possible difference in terms between vowel systems and syllable systems in this respect, see J. R. Firth, *TPhS* 1948, 139 (= *Papers in Linguistics 1934-1951*, 129). Frankly, 'weight' is a less appropriate notion than 'duration' in a verse system in which the values do not derive immediately from stress, as in modern English; but the clarity afforded by the application of this distinction between vowels and syllables may be allowed to carry the day.

long, which is followed by a string of two or more consonants (i.e. phonemes, x being a sign for a native two-phoneme string) — that syllable is heavy. The first presumption, therefore, is that the sC-string might be expected to play its role in this regulation. But if a stop precedes a trill or lateral continuant (r, l), the short vowel which stands before such a TR string ($T=$ any stop; $R=r$ or l) may be allowed to be the nucleus of a syllable which remains (and this must mean 'can still be pronounced as') a light syllable. The reservations will appear presently. On the face of it, the TR strings and the sC strings have in common the privilege of occurrence as word-initial: therefore they might be expected generally to behave alike. Or, a compromise is possible: in Greek some strings (δμ, δν, γμ, γν, γλ, and sometimes βλ) are metrically treated as, and only as, TT types, despite free distribution as word-initials of the TR sort. Latin sC strings could behave like that, in quantitative verse modelled on the Greek (and with Greek phonological rules borrowed to handle loans like *cycnus*). Thus there are three differ-ent behaviour patterns, each of which has, *prima facie*, much to commend it as the descriptive truth about sC. Yet the fact is that the sC strings shuffle uncomfortably between these clearcut types, in a sort of phonological limbo.

Let us reformulate the position in terms of linguistic taxonomic description. The TR strings may be listed as *br, cr, dr, fr, gr, pr, tr*; *bl, cl, fl, gl, pl*; and the sC strings as $sc(sq)$, (sm), sp, st.[2] Then a division may be proposed, according to the role of each exponent in syllabic structure, into *sequences* and *clusters*. These are diagnostically

---

[2] The strings *fl* and *fr* are included here for convenience. There is no proof of the syllabic division *ua-fri* etc. (i.e., in the case *-fR-, f + R→* sequence — a variation of rule 3 below). Also, a fricative value for T in TR appears nowhere else. Nevertheless, the first syllable of words like *refringo* is usually light, as a result of the morpheme boundary which gives *fr* word-onset status; and the succession $-\bar{V}\#fR$- demands cluster status, so that fR is clearly far more acceptable as a candidate for cluster status than is sC (see next footnote). For the purpose of the present calculations, then, initial fR can be subsumed under TR. For *sy-*, see footnote 7. The string *sm-* was included in the computer programme on the strength of its verse occurrence; it does not turn up initially in the prose works studied (being a non-native onset) and can for our present purposes be disregarded.

characterized by the absence and the presence, respectively of a light syllable as the ambience of a short vowel preceding the string in question (which is a cumbrous way of putting it, but anything terser is ruled out by the different boundary-position of the relevant syllable in the two cases). In syllabic terms, of the string $T + R$ in certain circumstances the T functions as the coda of a syllable which terminates after the T and is succeeded by another syllable of which R is the onset; in other circumstances the syllable-boundary of a coda-less syllable falls before TR, which then functions for these purposes as the indivisible onset of the succeeding syllable. In the first of these functions TR is a sequence, in the second a cluster.[3]

[3] *Onset, peak* and *coda* are here used as by Hockett (*A Manual of Phonology* [Indiana, 1955], 52; *A Course in Modern Linguistics* [New York, 1958], 85), but with the difference that INTERLUDES, in his special sense, are excluded because syllables must here be handled as isolates and yet exhaust the phonic material (and Latin, quite apart from the requirements of quantitative verse, has no unexplored syllabic frontiers other than the anomalous cases which are the subject of this enquiry). CLUSTER and SEQUENCE, as defined above, are employed in the manner established by Ernst Pulgram (*Phonetica* 13, 1965, 76ff.). STRING is intended as the neutral, unprejudiced term for potential clusters or sequences; and SUCCESSION means a string set within a relevant phonological environment (as '-$V \# sC$-' indicates sC in [-$V \#$ ( )-]. A syllable which has a coda is checked. For the general analysis of Latin syllables here presumed, at least for metrical purposes, no apology is needed; it has long been standard, if otherwise expressed. It is possible to cite the variants *pa-tris* and *pat-ris* as different structures $\langle K^r N + K^r N K^a \rangle$ and $\langle K^r N K^a + K^r N K^a \rangle$, with a variety of exponents at K^r so that at the outset of the second syllable CC and C respectively occur (for an explanation of this scheme, see J. C. Catford, *A Linguistic Theory of Translation* (London, 1965), 16f.). But it is less convenient thus to split the point at issue into a dual opposition ($\emptyset / K^a$ at an element in structure, and CC/C in the exponence of K^r). I emphatically reject the onset-less, coda-complex description offered by J. Lotz, 'Metric typology', in *Style in Language* (ed. T. Sebeok, Cambridge, Mass., 1960), 146, which obscures all the crucial distinctions examined in this paper, and *inter alia* fails properly to distinguish the light (t)*eg*(o) from the heavy (t)*ect*(um) — unless perhaps as 'halfchecked' as against 'fully checked' — and would otiosely differentiate the metrically identical (m)*e*(us) and (m)*er*(us).

Notwithstanding the Firthian and subsequent use of 'prosody' (and, later, 'conphonation', 'prosodeme', 'suprasegmental' — this last in the prosodic sense), the restriction of the term as in this chapter to relative syllabic weight and/or vowel length is traditional in classical studies and convenient here. See P. Maas, *Greek Metre* (trans. Lloyd-Jones, Oxford, 1962), 72 (though Maas

With these categories the formulation becomes:

(A) — for $T+T$ (here comprising strings of stops, stops plus s, ss,
    stops plus f, ff; and $R+R$ is to be included here): —
    rule 0: in the cases $-T\#T$-, $\#TT$-, $-TT\#$, $T+T \rightarrow$ sequence

— for $T+R$: —
    rule 1: in the case $-T\#R$-, $T+R \rightarrow$ sequence
    rule 2: in the case $\#TR$-, $T+R \rightarrow$ cluster
    rule 3: in the case $-TR$-, $T+R \rightarrow$ sequence OR cluster

(except that rule 3 may need amendment for application to a special
corpus: e.g. for Plautus and Terence it becomes 'in the case $-TR$-,
$T+R \rightarrow$ cluster'.[4] See also footnote 3, as to $-fR$-).

(B) — for $s+C$: —
    1. in the case $-s\#C$-, $s+C \rightarrow$ sequence
    3. in the case $-sC$-, $s+C \rightarrow$ sequence

(whereas Greek δμ etc. obey rule 0, as of course do all Greek sC
strings).

But a rule B2 (i.e. for the case $\#sC$-) cannot be generally and
economically formulated on the basis of a fixed treatment of the
string. What is worse, it cannot be formulated in terms of a free
variation, unlike rule A3 for $-TR$-. Classical scholars know this
well, but do not always find themselves able to cite the data correct-

---

strangely ignores non-poetic prosody). It must be remembered that the
prosodic rules for verse establish sequences which override junctural phenomena; this paper's task, in part, is to see if the same is true at all in prose.
[4] Morpheme boundary commonly interferes with phonological analysis. It
is clear that the type *refringo*, *recludo* has a light first syllable more often than
not (for some exceptions see E. J. Kenney, *Cl. Rev.* n.s. xv (1965), 188 fn. 1;
add specialities like *recclusit* Plaut. *Capt.* 918); conversely, the type *abripio*,
obligo is invariably heavy in its first syllable (some Plautine occurrences are
equivocal but a light value can nowhere be proved). Therefore these two
successions are to be read as *re # fringo* etc., *ab # ripio* etc.; and they become
subject, respectively, to rules A2 and A1. (It may be that *adripio* etc. were early
realized as *arripio* etc. — see Allen, *Vox Latina*, 22 — and are to be assigned to
the RR ($= TT$) group. The only curiosity is the deviant tendency within the
refringo type).

ly.[5] For the comedians clinching evidence would be difficult to secure, and seems not to exist. A clustering of $\#sC$- would be proved only by the occurrence of a metrically light syllable (a) where it is *de rigueur* (and that means, for the only sufficiently common metres, iambic senarii and trochaic septenarii, at no other place than the penultimate syllable of the verse; or, for iambic septenarii, nowhere but at the penultimate syllable before the diaeresis which follows the fourth foot, provided there is such a diaeresis in the given verse, otherwise a heavy syllable is allowed) — and (b) where no interference, like the possibility of *Iambenkürzung*,[6] offers an alternative source of 'lightness' (e.g. at Ter.

---

[5] Of these classical data the only adequate presentation so far is that by H. M. Hoenigswald, "A note on Latin prosody: initial *s* impure after short vowels", *Trans. Amer. Philol. Ass.* 80 (1949), 271-280. There *spero* is credited with at least 12 Plautine occurrences which do not make the preceding syllable heavy: but in fact such cases, like those of *quia⌣stare* (*Mil.* 1260), *ita⌢statim* (*Am.* 276), *neque⌣speraui* (*Rud.* 1195) etc. are so placed metrically that they must involve two consecutive short vowels by 'resolution', and iambic shortening cannot then be ruled out (see footnote 6). Still, the anapaestic *sed erile⌢ scelus* (*Rud.* 198) argues cluster status. But the reader is recommended to Hoenigswald's diagrammatic display of what I call 'rules' (p. 276), and to his list of all the Latin poetic passages relevant to the $\#sC$ question. He also exposes Kolař's claim for 'lightness' before $\#$ cκ in Homer and Hesiod (it is an exceptional device, to cater for the words Σκάμανδρος, σκέπαρνον and σκίη; one may compare Ζάκυνθος etc.). Hence he rightly removes Catullus's *unda Scamandri* (64, 357) from consideration: it is a mere rewrite of the end of a Homeric verse (*Il.* 5, 77). It would be better, however, not to accept as he does the three apparent cases of $-V\#sC$- (with V short) giving a heavy syllable *without ictus* in classical and silver Latin verse (this affects Hoenigswald's whole solution of the problem; see below). O. Skutsch (*Cl. Quart.* n.s. x (1960), 197 fn. 5) reasonably objects to Martial 5, 69, 3 *quid gladium demens Romana stringis in ora* on the ground that *Romana ora* is impossible Latin for 'the mouth of Rome'; and likewise rejects *per silentium* the Grattius example *post ubi proceris generosa stirpibus arbor/se dederit* (142-143); and certainly the conjecture *generosam* restores syntactical as well as metrical normality. Interesting, in view of the discussion below, is Skutsch's ruling (*Cl. Quart.* xlii [1948], 95) that Ennius accepted a short-vowel heavy syllable in this succession 'in the fall' i.e. even without ictus (so *Ann.* 100 *stabilita scamna solumque*). This makes Ennius a lone, pioneering, figure.

[6] This is the lightening of a heavy syllable, but rarely one with a long vowel nucleus, which is itself preceded by a light syllable and flanked by verse ictus. Whatever the phonic nature of the ictus may be, it is probable that it conditions the process unaided. Apart from the quite separate accent effect in common

Pho. 146 the scansion *nisi ˜spem* tells us nothing of the basic syllabic function of *sp-*). I find no monosyllables like *scis, stas* or *spes* in the relevant positions.

Ennius seems to have applied the rule 'in the case $\#sC$-, $s+C\rightarrow$ sequence' (see footnote 5). Subsequent poets, apparently faced with an unpalatable decision, sprang two surprises. They distinguished between occurrences where the verse ictus fell on the crucial syllable and occurrences where it did not ('rise' and 'fall', some call these positions), and accepted the Ennian ruling in the former case but rejected it in the latter (or else avoided the choice). This introduction of a further dimension would be curious enough by itself: appeal to ictus-conditioning in the choice of prosodic alternants is normally confined to phenomena of low frequency (e.g. *grauidus autumno* at Virgil, *Geo.* 2, 5, where either the heavy/light opposition is suspended or one may say that a METRICAL variation is admitted), or is combined with other stimuli (Virgil's spondaic close here, or *Iambenkürzung* or the like). But the oddity increases with the second innovation: no poet at all (as Hoenigswald's paper really makes clear: see above fn. 5) permits himself BOTH sequence AND cluster treatment of $\#s+C$. And this despite the poets' regular acceptance of the ictus-condition which, one would have thought, provides a guiding principle for generalization and rids this variation of all recurrent onus of choice and personal malaise. Thus the rule 'in the case $*\#sC$- (where $*=$ictus), $s+C\rightarrow$ sequence' appears in Catullus, Cicero, Tibullus, Grattius, Seneca, Lucan, Statius, Silius Italicus, Juvenal, Martial and *Aetna*; whereas 'in $\stackrel{*}{-}-\#sC$- or $--\#sC$-, $s+C\rightarrow$ cluster' is applied by Lucilius,

---

iambic words (*bénĕ, módŏ* etc.) in speech (which of course affects the forms in comedy), it seems to me that in the usual verse incidence the distribution of the affected syllables, in relation to word boundary and word accent, rules out word accent itself as the motivator. (But this is no place to rehash a complex and much debated problem; the data can be found in W. M. Lindsay's introduction to his edition of Plautus' *Captivi* [London, 1900; repr. Cambridge, 1961]; or his *Early Latin Verse* [Oxford, 1922]; cf. W. A. Laidlaw, *The prosody of Terence* [London, 1938] — where [despite their overprizing of accent] references will be found to the interpretation, less fashionable now but more common among the older German commentators, which I prefer; see also *Phonetica* 15, 1966, 48f., for some reasons).

Lucretius, the author of *Culex*, Virgil, Horace, Propertius, Manilius and Phaedrus. The Montague-Capulet effect is striking. Distaste for the entire succession is clear, and the sole occurrence in Virgil (*Aen.* 11, 309) interposes a sentence boundary ... *ponite. spes sibi quisque* ..., which may argue it out of court as worthwhile evidence. One notes the repugnance of some poets towards clustered *sC*; as arresting is the position of others (those of the second list above), who admit that an undeniable word-initial string deserves cluster-status but who obstinately refuse, despite available circumstantial control, to allow *sC* to enjoy two kinds of syllabic function in their idiolect.

Hoenigswald's solution to this problem is to regard the avoidance of the impasse, and the consistent loyalty to one or the other 'rule' (if avoidance is not possible), as a sign that the Latin poets were conscious of a conflict. The tug-of-war was between Roman phonological tradition, including prose syllabification, and Greek metrical doctrine. The first forced them to diverge from the Greek model (the model of all their quantitative verse); the second compelled them to pronounce a sound-succession in a thoroughly non-native way.[7] Therefore they either admitted the Greek practice

[7]   *TR* strings were probably ambivalent for them in native speech, as is shown by the readiness of poets to accept sequence value of *TR*; cf. S. Timpanaro, *Riv. Cult. Class. Med.* 7 (1965), 1075 ff., though one or other status may have prevailed in fashion. The *sʉ*- string is always a cluster if initial, not so much because of its absence in Greek (Hoenigswald) as because (*a*) local variants like *sauium* suggest a simplified pronunciation, and (*b*) it fell together, no doubt, with *qu*, which had both a two-phoneme and a one-phoneme origin (**kw, *kʷ*) but levelled itself out as a single phoneme (cf. post-Lucretian verse) — although in very late Latin verse *qu* once again becomes a sequence. Hence *sʉ* is not included among #*sC*- exponents.

    In Homer *TR* is usually a sequence, (for the exceptions see P. Chantraine, *Grammaire Homérique* I, [Paris, 1958³], 108 f.), even to the extent of occasional structure-blind scansions like με πρότερος (*Il.* 3, 351). In Lesbian poetry, outside abnormalities usually of Homeric origin, it is a thoroughgoing sequence. In Attic verse only -*T* # *R*- imposes heaviness; -*TR*- moves towards being an optional cluster (and in comedy, barring parody of tragedy, it is always a cluster). A preceding morpheme boundary accelerates the process; after the still largely separable augment *TR* is always a cluster, as after word boundary, all apparent exceptions being restricted to such basically non-Attic verse forms as tragic lyric. But *sC* is regularly a sequence like the δμ group, despite word-initial status, as is also true of κτ, πτ. But it is to be noted that Mycenaean (heavy) as a artificiality in cases where the verse beat might be permitted to override phonological niceties, or else they insisted on Roman phonology (light) where the verse could accommodate it.

There are, however, several objections to so simple an answer. It is true that a poet who chose to be Roman at all costs in this matter (and joined 'list 2') could not use the relevant syllable as a heavy one, unless he regarded the verse beat as excusing Hellenism; and, by themselves, the poets of this group give no warrant for regarding the verse beat as a factor at all in the question. They only had a light syllable to play with. But, the 'list 1' poets, because they did not extend the use of the 'non-Roman' heavy syllable into positions without ictus, must have taken the beat as a necessitous expiating dispensation, so to speak.[8] Therefore nothing prevented them from remaining 'native' and admitting light syllables of this pattern 'in the fall', where the beat is absent. Yet they did not admit them. Conversely, if they felt themselves 'sold to Greece' by their behaviour under the influence of ictus, nothing prevented their wholesale use of heavy syllables with this phonological succession at all possible positions in the verse scheme. But this does not occur, either. Moreover, medial *sc* perhaps attracted length before it (cf. Aulus Gellius, vii 15), which obscures the issue. And again, to assign sequence status to medial *TR* is a Grecism itself, yet classical Latin poets show no hesitation or tenderness in accepting this licence *ad libitum*. Hence a deeper search is called for. A solution is still to be found which will account for the co-existent features, of consistent individual limitation, and national uncertainty and distaste for decision, which characterize these

---

spelling suggests an occasionally clustered *sC*, in that, in some strings which could be word-initial, /s/ is graphically indispensable (*dosomo* etc.) and is therefore not a coda. (This is the argument of F. W. Householder Jr., "A morphophonemic question and a spelling rule", *Mycenaean Studies* [Madison, 1964], 71-76, esp. 73. A coda is omitted; unfortunately the converse does not hold; an omitted /s/ need not be a coda [cf. *pema* etc.] for clustering need not ensure graphic representation [for a medial case, cf. *tosodepemo*]).

[8]   As may be seen from the reference in fn. 6, ictus is more likely (than accent) to be the weight-conditioning factor where syllabic structure suffers interference: therefore it might of itself enforce sequence-status of *sC* in these occurrences under review. Then the 'list 2' poets become anomalous once more.

consonant strings in verse authors. It must also take account of the probable PIE elision of prefixed /s/ before initial /p/, /t/, etc. (so called 's-movable'), which pushes dislike of initial *sC* clusters back into PIE (Siebs, *Kuhns Zeitschr.* 37, 277ff.).

One or two irrelevant details may now be cleared away. It is true that some other sequences than those cited are found word-initially; but these are either archaic or loans or proper names (on which see chapter 3) and are infrequent. They are *cn-, gn-* [ŋn-], *ct-, tm-, mn-, x-, z-* (although there is some indication that this was equatable with 'voiced *s*', hence hexameters often end with *Zacynthus*; or compare Juvenal's *ponere zelotypo* ... [5, 45]),[9] *pt-, ps-*. In addition, *sm-* belongs here but is for convenience included among the *sC* categories. Again, some *TR* strings are treated as sequences even in the face of 'rule A 2' above, that is, in the case #*TR*-; in the succession *-quĕ*#*Tr/l-* (with ictus on *-que* and with a second *-que* following, and with many concomitant signs of Grecism) syllabic weight is a Homeric inheritance, as also in *-quĕ* # *x/z/st/mn-* etc. Equally foreign (based on Greek sound history), and conventionally tolerated, is a like effect before a single initial continuant, *l/r/m/n/s/u-*; it is also much rarer. Rarest of all is a rash extension of the process by replacement of the initial continuant by *T-* (*telasque calathosque*, Ovid, *Met.* 4, 10 — somewhat excused by earlier *metallique caculaeque*, Accius, *Ann.* 1 W. Conversely, *tr* as initial sequence in Catullus 4, 9 *Propŏntidă trucĕm* ... (cf. 4, 18; 29, 4; Tib. 1, 6, 34) shows a similar handling of *͝*#*Tr/l-* without limitation to preceding *-que*; and one example (Virgil, *Aen.* 3, 464 *dona dehinc auro graviă sectoque elephanto*-so mss.) betrays the same usage in *͝*#*s-* (for no other initial, isolated continuant functions thus). These obvious loans and infrequent experiments need not detain us.

To explain the behaviour of the #*sC* strings it is useless to presume a free variation in every Roman idiolect; the consistency of individual poets (which is not conditioned by genre, as a glance at the two lists reveals) indicates a refusal to vary. We have already seen the objection to supposing a fixed native usage (clustering).

[9]   For a similar treatment in Greek see P. Maas, *Greek Metre*, 75.

Free variation in *langue* with exclusive selection in *parole* (in the Saussurian sense of this distinction) is more attractive; but a poet has to acclimatize himself and his readers to so much that is unusual, and even artificial, that one wonders if he is likely to boggle at sporadic switching to a merely unfavoured usage which is itself frequently attested among speakers of his own language. Nevertheless the truth must be in one or other of these two latter explanations — unless we uncover coexistent competitive usages in *langue*, which is not impossible.

That prosodic uncertainty may indeed correlate with phonetic speciality is shown by the classical behaviour of *qu*, which derives equally in Latin from a single PIE phoneme (*quis* etc.) and from a sequence of two phonemes (*equos*) in PIE. Hoenigswald (274 fn. 18) rules out a unit-phoneme status. But Lucretius' metrical usage (*lĭquidus* etc.) may mean not $\bar{\imath}/\bar{\imath}$ variety but a shift towards generalized cluster value (*equ-* is probably a heavy syllable at Plaut. *Capt.* 31, but $qu = C$ for classical poets after Lucretius), and that at the very time when -*TR*- was moving in the opposite direction (the comedians' invariable clustering of -*TR*- gives way to optional cluster/sequence status). So determined a move towards cluster status argues that phonological oddity should have a basis in phonetic oddity; and Allen (16 ff.) shows that the balance of phonetic evidence is in favour of the value [kʷ] for this digraph. Now a similar articulatory overlap in *sC*, apprehensible even to untrained speakers, may be the cause of natives feeling uneasiness over initial *sC*, where the pronunciation problem, lightened elsewhere by adjacent vowels, is sharpened by the preceding juncture.[10]
But the absence of direct phonetic comment by ancient authorities

[10] H. M. Truby, "Pleniphonetic transcription in phonetic analysis", *Proceedings of the Ninth International Congress of Linguists* (The Hague, 1964), 101-108, with a wealth of mechanical corroboration, has shown (104) that e.g. [pl] operates in many, probably most, articulations as a largely simultaneous production (with pre-release overlap) of bilabial plosion and lateral resonance. The *TR* strings are probably all articulatorily distinct in this respect (i.e. naturally clusters) from the *sC* strings other than [st]. This is another reason for doubting a simple, fixed 'Roman' clustering of #*sC*-. Reduplication by whole clusters underlies *steti*, s*popondi*, but the picture is marred by the type *sisti* and the absence of **sCVsC-* (cf. Got. *skaiskaiþ*).

on sC makes it essential to search for clues to its nature in examples of actual use, purely graphic though these are; and to do so in prose texts, to evade the unnatural element of poetic language as well as the built-in 'solutions' which poets display.

Besides, apart from the metrically slanted and largely opaque testimony of the comedians, the nearest we can come to ordinary Latin speech is via the prose corpus of historians, orators, letter-writers, gazetteers, novelists and so forth. These stand on a cline of selfconsciousness, from full sophistication to extreme insouciance. But what is informal is comparatively late and small in quantity, and it is hard to identify a standard or received speech-form between the various registers even when the whole spectrum is accessible. Still it may be useful to extricate the occurrences of $\#sC$ strings in classical prose authors, in the hope of unearthing some co-present phenomena which may point to an answer to the poetic problem. Prose will only offer a solution, however, if repetitious examination of the texts, with progressive shifting of environmental variables, ultimately calls the analyst's attention to a suggestive pattern of co-occurrences. This complex and long term process (which is merely adumbrated here), and not any difficulty of recognition or summation, enforces the recourse to a computer.[11] The primary end is not the answer, but the experimental and unpredictable reshaping of the problem.

II

At this point, therefore, a programme-series was written[12] for the digital computer. The aim was to test for disinclination in prose

[11]   See T. Sebeok, "Notes on the Digital Calculator as a Tool for analyzing Literary Information", *Poetics* (Warsaw Conference, 1960) (The Hague, 1961), 571-590, especially the valuable remarks on machine 'browsing' (589). Much mere counting has been done 'by hand' on classical texts: we know, for instance that Ovid has 2,646 examples of $\#sC$-, $\#Cs$-, $\#z$, with only four short vowels preceding (of which 2 cases are textually doubtful and 2 are Greek loans).
[12]   With technical guidance from Dr. J. Hawgood and Mrs. E. J. Templeton, for which I am very grateful.

writers (of various registers) to assign inescapably to $s + C$ the cluster-status to which its word-initial distribution entitles it. The symptoms are imagined to be these: (1) a greater frequency of $\#sC$ in successions where a phonic transformation into $-s\#C-$ is easy, so that /s/ becomes a coda or, like the /p/ in *decerptus*, a post-coda; (2) a gradience of frequency in these terms, over the different authors. This latter diagnostic will separate the sound-conscious composers from the rest, but with 'shading'. It may provide a cline similar, in the placing of individual authors on it, to that of the known grading of authors in respect of general RHYTHM-consciousness; then the disinclination to cluster $s + C$ may be a fact of the language. Indeed it will be so, unless the 'rules' of rhythm prove to be basically Greek in origin (as with poetic quantitative metre) in which case the disinclination will be non-native, and Hoenigswald's theory will be strengthened. But there is no prima facie case for expecting an identity of verse-prosody and prose-prosody (any more than for presuming an identity of verse-prosody and, for instance, accent-prosody, which are clearly and certainly different in Greek).

Many by-results may emerge. Judgements of prosodic likeness ("Cicero is more 'Virgilian' in his speeches than in his treatises", *exempli gratia*), whether between authors or parts of one author's corpus, may become possible. More importantly, a poetic prosodic usage may be shown to be not a sign of phonological autocracy in an unrepresentative sector of the language, but to have one or more correlates in prose (and SOME prose must be designated, for purposes of control, as the basic linguistic data-source, suffering minimal interference).

The orthography of Latin is on the whole closely phonemic, and little trouble occurs in the conversion of coarse phonetic enquiry into graphic recognition and sorting. The sC 'pseudoclusters' are tested against the behaviour of the 'real' TR clusters. The latter should prove to be treated alike by all prose authors; the picture of sC occurrence should, by comparison, be confused (answering to symptoms (1) and (2) above). Apparent phonic transformation (/s/ → coda) may be isolated by dividing the relevant successions into five basic classes, according to the nature of the element preceding $\#$. These set $\#sC$ after respectively:

(i) strong pause (e.g. sentence-boundary): marked by punctuation other than comma.[13] (Here a factitious shift of $\#$ is either improbable, or, in paragraph-initial cases, frankly impossible).

(ii) consonant

(iii) -*m*

(iv) vowel. (Here the difference between final and initial status is obscured, in respect of individual elements in the succession, by the potential submerging of normal juncture by sandhi-treatment — as if, e.g. *nulla $\#$ spes → nullaspes → nullas $\#$ pes*.)

(v) [s] (= -*s* or -*x*). (Here the strident continuant physically obscures the positioning of $\#$ — as if, e.g. *nullus $\#$ scit →* [nullus: cit], and phonic reinterpretation is possible — here into *nullus $\#$ cit*.)

Of these classes, (i) is essentially cluster-forcing, and one would expect sound-conscious authors to avoid it as an environment for *sC*, without prejudice to the pattern and placing of such avoidance in their work; (iv) and (v) make sequence status of *sC* possible; (ii) appears to be close to (i), but a re-assignment may be needed if the common medial stringing of *CsC* (*abstinet* etc.) outweighs the prima facie unlikelihood, in this succession, of '$\#$ shift'; (iii) may behave as (ii) or as (iv),[14] and it will be a further merit of this programme if its results permits a decision on this very point.

---

[13] A comma tends to be a merely subjective indicator, corresponding to no necessarily present phonic feature, and reflecting an editor's personal calculus of constituent boundaries within a more or less unified grammatical structure.
[14] It is a commonplace of Latin metrical prosody that in the succession -*Vm $\#$ V*- (*V* before *m $\#$* is always short) the presence of the -*m* is immaterial, precluding neither hiatus nor elision (or crasis). As the heaviness of syllables of the form -*Vm $\#$ C*- may in turn be attributable to a retention of the full contoid [m], the loss before a vowel may be ascribed to incomplete lip closure, or the like, in that environment. But the heaviness of -*Vm $\#$ C*- may rest on a compensatory dureme (or a phonological realization of the phonetic fact that nasalized vowels are regularly of longer actual duration than non-nasalized equivalents); hence there is no hindrance to our explaining the apparent behaviour of -*m $\#$* in each environment (and any environment in classical Latin) on the basis of an invariable nasalization of the preceding vowel; then *m* itself loses consonantal status. This could result from a generalization of what was the original product of the succession -*Vm $\#$ C*- alone — cf. the Skt. incidence

The programme of counting occurrences of $\#sC$ and $\#TR$, and sorting them according to these five succession-categories, was then first applied to the following texts: Sallust, *Jugurtha* ch. 85 (speech of Marius); *ibid.* ch. 86-96; Cicero *I Philippic*; Livy I 23-31. The tables of results are these (the items are so uniform as not to need e.g. χ^2 summation): —

Figure 1

1. Sallust: *Jugurtha* ch. 85

punctuation precedes initial	$=\ \ 90$
final consonant precedes initial	$= 219$
final *m* precedes initial	$= 195$
final vowel precedes initial	$= 453$
final *s* or *x* precedes initial	$= 198$

	sc/q	sm	sp	st	br	cr	dr	fr	gr	pr	tr	bl	cl	fl	gl	pl
-Ø#	1	0	0	0	0	0	0	0	0	3	0	0	0	0	0	1
-C#	1	0	0	0	0	0	0	0	0	8	0	0	0	0	0	2
-m#	2	0	0	1	0	0	0	0	0	2	1	0	0	1	1	1
-V#	1	0	1	0	0	0	0	1	1	12	1	0	3	2	2	5
-s/x#	0	0	0	2	0	1	0	1	0	3	0	0	0	0	1	2

initial strings of type *sC* as fraction of all initials $= .00779896$
initial strings of type *TR* as fraction of all initials $= .04766031$.

2. Sallust: *Jugurtha* ch. 86 to 96

punctuation precedes initial	$= 106$
final consonant precedes initial	$= 371$
final *m* precedes initial	$= 271$
final vowel precedes initial	$= 742$
final *s* or *x* precedes initial	$= 384$

---

of -$m\#V$- and -$\dot{m}\#C$, and the Latin treatment of preclassical -$\breve{V}s\#C$-, -$\breve{V}s\#V$- ($> -\breve{V}\#C$-, -$\breve{V}s\#V$- respectively); cf. also such hints as to final -m as the written evidence offers, as in the Scipionic epitaph *CIL* I², 7: *Taurasia Cisauna Samnio cepit/subigit omne Loucanam opsidesque abdoucit*. After levelling, -$Vm\#$ will then operate as -$\breve{V}\#$ in any sound-conscious author.

	sc/q	sm	sp	st	br	cr	dr	fr	gr	pr	tr	bl	cl	fl	gl	pl
-Ø#	0	0	0	0	0	0	0	0	0	0	0	0	0	0	0	0
-C#	1	0	1	3	1	0	0	1	0	15	0	0	1	2	1	5
-m#	0	0	0	0	0	0	0	3	0	14	1	0	0	0	1	3
-V#	1	0	2	4	0	0	0	1	1	24	1	0	1	1	5	6
-s/x#	1	0	0	1	1	2	0	2	3	12	2	0	1	0	1	1

initial strings of type sC as fraction of all initials = .00747464
initial strings of type TR as fraction of all initials = .06033102.

3. Cicero: *First Philippic.*

punctuation precedes initial	= 335
final consonant precedes initial	= 842
final m precedes initial	= 617
final vowel precedes initial	= 1296
final s or x precedes initial	= 606

	sc/q	sm	sp	st	br	cr	dr	fr	gr	pr	tr	bl	cl	fl	gl	pl
-Ø#	1	0	0	0	0	2	0	0	0	3	0	0	0	0	0	0
-C#	0	0	1	1	1	3	0	0	6	20	3	0	1	0	4	2
-m#	1	0	4	1	0	0	0	3	1	20	0	0	1	0	5	3
-V#	3	0	1	6	0	1	0	1	6	38	2	0	2	2	2	9
-s/x#	3	0	1	1	1	2	0	1	2	9	5	0	2	1	2	5

initial strings of type sC as fraction of all initials = .00649526
initial strings of type TR as fraction of all initials = .04627875.

4. Livy I ch. 23 to 31.

punctuation precedes initial	= 250
final consonant precedes initial	= 665
final m precedes initial	= 527
final vowel precedes initial	= 1080
final s or x precedes initial	= 515

	sc/q	sm	sp	st	br	cr	dr	gr	fr	pr	tr	bl	cl	gl	fl	pl
-Ø#	0	0	0	1	0	0	0	0	0	8	0	0	0	0	0	1
-C#	0	0	5	1	0	4	0	1	1	14	8	0	2	1	0	4
-m#	0	0	6	3	0	5	0	1	1	10	10	0	3	1	0	1
-V#	1	0	7	7	0	3	0	8	1	23	7	0	3	3	6	3
-s/x#	3	0	6	2	0	0	0	1	2	10	4	0	0	0	1	3

initial strings of type sC as fraction of all initials $= .01383399$
initial strings of type TR as fraction of all initials $= .05072464$.

From the outputs of this first scanning, and the application of crude arithmetic, some interesting observations can be made. The eleven narrative chapters of *Jugurtha* do not offer a suggestive phonic pattern. The contrasting environments $-C\#$ and $-V\#$ admit the TR strings at the rate, respectively, of $1:14.27$ and $1:18.63$ (TR strings: all initial strings). The sC types occur at the rates of $1:74.2$ and $1:106$. The greater readiness of TR types to form an onset in (of the two environments) an apparently unfavourable, cluster-forcing, sandhi position is thus nullified (as a diagnostic) by the similar comparative readiness of the sC types. (It is a curious nuisance that in the more crucial post-punctuation position no example of either type occurs: Sallust is obviously restrictive in his choice of sentence openers.) In the $-s\#$ environment the occurrences of all strings: TR strings: sC strings $= 384:25:2$, which seems to indicate a non-sandhi treatment, as the total occurrences $(1674:113:14)$ predict the figures $*384:25.92:3.21$, and sC strings seem somewhat shy of what ought to be their most acceptable sandhi position. They may perhaps be countenanced as clusters, needing no phonetic salvation.

The speech of Marius has some *ars*, yet the speaker parades his lack of education; therefore rhythmic awareness and indifference are equally likely. In fact, the sC strings occur (though such few instances are scarcely evidence) with no comparative reservation as between sandhi and non-sandhi positions. In $-\emptyset\#$ and $-s\#$ they figure (as compared with all strings) at $1:90$ and $1:99$, in $-C\#$ and $-V\#$ at $1:219$ and $1:226.5$. And the $TR:sC$ ratios, as the reader can readily see, are chaotic and unhelpful.

The *First Philippic* is more informative. The occurrence-rate of TR (: all strings) after $-V\#$ is $1:20.57$, after $-C\#$ and $-s\#$ combined it is $1:20.9$ — the expected neutrality. But sC after $-\emptyset\#$ and $-C\#$, the presumed non-sandhi positions, occurs at $1:335$ and $1:421$ whereas after $-V\#$ and $-s\#$ it shows the 'sandhi-rates' of $1:129.6$ and $1:121.2$. This latter comparative frequency of appearance points to phonic unhappiness in any attempt to cluster sC unless the clustering can be nullified by a potential shift of $\#$, and by transformation of the string into a sequence (as if $-s\#C-$). Cicero is here euphonically(?) or rhythmically(?) aware, and perhaps Ennian in solution.

To be sure, both the TR and the sC strings treat alike the environments $-V\#$ and $-s\#$ (the figures being, for all strings: TR strings: sC strings, respectively 1296:63:10 and 606:30:5). The former are indifferent to any distinction between these positions; the latter find a vowel final and a sibilant final equally conducive to their own sequence status. But there is a discouraging feature: after $-\emptyset\#$ and $-V\#$ no variation is looked for in the incidence of TR. Yet the figures are, respectively, 1:67 and 1:20.57, which appears to indicate a preference for TR sequence status, a skewness which also appears elsewhere, more significantly (see below).

The nine Livian chapters show some features of interference. The incidence of $-m\#tr-$ is high, as is $sp-$ overall; the total of $sC-$ occurrences (138 per 10,000) stands to that of $TR-$ (507) in the ratio 1:2.71 as against the range elsewhere of 1:4 to 1:8. Still, the Ciceronian picture is largely repeated, as one would expect in an equally (though in detail differently) self-conscious author. TR neutrality appears in the occurrence-rates (TR:all initials) 1:18.47 after $-C\#$ and 1:18.95 after $-V\#$ (where 1:24.52 after $-s\#$ shows no special liking for this position). The preference of sC for sandhi treatment is obvious from the proportions 1:46.82 after $-s\#$, 1:72.00 after $-V\#$, 1:110.83 after $-C\#$ and 1:250 after a punctuation pause. The small totals of both sC and TR after a punctuation pause show, in fact, for what it is worth, a 1:9 ratio to each other against the overall ratio of 1:2.71 — which could argue a strong comparative reluctance to the clustering of sC strings. For Livy, then, word-initial occurrence of sC does not override a preference for treating the string as a sequence.

In these primary calculations the second class of successions, those where a consonant precedes the word boundary, have been taken closely together with the first class, where punctuation-pause precedes. Now it is quite arguable that no inescapable evidence of

the existence of a word boundary, or of the placing of word boundary characterizes this second class any more than in *[nullaspe:s]
or *[nullas # pe:s] or *[nullus:cit], the 'reinterpretations' cited above.
That is to say, as final *C* here comprises *b, c, d, l, n, r, t* (*f, p* not
occurring word-finally in these authors), and as all these readily
stand before *s within* a word (allowing for neutralization of voice-
oppositions there, like *b/p, d/t*), it follows that e.g. *adscribo* might
interfere with *ad # scribendum* and remove all sense of word-
initial clustering of *sC*; or *totiens # cadit* might prevent the actual
position of word boundary from inducing such a sense of initial
clustering in *tibicen # scandit*, and so forth. It is therefore worth
having a recount, this time taking classes 2-5 together as against
class 1. A somewhat unexpected picture emerges:

Text	all initials: $TR:sC$
1. In Sallust (speech of Marius):	
in environment classes 2-5:	= 1065: 51: 8
the expected figures, in ratio,	
in class 1:	= *90: 4.31: 0.67
the actual figures in class 1:	= 90: 4: 1
2. In Cicero, *I Philippic*:	
in classes 2-5	= 3363: 166: 23
expected figures in class 1	= *335: 15.09: 2.21
actual figures in class 1	= 335: 5: 1
3. In Livy, I 23-31:	
in classes 2-5	= 2787: 146: 41
expected figures for class 1:	= *250: 13.11: 3.68
actual figures for class 1:	= 250: 9: 1

No pattern of avoidance of class 1 is seen in Sallust. In Livy
the reduction of -Ø # *sC*- successions from *3.68 to 1 is consistent
with that author's unease at clustered use of *sC* strings. But Cicero's
usage is remarkable. First, an *sC* reduction after a punctuation
pause from *2.21 to 1 is much less than one expects arithmetically,
but could not be greater without the complete absence of *sC* in that
position; which would scarcely be helpful. It is useful therefore to

adduce here the figures, achieved by the same computer programme, for Cicero's oration *pro Caelio* (for the full results, see figure 2):

4. Cicero, *pro Caelio*
  in classes 2-5:   = 7615: 322: 80
  expected figures for class 1:   = *570: 24.10: 5.10
  actual figures for class 1:   = 570: 8: 1

here the reduction is, gratifyingly, of the order of $5 \to 1$. But what of the equivalent reduction of the incidence of *TR* after -Ø#? In the *First Philippic* this is $15.09 \to 5$, in the *pro Caelio* $24.10 \to 8$; that is to say, in Cicero's speeches *TR* is three times more reluctant to be an undeniable cluster than one might reasonably expect. (And one may note that in the pages of pure narrative in Sallust none of these initial strings *at all* occurs after -Ø#, although common sentence openers have *sC* and *TR* strings in normal ratio — e.g. *scilicet, praeterea.*)

Figure 2

Cicero *pro Caelio* (omitting ch. 16 — which mainly comprises quotations)

  punctuation precedes initial   = 570
  final consonant precedes initial   = 2066
  final *m* precedes initial   = 1444
  final vowel precedes initial   = 2825
  final *s* or *x* precedes initial   = 1280

	sc/q	sm	sp	st	br	cr	dr	fr	gr	pr	tr	bl	cl	fl	gl	pl
-Ø#	0	0	0	1	0	1	0	1	1	4	1	0	0	0	0	0
-C#	8	0	1	9	1	13	0	2	6	34	5	0	8	5	4	7
-m#	5	0	5	5	2	10	0	6	2	24	8	0	2	2	1	4
-V#	12	0	11	13	0	19	0	6	11	62	14	0	1	5	3	5
-s/x#	4	0	3	4	0	11	0	4	6	18	0	1	3	3	2	2

initial strings of type *sC* as fraction of all initials = .00990704
initial strings of type *TR* as fraction of all initials = .04036203.

The *pro Caelio* offers an unpredictably large gap between *sC* incidence after punctuation-pause and *sC* incidence after a final consonant (1:570 against 1:115, for sC: all initials so placed). The latter figure is out of line with the *First Philippic*, but less unlike Livy's usage. Where in Livy sC strings occur as a fraction of all initials at .0138 but as a fraction of initials after -C# at .0090, in *pro Caelio* the equivalent figures are .0099 and .0087 (*First Philippic* .0065 and .0024); but the *pro Caelio* stands alone in the width of its gap here, as also of the gap between the incidences after Ø# and C# respectively; and thus it adds support to the notion of a watershed, as noticed in the preceding discussion, between the -Ø# environment and all others. With the *pro Caelio* figures for -Ø# now available, the rarity of any consonant string in this environment can be appreciated:

Cicero, *I Philippic*:
sC as fraction of all initials:- overall = .0065; after Ø# = .0030
TR as fraction of all initials:- overall = .0463; after Ø# = .0149

Cicero, *pro Caelio*:
sC as fraction of all initials:- overall = .0099; after Ø# = .0017
TR as fraction of all initials:- overall = .0404; after Ø# = .0140

Livy I 23-31:
sC as fraction of all initials:- overall = .0138; after Ø# = .0040
TR as fraction of all initials:- overall = .0507; after Ø# = .0360

The minor anomaly (i.e. the frequency of sC after -C#) in the *pro Caelio* results is, however, offset by another suggestion, over Cicero and Livy together, of the 'verse-consciousness' of these authors. Let us call the environments -Ø# and -C# the 'NS' positions (i.e. those where initial sequences cannot rely on sandhi effects for phonic unobtrusiveness) and the environments -V# and -s/x# the 'S' positions (where sandhi does allow easy sequence-treatment). It is better to disregard the controversial -m# environments for this test; but -s/x# need not be subtracted (on the grounds that they particularly favour sC strings in sandhi) because sTR is a common, euphonic string, and we are in any case slanting the examination towards sC behaviour.

Now it may be seen how frequently any word-initial occurs as between these positions. Or we can, in effect, measure how much more frequent the 'S' positions are than the 'NS' positions as stretches preceding 1) all initials, 2) *TR* initials, 3) *sC* initials. (It is a natural characteristic of the language that the 'S' positions are always absolutely the more frequent.) The figures follow:

Sallust: *Jugurtha* 85:

all initials in 'S'/'NS' positions $= 651/309$ ($= 2.11$)
TR initials in 'S'/'NS' positions $= 35/14$ ($= 2.5$)
sC initials in 'S'/'NS' positions $= 4/2$ ($= 2$)

Sallust: *Jugurtha* 86-96:

all initials in 'S'/'NS' positions $= 1126/477$ ($= 2.36$)
TR initials in 'S'/'NS' positions $= 65/26$ ($= 2.5$)
sC initials in 'S'/'NS' positions $= 9/5$ ($= 1.8$)

Here there is an astonishing indifference of *sC* strings to those environments which apparently assist them to operate as sequences. This fact permits us to read them as clusters no less readily than the *TR* strings. In fact, they seem to have a greater right to cluster-status than the *TR* strings (the clusters κατ' ἐξοχήν, one would have thought); it may well be that the whole incidence is random. With the other authors the position is quite different:

Cicero: *I Philippic*:

all initials in 'S'/'NS' positions $= 1902/1177$ ($= 1.62$)
TR initials in 'S'/'NS' positions $= 93/45$ ($= 2.0\overset{.}{6}$)
sC initials in 'S'/'NS' positions $= 15/3$ ($= 5$)

and Cicero: *pro Caelio*:

all initials in 'S'/'NS' positions $= 4105/2636$ ($= 1.56$)
TR initials in 'S'/'NS' positions $= 176/93$ ($= 1.89$)
sC initials in 'S'/'NS' positions $= 47/19$ ($= 2.47$)

where *sC* strings are forced, apparently in order to operate preferentially as sequences, to occur predominantly in 'S' positions.

Livy I 23-31:

all initials in 'S'/'NS' positions = 1595/915   (= 1.74)
TR initials in 'S'/'NS' positions = 78/45   (= 1.73)
sC initials in 'S'/'NS' positions = 26/7   (= 3.71)
which shows the same sC sandhi preference.

Finally, the behaviour of $-m\#$ is worth examining (in view of the discussion of the phonetic nature of $-Vm\#$ in footnote 14). The relevant figures will be those for $TR : sC$ incidence after $-C\#$, $-V\#$, $-s/x\#$ and $-m\#$ in the authors who show cluster vs. sequence treatment of TR vs. sC (Cicero and Livy). These are:
TR outnumbers sC in the following ratio:

	after $-C\#$	after $V\#$	after $s/x\#$	after $-m\#$
Cicero, *I Philippic*:	20	6.3	6	6.6
Cicero, *pro Caelio*:	4.72	3.5	4.55	4.06
Livy, I 23-31:	6	3.8	1.91	3.5

Compare the plotting of $-m\#$ in relation to $-C\#$ and $-V\#$ in figure 3 (p. 214).

The curiously high number of $-C\#sC$ occurrences in *pro Caelio* masks the greater closeness, even there, of $-m\#$ behaviour to $-V\#$ behaviour. Otherwise the conclusion seems to be that preconsonantal $-Vm\#$ is realized as $[-V\#]$ or $[-V:\#]$ (one cannot say whether with or without a nazalization prosody) in the more polished style of mid and late first century (56-25 B.C.) prose.

III

None of these analyses suggests an obvious clue to the phonological 'feel' of sC- for a Latin speaker. All that can so far be deduced is that conscious euphony and a clustering of sC were incompatible. It remains possible at this point, before more detailed search is made in texts which are free from artistic interference, that the euphonic principle is identical with the rhythmic impulse, and that the rhythmic impulse is itself based on an inheritance of Greek

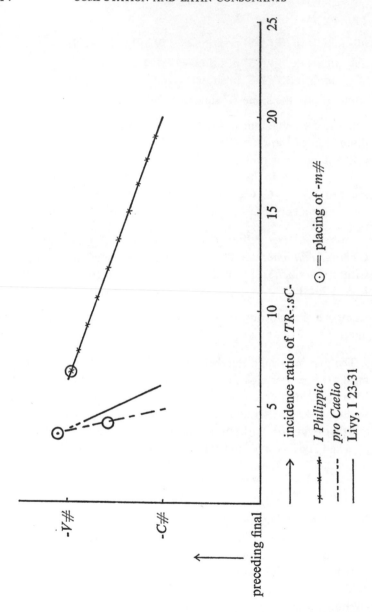

Figure 3

metrical architecture. It is reasonable to suppose that free variation, as between sequence and cluster status, ceased to be a possibility once a speaker or writer had to make up his mind as to
the regular weight of syllable-types.[15] For this reason it is clearly
worth examining texts, if any can be found, which exhibit co-
existing rhythmic and non-rhythmic sectors (but no other variation
of style or register). The solution would then seen to lurk in
comparison of, for example, the *clausulae* (rhythmic 'closing sections') in Cicero's speeches with the utterance-remainder in the
same works. That rhythmic closures may be sought elsewhere
than at the ends of 'cola' (and 'commata') is a thesis which has
always resisted systematic demonstration; it may be disregarded.
But that it is difficult to determine the boundaries of a colon or
a comma (in the technical sense) — because these are rhetorical
units by no means coterminous either with grammatical units or
with the conventionalized 'units' of punctuation[16] — is a more
real difficulty. One must look at all sentence-endings, but not
neglect the closing syllables of any contextually self-contained
'immediate constituent'. The value of this particular analysis would
be twofold:- (*a*) a behaviour-pattern is predictable, in that in
clausulae, if anywhere, either the status of *sC* must be decided
or else *sC*- initials resolutely avoided after -$\bar{V}\#$; (*b*) by varying
the weight-value assigned to syllables of the type -$\bar{V}\#sC$-, if any
do turn up, one may

---

[15] The absence of any metrical need to reach a decision (because the literary
verse is non-quantitative) may explain such effects as the seemingly arbitrary
assignment of sequence or cluster status to *st* in Middle English; this would in
its turn appear to underlie the divergence in the sound histories which produced
priest versus *breast*, each from earlier $\# Cr + éo + st \#$.

[16] One may note that R. G. M. Nisbet, in his edition of Cicero, *in Pisonem*
(Oxford, 1961), introd. xviii, marks as many as thirty-two cola (and notes
deliberate rhythm in twenty-eight of them, including only the four major
metrical patterns) in sections 1, 1-2 alone. Among the rhythmically marked
ends of cola, thirteen occur before a modern comma in his text (and two other
cola-ends are similarly placed), while two metrically marked stretches which
are not cola-ends occur likewise before a modern comma. Three metrical
cola-ends occur before no punctuation sign at all; and two successions, metrically marked but not noted as cola-ends, also occur without punctuation.

(i)   significantly corroborate the frequency of 'favoured' *clausulae*.
or (ii) significantly increase the frequency of merely 'accepted'
clausulae.
or (iii) establish as sought *clausulae*, within the metrical schemes
already fixed, several colon-endings previously regarded as non-
rhythmic.

It is unlikely that the number of cases will be so great as to permit
the shift of a *clausula* from the class 'avoided' to the class 'favoured'
or vice versa, or introduce a new rhythmic pattern into the whole
discussion. Here, however, is a further attractive field for computer
search, which would seem best dug over by a programme designed
first to pick up $-\bar{V}\#sC-$ syllables embedded in strings of up to fourteen syllables (i.e. seven relevant environments of preceding plus
succeeding syllables, running from 0 ... 7 to 6 ... 1 — for the
$-\bar{V}\#sC-$ syllable cannot itself be final — thus permitting any placing
of the crucial syllable within a string of eight of those co-occurring,
eight syllables being the longest relevant string admitted in the
generally accepted inventory of these metrical patterns). There
are, however, difficulties in programming syllable-recognition, not
least the different values of successive graphic 'vowels' (e.g. $a + e$ in
aera/*aëra* = 'bronzes'/'air', or in *aeuos*/*aëneus* = 'age'/'brazen', or
Aenus/*aënus* = proper name/'brazen' — with different respective
syllable-tally in each pair). Therefore it seems better to pick out
sign-successions, setting the succession $\# + s + C$ in environments
of, say, up to forty signs including $\#$ and punctuation marks, the
latter being highly relevant in establishing possible *clausula*-
positions. The number of occurrences, even with overlaps where
punctuation is not present as a fixer of utterance-position, will
not be so great in any text as to make impracticable the use thereafter of 'hand' methods in varying the syllabic weight (failing a
weight-sensitive programme) and logging the metrical shapes
which result.

Other tests of this kind may readily be devised by analysts seeking
to probe further into the *parole*-status of these consonant strings
in Latin; and the tentative results given in the pages above may

or may not be significantly altered or corroborated by applying the same type of programme to more and more texts. One last enquiry directed to these present texts may be briefly mentioned: namely whether the apparently non-segmental status of the element designated by *m* (see above, and fn. 14) may also be attributed to that designated by *n* — this in view of the seeming nasalization (or some replacement process) which transforms *censor* into *cēsor* or produces such hyper-corrections as *thensaurus*.[17] The prima facie case is in favour of a segmental consonantal value for final -*n*. No elision occurs in verse in successions like *carmen et error* or *nullum numen habes*, nor does early non-standardized orthography hint at any segmental loss. It happens that the ratio of -*n#* to all other word-final successions (and punctuation pauses) is such as to predict, in four of the above texts, an incidence of -*n#sC*- and -*n#TR*- so minimal as to be useless for computation. But the figures for the *pro Caelio* give a slight hint. They are:

final *n* precedes initial: 406
-*n#* before

sc/q	*sm*	*sp*	*st/*	*br*	*cr*	*dr*	*fr*	*gr*	*pr*	*tr/*	*bl*	*cl*	*fl*	*gl*	*pl*
2	0	0	1	0	5	0	0	1	6	0	0	0	1	2	1

The fraction of *TR* initial strings in all initials, in this speech, is .0404, that of *sC* initials likewise compared is .0099. These figures would forecast, for an overall occurrence of 406 for -*n#*, that the incidence of -*n#TR*- and -*n#sC*- should be, respectively, 16.4 and 4; they in fact occur 16 and 3 times. If the occurrences after -*V#* are noted (all initials $/TR/sC = 2825/126/36$) and scaled to the total occurrence after -*n#*, the predicted equivalent figures for cases after -*n#* become *406/18.1/5.2. If a similar calculation is applied to the incidences after -*C#*, (all initials $/TR/sC = 2066/85/$

---

[17] On this whole complex matter of the true nature and interrelations of *Vns/f*, *V:s/f*, *?V:ns/f*, see my 'Phonetic information and misinformation in dead languages', *Proceedings of the 5th Internat. Congress of Phonetic Sciences*, (Münster, 1964), Basel, 1965, 235-238.

18), the prediction for cases after -$n\#$ becomes *406/16.7/3.5. The actual figures of 406/16/3 thus support the contention that, for Cicero at least, final n is a segmental consonant; or, to put it more soundly, the fact that the range of incidence figures arrived at by equating -$n\#$ with -$C\#$ is also very like both the range calculated from the overall occurrence of -$n\#$ (*406/16.4/4) and the actual incidence proves, negatively but importantly, that -$n\#$ does not drift towards behaving like -$V\#$. To be sure, such a tiny sample means nothing of itself; and if this pilot study as a whole gives no more than hints on possible future procedures, one will be satisfied.

INDEX OF MODERN AUTHORITIES